The Crimson Thread

IDEAS FOR AUSTRALIAN SOCIETY

THE HENRY PARKES ORATIONS
2001–2014

THE HENRY PARKES FOUNDATION

ETT IMPRINT

Published by ETT Imprint, Sydney Australia,
in association with the Henry Parkes Foundation.

First published 2015.

**National Library of Australia
Cataloguing-in-Publication entry:**

The crimson thread : ideas for Australian society :
the Henry Parkes orations 2001–2014 / The Henry Parkes Foundation.

ISBN 978 1 87589 299 0 (hardback)
ISBN 978 1 87589 296 9 (paperback)
ISBN 978 1 87589 297 6 (eBook)

Includes bibliographical references and index.

Parkes, Henry, Sir, 1815–1896
Speeches, addresses, etc., Australian
Australia – Politics and government.

808.85

Design: Alison White Designs Pty Ltd
Editing: Catherine Gray
Index: Jon Jermey

Contents

	Introduction *Brian H. Fletcher, Inaugural Chair, Henry Parkes Foundation*	*1*
Susan Ryan	**Priority public: the supreme legacy of Henry Parkes** *27 May 2001*	*5*
Gordon Samuels	**Australia in the 21st century: living in peace and freedom?** *24 October 2001*	*13*
Neal Blewett	**A presidential republic or a republican president?** *26 October 2004*	*29*
John Faulkner	**Apathy and anger: our modern Australian democracy** *24 October 2005*	*49*
Helen Irving	**The crimson thread: what unites Australians today?** *28 October 2006*	*59*
Geoff Gallop	**Whatever happened to Australian radicalism?** *20 October 2007*	*73*
Linda Burney	**Weaving the Australian tapestry** *17 October 2008*	*85*
John Bannon	**National questions and local matters: Australia's Federation then and now** *24 October 2009*	*97*
Lyndsay Connors	**Public education and the common wealth: towards sustainable democracy** *29 October 2010*	*109*
Philip Laird	**Railways in Australia: Federation unfulfilled** *22 October 2011*	*123*
George Williams	**Social justice through constitutional change: mission impossible?** *24 October 2012*	*139*
Ted Mack	**State of the Federation** *26 October 2013*	*155*
Marie Bashir	**The enduring legacy of Henry Parkes** *25 July 2014*	*175*
Henry Parkes	**The Tenterfield Oration** *24 October 1889*	*185*
	Acknowledgements	*193*
	Bibliography	*194*
	Index	*196*

'One hundred years ago, flawed as we were,
Australians did create a society characterised
by an egalitarian ethos, and an effective attention
to the needs of individuals and communities
through a strong and well resourced public sector.
For the mass of people, Australia was the best
and fairest country in the world.

We can thank Henry Parkes for some of that.'

The Hon. Susan Ryan AO

Introduction

HENRY PARKES has always figured among the heroes of the nation, but these days the average Australian may be only superficially aware of his many contributions to their country. Interest has turned in directions that lead away from men of Parkes' style and calibre. Social history with its emphasis on the lives of ordinary men and women has supplanted political history, and the era of British dominance, when Australia was divided into a congerie of colonies, has been marginalised and even vilified. Parkes' reputation has suffered from this and he has become identified with an era which many consider best forgotten. This is to overlook the fact that his legacy was of enduring value and that he contributed much to the shaping of the nation in which Australians are privileged to live.

A desire to address this perception brought together in 1996 a small group of men and women who met at Sydney University, shortly after celebrations had been held at Faulconbridge in the Blue Mountains to commemorate the centenary of Parkes' death. The meeting was exploratory and its object was to examine whether steps might be taken to restore Parkes to his rightful place among the founders of Australia. The group included descendants of Parkes along with leading historians and others who recognised the importance of undertaking such a task.

It was agreed that efforts should be made to establish a Henry Parkes Foundation and a working party was established to examine the practicalities and sort out the complex legal issues involved. After lengthy deliberations a constitution was finally approved in December 1998 and the Henry Parkes Foundation was born. Family pride influenced Parkes' descendants, who worked with great enthusiasm and commitment. But like the other early contributors to the Foundation they were conscious of the fact that Parkes was not only a man of stature who deserved remembering for his own sake, but that he also espoused beliefs and ideals which were of value to the present generation. A new sense of national identity was being shaped in Australia and this would be the poorer were the beliefs of men such as Parkes to be overlooked. He was instrumental in forging what are sometimes referred to as the core values of the nation.

The Foundation, therefore, looked not simply to the past but to the future. It was not to be a museum-piece but a vibrant organisation that sought to act creatively and constructively in the interests of the nation. Conscious of the need to reach into the minds of the younger generation, the group initiated conferences of school children, selected by schools from all over New South Wales, who assembled annually from 1999 to 2010 in Parliament House, Sydney, to discuss social and political issues of current concern. In this environment they were exposed to the realities of parliamentary government and were also able to engage in debate and develop their own ideas, which they then shared with the communities from which they were drawn. The intent was to foster a sense of engagement with political processes and an awareness of the potential for change and reform through the framework of our parliamentary democracy.

In the background was the example of Henry Parkes himself. As Professor George Williams states in this volume: 'Across many fields, Parkes was a reformer, and an extremely successful one at that. He demonstrated the qualities needed to achieve social justice in a tumultuous and unforgiving political process. He showed that this can be realised when it is backed by a clear vision, sound political judgement, persistence and a willingness to convince the community of the need for change.'

Parkes' ideas had been shaped in the crucible of 1830s English radicalism, a movement to which he was instinctively drawn as a result of his humble beginnings and early struggles. Like so many of his compatriots he experienced the disadvantage of living in a class-bound, exploitative society, which offered little opportunity for advancement. His ambitions thwarted, he joined the flood of aspirants seeking a better life in the British Empire, arriving in Sydney with his wife Clarinda (née Varney) in 1839. Success did not dim his political ideas, which were directed towards the creation of an open society in which all could advance regardless of class. Blocking such a goal was the conservative landed gentry out to perpetuate its own influence, but by joining in the struggle against this group he sharpened his beliefs and made a name for himself both as a politician and a journalist. Even more was to come after 1856 when the colonists became semi-independent and a new system of government that transferred power to the middle class was established, providing Parkes with the opportunity to enter politics and serve as premier on no less than five occasions.

A firm believer in parliamentary government, which he did much to fashion, Parkes worked to break the power of the landed gentry. He advanced the cause of democracy, and strongly upheld the rights of the individual as well as the rule of law. Straitened family circumstances in England had denied him more than the most rudimentary education and forced him to engage in paid employment from an early age. His intelligence and drive helped compensate for his lack of schooling but from an early age he was aware that countless members of his class were denied through lack of education the essential means of realising their potential. In New South Wales, elementary schooling was for long the preserve of the Church of England and to a lesser extent other denominations. They lacked the means to meet the rising demand of an expanding population, necessitating state involvement, which Parkes favoured.

He worked hard to bring education under the state, his efforts culminating in the famous 1880 *Public Instruction Act* which laid the foundations for a system of 'free, secular and compulsory' education controlled by the state. In taking this initiative Parkes sought to eradicate the evils of sectarianism by bringing children of all faiths together at a time when their minds were being shaped. In these and other ways he stands out as a man of creative mind which found further expression in his recognition that the future lay with the formation of a nation governed federally. His famous Tenterfield Oration helped ignite a hitherto simmering movement and gave him national status.

It is this great speech that has provided the impetus for the second of the Foundation's main areas of activity – the annual Henry Parkes Orations, held since 2001 around the anniversary of the Tenterfield Oration, and now gathered together into this volume. The Foundation's aim in instigating this series was to offer a platform for distinguished Australians to consider contemporary issues in the context of Parkes' vision and achievements. Selection of topic was left to the individual speaker, and the result is a diverse collection ranging across the shape of federal government, the form that might be taken were a republic to exist, the commitments that bind Australians together, the continuing importance of public education to a healthy democracy, the challenges of a national railway system, social justice and constitutional reform.

What is striking is the freshness and independence of the ideas to which expression is given and the spirit of enquiry and questioning that underlies them. References to Henry Parkes may be frequent but his role is mainly as a catalyst who stirred in the mind of the speakers challenging thoughts about issues of contemporary concern. This is essentially an 'ideas' book written in a way that is readily understandable and calculated to encourage reflection.

It is a true feast for those committed to keeping Australia at the forefront of liberal democratic nations, and is particularly germane to an age in which personal ambition and the search for power and wealth seem to have replaced the ideologies which once inspired politicians and citizens alike.

Emeritus Professor Brian H. Fletcher
Inaugural Chair, Henry Parkes Foundation

March 2015

"For a democratic society to prosper, it must be built on an education system of the highest standard, open to all without fees or religious tests, accessible wherever school age children live. A public system was the right priority for the founders of our nation a hundred years ago. It is the right priority now."

Priority public: the supreme legacy of Henry Parkes

Susan Ryan
25 May 2001

An address commemorating the 186th birthday of Henry Parkes and his first entry into Parliament, in the Strangers' Dining Room of the New South Wales Parliament.

PARKES' OWN STORY is the story of Federation. His political tenacity and driving ideal of a unified nation were crucial to the achievement of the Australian Commonwealth. His personal story, an unsettled childhood of struggle and deprivation, no formal education, emigration from Birmingham via London to Sydney to face more years of poverty and defeat before emerging as a leading political figure, epitomises what the new colonies could offer the immigrants.

That Parkes, without money or connections, responsible for a large family and many failed business ventures could become premier of New South Wales five times is a reminder of the openness of the new social environment that was created here. It was the result of a mixture of necessity and idealism.

In contrast to the England of the industrial revolution, where class, religion and geography were all grounds for discrimination against the mass of people, the colony of New South Wales, in order to survive and prosper needed to reward ability, pragmatism and energy from wherever it emerged.

Hence Henry Parkes became a Father of Federation, and the designer of this state's great public education system. His achievement in education, for which we honour his memory tonight, was not inevitable. Things could have worked out differently, and worse.

Before Henry Parkes had become a person of power and influence in New South Wales, class, race and religious prejudice had already taken root in the colony. The few established denominational schools reflected these old-world values and were supported in general by the colony's rulers. The attractively egalitarian aspects of life that provided opportunity to Henry Parkes and his ilk had sprung up in the colonies along side of and in conflict with the old attitudes of exclusion. Egalitarian sentiment alone was not going to be sufficient to provide the building blocks for a modern democracy. For that great task more was needed.

I want to argue that a strong, robust, inclusive democracy, what I term a social democracy, needs a particular foundation. That foundation has to be a public education system. Parkes believed this, and he established such a system.

It is worth contemplating the significance of this achievement, particularly now when the leaders of our community, and many members of it, seem to have lost a sense of the importance of affording the highest priority to the public system.

In celebrating one hundred years as a federated nation, we find ourselves doing what is unusual for Australians, giving some thought to our nation's history and those who shaped it. Perhaps our current focus on the events of Federation will refresh the memories of our policy makers and remind them of why a hundred years ago in education, priority was given to a public system.

In my own case, the Federation festivities have provided me with many reminders. Although always proud of Australia's democratic traditions, I have never felt any particular pull to the events and personalities that led to the decision that the colonies would federate and form the Commonwealth of Australia. I have been surprised to find myself increasingly engaged by this collective consideration of the origins of our nation. I have started to think about not so much the federal arrangements in themselves (which I must confess caused me many frustrations when I was a Commonwealth minister), but how it was that through this rather clumsy constitutional machinery Australia became one of the first social democracies in the world, and has remained one of the most robust, inclusive and successful.

Such high praise is justified in my view by our early adoption of universal franchise, the extension to women of the right to vote and to stand for parliament,

SUSAN RYAN

The Hon. Susan Ryan AO was appointed as Australia's first Age Discrimination Commissioner on 30 July 2011 for a five-year term. She has also been the Disability Discrimination Commissioner since 12 July 2014. Up until her appointment as Commissioner, Susan had chaired the Australian Human Rights Group since 2008 and the Australian Human Rights Act Campaign Inc. since 2005. She held senior roles in superannuation bodies and governance positions at the University of New South Wales including Pro Chancellor. From 1975 to 1988, Susan was Senator for the ACT, becoming the first woman to hold a Cabinet post in a federal Labor government. She served in senior portfolios in the Hawke government as Minister for Education and Youth Affairs, Minister Assisting the Prime Minister on the Status of Women and Special Minister of State. In 1990, Susan was appointed Officer of the Order of Australia for her contribution to Parliament.

and the rapid move to the provision of universal education. The forward looking section in the Constitution, section 116, that prevented the establishment of any religion, kept church and state separate and guaranteed our secular system of government, should be recognised as contributing greatly to the capacity for social harmony in the newly created democratic nation.

Of course I must qualify my congratulations to Australia. Much has been said recently about the wrong and destructive decision to exclude Aboriginal Australians from this otherwise glorious start to our national democracy. The hurt and dispossession resulting from this exclusion, backed up by decades of harsh and wrong-headed policies remain a hundred years later our most urgent moral issue. One of the first legislative acts of the new federal parliament was to exclude Chinese and other Asians on racial grounds. It has taken us nearly one hundred years to reverse fully this terrible discrimination. So we are flawed and were flawed from the start.

Today, however, in the 186th year of his birth, we honour Henry Parkes, the Father of Federation. It is an occasion for celebration. One hundred years ago flawed as we were, Australians did create a society characterised by an egalitarian ethos, and an effective attention to the needs of individuals and communities through a strong and well resourced public sector. For the mass of people, Australia was the best and fairest country in the world. We can thank Henry Parkes for some of that.

My address to you is called 'Priority Public'. Many of you will recognise this as the theme adopted by a group of citizens alarmed at the decline in support for public education from governments and the community. In this election year Priority Public will campaign to remind politicians and their fellow citizens of a central principle understood, advocated and after much conflict, implemented by Henry Parkes.

The principle is this: for a democratic society to prosper, it must be built on an education system of the highest standard, open to all without fees or religious tests, accessible wherever school age children live. A public system was the right priority for the founders of our nation a hundred years ago. It is the right priority now.

A community debate around the principles of priority public, if it is to produce worthwhile results needs to engage all political parties. I am not a High Court judge nor ever likely to be, so speak to you now free of the fear of prime ministerial rebuke. I am free to report to you how encouraged I was to read of Judge Michael Kirby's strong, intelligent and heartfelt advocacy of public education.

The benefits to society in general of the kind of education Judge Kirby had enjoyed should be apparent to all. It seemed to me strange and worrying that his principled advocacy of this essential element of democracy was attacked as inappropriately 'political'. Surely every political party knows, every leader knows, that the majority of children are educated in the public system, as they have been for one hundred years. It is through the public system that standards are set, curriculum developed, teachers trained, students examined and the broader requirements of business, the professions and community met.

Public education is the theme. Other options outside the state system are variations on the theme. Some variations are more successful than others, some more supportive of democratic values than others. All alternatives depend in one way or another on the public system. For many years now they all have claimed they can survive, in the manner to which they have grown accustomed, only with massive injections of public funds.

This situation has produced the unfair and damaging outcomes of reduced opportunities for many children in public education. A reduction in support for our public schools and universities has been tolerated, even reinforced for many years by both sides of politics.

Despite the Prime Minister's reaction, Judge Kirby's remarks do not apply to only one side of politics. I know very well that a drop in support for public universities and schools has not been 'party political'. Sad as it makes me to admit, Labor as well as Coalition governments can be faulted. Labor I believe allowed the infatuation with economic rationalism to undermine our democratic position on access to universities. Labor, temporarily I hope, put aside our traditional view that funding access to university on the basis of a student's intellectual capacity, not the capacity to pay, was the most important investment a government could make in the nation's intellectual infrastructure. Labor, while properly acknowledging parents' rights, diversity and the correctness of a needs-based approach to funding schools outside the public system, took its eye off the ball when the last schools funding formula was passed into law by the federal parliament.

In this state of New South Wales, while the rhetoric and indeed often the performance is good, planned closures of inner city schools are hard to reconcile with the principle of provision of equal opportunity to all through the public system. It seems, however, that a future Beasley government will be keen to rectify past policy faults, and here in New South Wales, a parliament that has just dedicated a room to the memory of Henry Parkes will surely not permit further erosion of the state's schools.

Coalition parties appear to have much more difficulty with the principles of priority public. A stark comparison from recent budget decisions demonstrates the problem. The legacy of the Howard government will have been to so reduce the operating grants from the Commonwealth to public universities, and to have transferred so much public funding to private schools, that the level of government funding for all of our public universities is now virtually on a par with the level of funding from the Commonwealth alone to private schools. The Commonwealth is the sole provider of public funds to universities. State governments give substantial additional funds to private schools as well as fulfilling their constitutional responsibility to provide public schools.

This is as stark a picture as I can draw of a government getting its priorities wrong. It is time to look again at what Parkes contributed to our national well-being by getting education priorities right.

In acknowledging the great and enduring contribution of Henry Parkes, I don't wish to romanticise his motives, or sanitise his attitudes. He was a man of his time and background, and like all of us, perhaps especially those of us who exercise political power, not without human flaws. He did indeed hold dear the centrality of public education to providing opportunity to all and building an enlightened society where ability and energy rather than privilege would be rewarded.

He was at the same time deeply affected, apparently to the point of paranoia, by the religious and cultural divisions that obstructed enlightened policy making in the colony well before Parkes gained political power. Anti-Irish and anti-Catholic sentiment prevailed in New South Wales and Parkes absorbed it. His over-reaction to the attempted assassination, by a deranged Australian of Irish birth, of Alfred Duke of Edinburgh in 1868 at Clontarf, was not Parkes at his most statesmanlike. But given the depth of religious and cultural divisions, very real problems not of his making, it is understandable that Parkes saw a 'national' or public school system as offering much more than the denominational alternative to social harmony.

As well, he was aware that a unified system would make better use of the always-scarce education funds. His principles and the frustration he felt in trying to implement policies that reflected them are well expressed in the following extract from the parliamentary debate on his 1866 Public Schools Bill. In introducing his bill, Parkes declared that while more than half the children in the colony received no education at all, there were 26 places where two or more schools existed to serve fewer than 100 pupils. He blamed the clergy, of all denominations, for this disparity of provision.

> *...if in a locality where there is only a sufficient number of children to form one good school they (the clergy) would consent to their children being educated side by side, extravagance would be avoided and the means of education would be extended to a number of other children who, while ministers of religion were cavilling over a division of the spoils, were left to moral destitution – to the gaols, and unfortunately to the gallows.*[1]

After one hundred years, things have changed. Or have they? The outcome of the 1866 debate, as has become best practice in Australia's policy making for a pluralist society, was a compromise, but a good one. Parkes' biographer A. W. Martin, to whom I am indebted for my knowledge of Parkes and these events, wrote:

> *In effect, the new Act deferred to the preference of many colonists for denominational schools and guaranteed continued funding for them, but under conditions designed to improve their quality, to moderate clerical control of them and prevent such multiplication of their numbers as would adversely affect the spread of public schools.*[2]

In a later development however, in 1880, Parkes caused the repeal of the 1866 Act, and its replacement by the *Public Instruction Act* of 1880, which removed some of the compromise features. Control of the education system was transferred from the Council of Education to a new Ministry of Public Instruction; State Aid to denominational schools was ended. Education for children between the ages of six and 14 made compulsory. That last measure is surely one of the earliest commitments anywhere to universal education.

State Aid to the private schools did come back on the agenda. The policy of funding these schools according to need, introduced by the Whitlam government and further developed and stabilised by the Hawke government while I was the responsible minister, was and remains the correct policy for our pluralist democracy. Needs-based funding of private schools does not undermine the policy of according the top priority to public education.

I conclude by congratulating the Henry Parkes Foundation for their excellent current work in education, and express the hope that at this time, auspicious because it is both our celebration of Henry Parkes' work, and a centenary of Federation, we may see a renewed commitment throughout our community to the principle of public education as the foundation of our Australian democracy.

Notes:

1 A. W. Martin, *Henry Parkes: A biography*, Melbourne University Press 1980, p. 224.

2 ibid, p. 225.

"What we hold in common in Australia is a civic faith … represented by adherence to the rule of law, parliamentary democracy, the right of free speech, the notions of tolerance and fairness, a preference for equality rather than privilege and a readiness to help one another."

Australia in the 21st century: living in peace and freedom?

Gordon Samuels

24 October 2001

Sir Henry Parkes Memorial School of Arts, Tenterfield NSW.

IN OUR CENTENARY of Federation year we have had the opportunity to look back over the history and events which have brought us to where we are now, to assess the strengths and weaknesses of our present situation, and to look forward to consider how, as a nation, we wish to proceed.

I want here to engage in a similar exercise. In order to maintain focus upon the man whose memory we honour, I will examine some aspects of the federation movement, and then consider in a general way what Parkes' response might be to Australia in the 21st century – its institutions, attitudes and general social structure, and to the immense changes which have taken place in the Australian community since his day.

In his collection of verses called *Fragmentary thoughts* there is a poem called 'The flag', which has these lines:

God girdled our majestic isle
With seas far reaching east and west
That man might live beneath this smile
In peace and freedom ever blest.[1]

Hence my title 'Australia in the 21st century: living in peace and freedom?' The question mark is there to enable me to enquire whether Parkes' vision of Australia's destiny has been realised; and whether Parkes would have greeted with sympathy and approval the Australia and the Australians whom we know today.

PARKES' AUSTRALIA

Parkes, of course, did not live to see the consummation of the cause to which he had devoted a great part of his later years. When therefore I speak of 'Parkes' Australia' I mean, in a proleptic way, the country and its inhabitants as they were in 1901, and the nation and its people which Parkes envisaged as the desired fruits of federation.

Parkes' basic vision of Australia was of a loyal and devoted member of an empire upon which there appeared to be no prospect of the sun ever setting; and he yielded to none in his personal loyalty to the Queen.[2] Parkes saw Australians as almost wholly descended from the Anglo-Celtic heritage, and linked by that 'crimson thread of kinship' to which he famously referred[3] – as indeed in his day they were. In 1901, of the non-Aboriginal population, 95 per cent were either Australian-born or born in Great Britain or Ireland.

Parkes' attachment to the Empire connection was not solely the product of sentiment or emotion. It was generated also by apprehensions concerning the possible incursions of Russian naval vessels in the Pacific, and, later, by fears of French adventurism. These anxieties about the colonies' capacity to defend themselves against an external threat profoundly influenced Parkes' support for federation. In his Tenterfield address, a central theme was the report by the British Major General Sir Bevan Edwards into the organisation and efficiency of the military forces of the colonies. General Edwards advised that the forces of the various colonies should be federated together for operation in unison in the event of war 'so as to act as one great Federal army'.

Parkes dealt at some length with the desirability of what he called 'a great Australian army'. Concluding that this would require the establishment of a central executive government, he passed on to ask the celebrated question 'whether the time had not now arisen for the creation on this Australian continent of an Australian government, as distinct from a local government, and an Australian parliament'. His primary theme indeed was that it being essential to the preservation of the security and integrity 'of these colonies that the whole of their forces should be amalgamated into one great Federal army, feeling this, and seeing no other means of attaining the end, it seemed to him that the time

GORDON SAMUELS

Gordon Samuels AC CVO QC was governor of New South Wales from 1996 to 2001. Born in London in 1923, he was educated at Oxford. After serving in World War II, he was called to the bar and emigrated to Australia in 1949. Serving as a barrister in Sydney, Samuels was made a Queen's Counsel in 1964 and appointed as a judge of the Supreme Court of New South Wales in 1972, then a judge of the New South Wales Court of Appeal in 1974, serving until his mandatory retirement in 1993, aged 70. He became chairman of the Law Reform Commission of New South Wales in 1993, a position he held until he was appointed governor in 1996, and served as chancellor of the University of New South Wales from 1976 to 1994. He died in 2007 aged 84.

was close at hand when they ought to set about creating this great national government for all Australia'.

So Parkes' vision for Australia was essentially of a nation of Britons, maintaining links of loyalty to the Sovereign and the Empire, and protected by the ships of the Royal Navy.

One hundred years later this picture has been significantly altered. The Australian population is still predominantly British in origin, although significantly less so than it was at the time of Federation or just before. The Queen of the United Kingdom remains Queen and Head of State of Australia. But the old Empire has faded into the Commonwealth of Nations and the great change has been the shift in Australia's strategic alliance.

In December 1941, two weeks after the Japanese attack on Pearl Harbor and, incidentally, more than a month before the fall of Singapore, John Curtin made the declaration which was to sever Australia's strategic dependence upon the United Kingdom. He said: 'Without inhibitions of any kind, I make it quite clear that Australia looks to America, free of any pangs as to our traditional links or kinship with the United Kingdom'. In 1951 the American alliance was sealed by the signing of the ANZUS Treaty, whose 50th anniversary we acknowledge this year. Indeed, we have celebrated it by being the first of the two allies to invoke it.

There is, I think, an interesting parallel here. In September 1939 Prime Minister Menzies simply proclaimed that as Britain was at war, Australia was also at war; a conclusion which Parkes would no doubt have applauded. In September 2001, following the terrorist attack on New York, Prime Minister John Howard invoked Article 4 of the Treaty which provides that an attack on one party is an attack on both. But, curiously, he did not do so to summon US aid to Australia, but to pledge, and perhaps to authorise, Australia's support for the United States in any way within Australia's capability.

But, of course, it would be wrong to assign undue significance to anxieties about the defence of the continent as an element in the move to federation.

IDEALISM

Economic and fiscal considerations, and apprehensions about Australia's defence against foreign invaders, were certainly influences upon the federation movement. But it seems to me that historians such as John Hirst[4] and Robert Birrell[5] are correct in arguing that the movement was essentially informed by a kind of idealistic nationalism, which is strikingly exemplified in much of the large quantity of verse – not all of it of memorable quality – which was produced by supporters of the movement, including Parkes himself. The poets hailed the coming federation and attempted to assign an ideological basis for its inevitability. In his Tenterfield Oration, Parkes quoted from a poem by James Brunton Stephens, written in 1877, in support of the argument that federation was inevitable and imminent:

Not yet her day. How long 'not yet?' …
There comes a flush of violet!
And heavenward faces, all aflame
With sanguine imminence of morn
Wait but the sun-kiss to proclaim
The Day of The Dominion born.

It would be surprising these days to find verse introduced into a political speech.

Parkes himself regarded federation as inevitable, and in 1883 wrote to Lord Tennyson, with whom he had been staying in England, saying: 'The future of Australia in which you take so deep an interest will in a few short years surprise the world. The federation in some form or other, of the now existing colonies will come by natural processes'. It will be remembered that at Tenterfield,

Parkes, referring to the formation of the great commonwealth of the United States added: '... surely what the Americans have done by war, the Australians could bring about in peace'.

The poems written in the years approaching Federation provide the best guide to the notions and ideals which inspired the movement.[6] The general theme was that Australia had been called by destiny to federation. The land had but one natural boundary (this rather conveniently overlooked Tasmania) and was a unit 'girt by sea' as Peter McCormick wrote in 1878. The poem in which those words appear became our National Anthem almost exactly one hundred years later. The people who lived within these convenient national frontiers were, it was emphasised, of one race and spoke the same language.

I have already quoted Parkes' poem 'The flag', and there were many other such tributes, often equally dubious geographically, to an ideal land. The theme which runs through all these verses asserts Australia's destiny, ordained by God, and therefore advances federation as a sacred task uncorrupted by ordinary considerations of power or ambition. The terms employed often portray Australia – the country and its flag – as unstained by blood or the other consequences of domestic conflict. This, of course, ignored the frontier wars between the European settlers and the indigenous people which, by 1890 or so, had cost a significant number of lives. The notion of federation was perceived as a Holy Grail in the quest for which the people of Australia were excellent candidates. The poets commonly depicted Australia as a young virgin awaiting her arousal to nationhood.[7] This imagery conjures up not only the Sleeping Princess, but, more aptly perhaps, Brunnhilde, lying on the Valkyrie Rock (girt by flames rather than girt by sea), awaiting the advent of her liberating hero.

For poets such as Farrell and Banjo Paterson, and for that matter for a number of Australian historians of the period or later, the indigenous people simply did not exist, and the conflicts with the European settlers were airbrushed out of history. But the theme of these verses is devout, high-minded, concerned with the moral values which should inform the new polity; and celebrating a movement which had never been born in blood and strife, and would achieve its purposes by the peaceful realisation of manifest destiny.

In the event, the new national identity was established by the orderly, democratic processes of conference, discussion, compromise and the ballot box. There were, of course, disagreements and strong divisions over policy in the shaping of the new constitution. But there was nothing which could be regarded as civil turmoil or unrest or anything likely to stain with blood the pristine country of Farrell and Paterson. No possibility of blood on the wattle.

CITIZENS OF THE NEW COMMONWEALTH

Now, what sort of people were they, who, in 1901, became citizens of this new Commonwealth. I could really say what sort of men were they, because at that time women still played only a limited role in public life; and at public banquets were commonly confined to seats in the gallery, where they fluttered their handkerchiefs in support of the orators who performed prodigious feats at the end of the immense dinners which distinguished every major occasion.

But Parkes had declared for female suffrage in 1887;[8] and in 1889 at the banquet in Tenterfield, women sat down with men for the first time at a public banquet.[9] Thereafter, during the federation campaign places were regularly reserved for ladies at meetings.[10]

Now, the citizens of the new Commonwealth were overwhelmingly British. In 1901, 77.2 per cent of the Australian population, excluding Aboriginal people, were native born, and 18 per cent were born in Great Britain or Ireland. Of the remaining 5 per cent or so only 1 per cent had been born in countries which could be called Asian, these sources being India and China. In 1947, 90 per cent of the population were Australian born and hence less than 10 per cent were born overseas. Of those, 6 per cent were from the British Isles, and only 3 per cent from the rest of the world. The Aboriginal population was only 87,000, having risen from a low point of 74,000 in 1933. The Asian-born or Asian-descended population was even smaller;[11] so that Australia could claim immediately after the Second World War to be 99 per cent white and 96 per cent British,[12] although public statements often put the latter percentage higher'.[13] The major cultural differentiation was not primarily ethnically determined but was between Catholics and Protestants, although reflecting Irish and British origins in most cases.[14]

Hence, 50 years after his death, Parkes would have found the composition of the population of Australia recognisably familiar. This long period of demographic stasis was due to two primary factors. First, the comparatively low level of European immigration between the wars other than from the United Kingdom, and, secondly, to the White Australia Policy, to whose principles Parkes would have been entirely sympathetic, and which was formally established by one of the first legislative acts of the new Commonwealth Parliament.[15] This incorporated the infamous dictation test designed, not as a measure of literacy, but as a means of excluding all non-Europeans from Australia.

It is argued by some that the White Australia Policy, with its exclusion of non-whites from Australia was, at least in its early days, primarily designed to protect white employment, and the wage levels of native-born Australians and

European immigrants. No doubt this was an element in the adoption of the policy. But, fundamentally, it was central to building a white British Australia from which all others would be excluded;[16] thus preserving the unity and egalitarianism which could not be achieved in the face of the racial problems which had beset the United States and South Africa.[17] Parkes expressed his own view about the entry of non-whites in these terms: 'I contend that if this young nation is to maintain the fabric of its liberties unassailed and unimpaired, it cannot admit into its population any element that of necessity must be of an inferior nature and character'.[18]

The commitment of Parkes and his political contemporaries to the exclusion of non-whites from Australia largely reflected the values of their time, and their conviction that the rise of the new nation could be achieved only by maintaining the purity of the priceless heritage of their British ancestry. The crimson thread of kinship must be preserved; and with federation Australia 'would be admitted in the rank of nations, under the noble and glorious flag of the mother land'.[19] White Australia was certainly racist; but it must be acknowledged that it was designed to protect the establishment of Australia as a world in which the dignity of labour and a decent standard of living would be preserved and social harmony maintained.[20]

However, there is a fine distinction between out and out racism, that is the exclusion of those perceived to be inferior, and the purpose of constructing a society which will achieve harmony by the exclusion of those manifesting obvious ethnic and cultural differences. It is difficult to acquit White Australia of fundamental racism when one recalls that *The Bulletin* had 'Australia for the white man' on its masthead until 1961, when it was removed by its new editor, Donald Horne. The civic disabilities of non-Europeans imposed in 1903,[21] which prevented them from acquiring British citizenship in Australia, were not lifted until 1957.

White Australia was removed from the platforms of the Liberal and Labor parties in 1965 and formally abolished by the Whitlam government in 1975. It could not survive the need for Australia to develop and strengthen its relationship with its neighbours in the Asia-Pacific region.

EMERGING MULTICULTURALISM

From the end of World War II there commenced to gather force a considerable change in the ethnic composition of the Australian people. There was a very marked increase in the volume of immigration to Australia. Significant numbers of displaced persons and other European immigrants commenced to flow into

Australia, following the adoption of the immigration program of 1947. As James Jupp points out,[22] the new immigration policy restated the objectives of the old in endeavouring to maintain the British character of Australia, by emphasising the necessity that newcomers assimilate into the dominant local culture. Of course, until 1948[23] Australian citizenship did not exist; and Prime Minister Chifley became, on Australia Day 1949, the very first Australian citizen. The early immigration policy was to bring about as rapid as possible an assimilation of immigrants into one of the two contenders for the role of dominant culture; they would either become Australian or British.

However, assimilation simply did not work. The great majority of immigrants did not wish to relinquish their own distinctive ways of eating, dressing and looking at life, and those – at that stage the majority – who had no, or a very imperfect, knowledge of the English language could not successfully pass as locals. A rather droll and Orwellian acknowledgment that assimilation was no longer the policy of the government came in 1964 when the Assimilation Branch of the Department of Immigration was renamed the Integration Branch.[24]

As soon as Australia dismantled the White Australia Policy and opened its doors to an increasing flow of immigrants from the most diverse cultural, ethnic and racial backgrounds, and as soon as it was evident that the policy of assimilation had failed, it was obvious that it was necessary to establish a legal structure, and encourage a social response, which would ensure that immigrants were treated equally with other Australians and given a fair chance of realising their aspirations.

So, a year or two before the final demise of the White Australia Policy, there came the express declaration by the then Minister for Immigration that Australia was a 'multicultural' society. This statement, one of policy disguised as fact, formally embraced a social determination which was to have a profound effect upon the Australian community. It not only broadened the composition of its people, but sought to change the way in which the people regarded one another; and it inevitably eroded what had seemed to be until then an unassailably monocultural heritage. Its inevitable effect was to weaken Parkes' 'crimson thread of kinship'.

The concept of multiculturalism (a term, incidentally, which we borrowed from Canada) has not always been easy to grasp and define. At its simplest, it entails tolerance of difference, the right of migrants to maintain and pursue their own cultural identity, and an end to the automatic assumption of the superiority of a dominant host culture.

The Department of Immigration and Multicultural Affairs on its home page defines the term 'Australian multiculturalism' as one 'which recognises and celebrates cultural diversity. It accepts and respects the right of all Australians to express and share their individual cultural heritage within an overriding commitment to Australia and the basic structures and values of Australian democracy'.[25]

The policy of encouraging cultural diversity has produced great changes in the ethnic composition of Australia's population. 'Ethnic strength' is a concept which does more than count individuals from different genetic backgrounds. It takes account of intermixture of ethnic origins, by marriage for example, and represents the 'strength' of any particular ethnicity in the total population. In 1947 the ethnic strength of those of Anglo-Celtic origins was almost 90 per cent. In 1999 it was just short of 70 per cent – a considerable dilution.[26]

The effect of multiculturalism in Australia and the uncertainty it generates may be put in this way: 'A new nation has been created: just under six million immigrants have arrived in Australia since 1945 and the percentage of foreign-born residents is ahead of any other immigrant receiving country. But the question mark still hangs over whether the social reality has been embraced, or accepted under sufferance.'[27]

LIVING IN PEACE AND FREEDOM?

Now, let me at this stage return to my title, to my text as it were, and ask whether in this new nation, quite unlike any that Parkes imagined, we do live in the peace and freedom which he regarded as Australia's manifest destiny?

We live free of any external threat save that of international terrorism (which is, of course, an internal threat as well), which recent events have so tragically emphasised. We share a head of state with the United Kingdom, but we have been fully independent at least since 1986, when the Australia Acts vested the powers of the Queen in the state governors, abolished appeals to the Privy Council, and terminated any responsibility of the United Kingdom Government in relation to state matters.[28]

Our individual freedoms are preserved by our adherence to parliamentary democracy, the rule of law and the right of free speech. We have a generally adequate system of social services and industrial regulation, and a standard and availability of public education which, although often the object of lively criticism would, I think, have satisfied Parkes. We may say that we have freedom to live unfettered lives, to make our own choices, and to pursue our individual aspirations as successfully as our talents and determination permit.

So I think that we can probably render a favourable account to Parkes on the score of freedom. What about peace? We live at peace with other nations, and it does not seem probable that such tensions as inevitably do exist are likely to be translated into active hostility in the foreseeable future.

What then of the internal or domestic peace of the Australian community? Here there must be a substantial negative, arising from a phenomenon which Parkes would almost certainly never have considered. We cannot conscientiously assert that our society is a peaceful one until we have a solution to the wholly unsatisfactory state of relations between the indigenous and non-indigenous communities. The need for reconciliation, that is to say, to bring into harmony their different, and sometimes conflicting, cultural norms and aspirations, is a pressing social imperative. It requires the urgent substitution of action for the rhetoric which relieves but does not build.

We must bring to the task a greater degree of mutual candour and objectivity than that employed so far. Non-indigenous people must look steadily and without bias at the violent encounters and the destruction of traditional indigenous culture which the historical background, however conservatively assessed, really reveals. And Aboriginal leaders must accept honest and constructive criticism of their own position and arguments. To my mind, we must establish a workable accord within the frame of contemporary Australian society before we can claim that we live together in peace.

It remains finally to consider one further threat to the peace of our community. This is one which Henry Parkes would certainly have identified as a likely consequence of cultural diversity. The question is whether we can continue to maintain a place for separate and diverse cultural identities while maintaining also that degree of social cohesion without which any community may face the risk of practical disintegration.

SOCIAL COHESION

It has been said that there are three key concepts involved in the multicultural philosophy: maintenance of social cohesion, equality, and respect for cultural identity.[29] Equality speaks for itself; but 'respect for cultural identity' is a concept which for my own part I would query. You must respect the right of other people to be different; but you need not respect the essence of their different behaviour. You are required, however, to tolerate it; provided, of course, that it is not illegal or socially disruptive. I think that tolerance rather than respect is the key word in this context. It is, after all, naïve to imagine that members of different cultural or religious groups are to love one another;[30] but if they tolerate one another first, respect, at least, may follow.

It seems to me that the concept of social cohesion is the one which is problematic. Cohesion – that is sticking together – is obviously essential for the survival of any society. Equally plainly, that cohesion will be affected by the presence within the community of different and perhaps incompatible, and even hostile, cultural identities and practices. But the criteria of multiculturalism entail that room must be made for all of them.

Social cohesion requires that newcomers must learn to speak the language, be aware of and obey the laws and abandon social practices which are plainly contrary to Australian cultural values. The requirement that minority cultural groups should comply with Australian cultural norms presents a conflict which is not easy to resolve. Certainly no racism or discrimination is involved in disagreement, even of the most vehement kind; or in seeking to persuade others to modify or abandon certain of their cultural practices. At the same time the goal of cohesion should not be used to justify the imposition on a minority of the values of a dominant group. The problem is to differentiate between those values which are necessary for cohesion, and those which may be adjusted to allow for the tolerance of diversity.[31]

Social cohesion is commonly ensured by a sense of common identity or what has been called common belonging or self understanding.[32] This measure of self understanding defines the values which the members of the community hold in common, and which they wish to preserve; or, at least, those which they believe they hold in common and wish to preserve. As Donald Horne has suggested,[33] what we hold in common in Australia is a civic faith, which, I think, may be said to be represented by adherence to the rule of law, parliamentary democracy, the right of free speech, the notions of tolerance and fairness, a preference for equality rather than privilege and a readiness to help one another. These are values which are capable of adoption by disparate ethnic or cultural groups; and these shared standards will go a long way towards holding together the elements of our multicultural society.

EMOTIONAL KINSHIP

But adherence to these constitutional standards, which is essentially what they are, is to my mind insufficient to provide the whole of the social cement demanded. Cohesion needs some kind of perceived emotional kinship; 'such emotional symbols of collective identification as the National Anthem, the flag, national ceremonies, rituals and monuments to dead heroes'.[34]

Moreover, we need a common frame of reference, in which we can find the shared ideas, familiar values and responses which enable us to communicate with each other, and to care about and trust one another. The need for shared symbols, and the uneasiness which may be felt if they are lacking, has been well summed up by James Jupp in this way:

> *Australia 50 years ago was predominantly a British country and said so with pride, and now it's not, it's something else. But we haven't quite decided what else it is so we call it multicultural. The reason a lot of people are uncomfortable with it is because they are conservative – they want to conserve things as they were, and the thought there might be several million Australians who don't give a stuff about Don Bradman, and don't know who he was, will be shocking to them.*[35]

If one substitutes W. G. Grace or Darling for Don Bradman, the thought would probably have shocked Parkes. I confess it rather shocks me.

But this is, I think, an atavistic and somewhat irrational response and, in any case, the likelihood of this particular amnesia occurring is not overwhelming. The majority of those of our immigrants who come from India, Pakistan, Sri Lanka, Bangladesh and South Africa are committed to cricket and have certainly heard of Don Bradman. A lot of Scots, Welsh and Irish who have never been known for their devotion to the game, probably have not.

Resistance to change, in the context of social or community affairs often takes the form of what I might call the 'white picket fence' view of history, which is often accompanied by the 'white blindfold' view, and harks back to some imagined earlier time of peace, order and security. But the truth is that in the affairs of nations there has rarely if ever been such a time. In Parkes' day, for example, there was considerable sectarian animosity between Catholics and Protestants which reflected the deep divisions between the Irish and the English, convicts, settlers and native born. Parkes himself was largely responsible for promoting the Fenian conspiracy (which never in fact existed) in justification for the execution of the mad Irishman O'Farrell for the attempted murder of the Duke of Edinburgh in 1868.[36] Parkes spoke of Britons, but regarded himself as an Englishman.[37]

In the middle of the Waverley Cemetery in Sydney there stands an impressive stone and marble structure, erected by the people of Ireland and sympathisers in Australia, originally built in 1898, but with more recent additions, in memory of the Irish patriots, who died in the struggle against England.

We hardly regard this as a provocation or call to schismatic disunity, despite its trenchant criticism of our English ancestors. We are accustomed in Australia to the idea that one can be both Scottish and Australian, or Irish and Australian, or Chinese or Macedonian and Australian. Such multiple identities and sympathies are acceptable, provided that they do not involve conflicting allegiance, or prejudice overriding loyalty to Australia. They must not promote or permit the active persistence in Australia of hatreds generated in other places.

To describe a society as multicultural is not to imagine a federation of distinct and separate cultural groups, each living within its own boundary. Cultures change and evolve, both in their pristine and imported identities. In Australia there is a constant process of integration. The ethnic composition of our population is fluid and its character changes. At present, at least 60 per cent of the Australian people are ethnically mixed, while about 20 per cent have at least four distinct ancestries. 'In fact, the fastest growing ethnic group is not the Chinese, Lebanese, Filipino or any other rapidly growing immigrant group, but the category of people who are of mixed ethnic origins.'[38]

The fundamental rule of multiculturalism has been, and remains, to avoid discrimination against minority cultures. It is now firmly enshrined in our law. Multiculturalism, of course, may create another class of persons who feel the injustice of discrimination. Typical of this response is the criticism made by the poet, Les Murray, that multiculturalism denigrates the Anglo-Celts and the farming people, and 'the majority of Australians who are born in this country, those that have mainly British ancestry … '[39]

It is said that this response stems from the resentment of the once dominant Anglo-Celtic group at the erosion of their privileged position. I think rather that those in that group see themselves, with justification, as having been primarily responsible for the creation of modern Australia, and regard the tolerance of other and different cultures as a rejection of that undoubted achievement.

I do not myself believe that it is; but I imagine that Henry Parkes might have been inclined to think so. The Irish monument in Waverley Cemetery reminds us that years before Australia had heard of multiculturalism there were discords and frictions between the two major ethnic components of the European settlers. But the nation has survived, and grown stronger.

NEW PATTERNS OF DIVERSITY

We have managed our new phase of multiculturalism with considerable success. Despite some Hansonian hiccups our new nation is settling very well into its more diverse, and richer, pattern. We have never had the race riots which have recently disfigured both England and Germany, and this is a tribute to the generally tolerant and fair atmosphere of Australian society.

It is clear, I think, that our immigration program must and will continue, and that, accordingly, we must continue to accept cultural diversity, and to cultivate and exploit its undoubted benefits. There is no other way open to us. Our nation will change, and there will be more people with hitherto unusual names playing cricket for Australia. Our new sporting idols may be basketballers or soccer players; or, indeed, rugby stars because that is surely the international winter game of the future.

We can allay any apprehension that Parkes might feel by assuring his benevolent presence that even in 2025, on present indications, the ethnic strength of the Anglo-Celts will be a solid 62 per cent. I hope that, were he able to see it, Parkes would generally approve our Australia, and the standards and achievements of the nation he did so much to create.

I like to think that Sir Henry would have been as formidable on television as he was on the hustings. I feel sure he would have warmly embraced any community which was able to deploy the means of beaming him into every home across the nation.

Parkes was one of our greatest men. I am proud that I have been able to share in this tribute to his memory.

Notes:

1 Parkes, Henry, *Fragmentary thoughts*, S.E. Lees, Sydney, 1889.
2 See, for example, Parkes' remarks in June 1849 at the massive demonstration at Circular Quay against the continued landing in New South Wales of transported convicts: Robert Travers, *The life and times of Sir Henry Parkes*, Kangaroo Press, 2000, p. 53 (hereafter Travers).
3 At the dinner for the Federation Conference in Melbourne in 1890.
4 In Hirst, John, *The sentimental nation*, OUP, Melbourne, 2000 (hereafter Hirst).
5 In Birrell, Robert, *A nation of our own*, Longman, Melbourne, 1995 (hereafter Birrell).
6 Hirst, p. 15.
7 John Farrell, and Banjo Paterson, 'Song of the Future'.
8 Hirst, p. 83.
9 *Tenterfield Star*, 26 October 1889.
10 Hirst, p. 148.
11 Jupp, James, *Immigration*, OUP, Melbourne, 2nd edn 1998 (hereafter Jupp), p. 132 and Appendix IV, p. 192.
12 ibid.
13 Jupp, p. 132.
14 ibid.
15 *Immigration Restriction Act 1901*; repealed by the *Migration Act 1958*.
16 Jupp, p. 73. For a somewhat different view, see Birrell p. 12.
17 See, for example, Kelly, Paul, 'Pride of Race' in *The Australian*, 12 March 2001.
18 See Lyne, Charles E., *Life of Sir Henry Parkes*, George Robertson & Co, Sydney, 1896 (hereafter Lyne) pp. 476–7.
19 Lyne, p. 494.
20 Hirst, p. 22.
21 *Commonwealth Naturalisation Act 1903*.
22 Jupp, p. 134.
23 *Nationality & Citizenship Act*.
24 Jupp, p. 138.
25 And see the *Community Relations Commission & Principles of Multiculturalism Act* 2000 (NSW), s 3(b).
26 Price, Charles, 'Australian Population: Ethnic Origins' in *People and Place*, Vol.7, no.4, pp. 12 et seq.
27 Stevenson, Andrew, *Sydney Morning Herald*, 26 September 2001, p. 13.
28 *Australia Act, 1986* (Cwlth) passim.
29 By George Zubrzycki, the author of the pioneering report made by the Ethnic Affairs Council in 1977, *Australia as a multicultural society*.
30 cf *Donoghue v Stevenson* (1932) AC 562 at 580 per Lord Atkin.
31 Australian Law Reform Commission Report No 57, *Multiculturalism & the law*, 1992, para 1.23.
32 Parekh, Bhikhu, 'Defining National Identity in a Multicultural Society' in *People, Nation and State*, Ed. Mortimer & Fine, I B Tauris, London, 1999 pp. 66 et seq.
33 'Something Fishy in the Mainstream?', Barton Lecture No 1, 2001.
34 See note 32.
35 By James Jupp, Director of the Australian National University Centre for Immigration & Multicultural Studies.
36 Travers, pp. 162–6.
37 Travers, p. 91.
38 Price, Charles, 'Australian population: ethnic origins' in *People and place*, Vol. 7, No. 4, p. 12.
39 Quoted by Ellie Vasta in *The teeth are smiling (the persistence of racism in multicultural Australia)*, Ch. 3, p. 57.

"The first lesson is that if the people have got the bit between their teeth, then even a united stance by the political elite may be insufficient to prevent change, indeed in the present climate of opinion may even enhance its prospects."

A republican president or a presidential republic?

Neal Blewett

26 October, 2004

National Library of Australia, Canberra ACT

HENRY PARKES was one of the great figures of Australian politics. One measure of his greatness is that on nearly all the great issues that face this country he had something to say. Not infrequently, as in the case of the current subject, the republic, he can be found on both sides of the argument. He was at one time an enthusiastic supporter of the reverend John Dunmore Lang, our first notable republican, though he soon became disillusioned with both Lang and his republic.

Now to the terminology used in this lecture: The 'republican president' of the title is shorthand for 'a-republic-with-a-president'. 'Ah, but don't all republics have a president?' comes the query. At this stage I will cite the Humpty Dumpty justification: 'When I use a word it means just what I choose it to mean – neither more nor less.' By 'a-republic-with-a-president' I mean a republic in which the president is merely a political bit player, called upon only rarely and occasionally to play a political role. And by 'a presidential republic' I mean a republic in which the president is the key political actor, playing a day-to-day political role.

Obvious examples of republic-with-a-president systems are Germany and Italy; the classic example of the presidential republic is of course the United States.

It is important to stress that the essential distinguishing mark between a republic-with-a-president and a presidential republic is the nature of the political role of the president. In both systems the president performs similar ceremonial functions as head of state. While it is probably necessary for the president in a presidential republic to have some clear mandate, usually through popular election, presidents in a republic-with-a-president can also be popularly elected. For example Ireland, Iceland, Portugal and Austria are all examples of republics in which the president is merely a political bit player yet is elected by popular election. I stress again that it is the political function that distinguishes the two systems: in the presidential republic the president is at the heart of the political executive, indeed often *is* the political executive, a day-to-day player in politics; whereas in the republic-with-a-president the president is merely a minor political actor, the role of the day-to-day political executive being performed by someone else, usually the prime minister and Cabinet.

At this point I suspect that the political scientists among you are muttering 'Why does he go on with all this "Alice through the looking-glass" nonsense? What he means by a "republic-with-a-president" is what we simply call a "parliamentary republic". So what he really is talking about is a parliamentary republic versus a presidential republic.' They are of course right and I will soon abandon the clumsy term 'republic-with-a-president' in favour of the term 'parliamentary republic'.

But there was a purpose in this clumsy terminology, this 'Alice through the looking-glass' approach. If we frame the debate as parliamentary republic versus presidential republic then at least in British Commonwealth countries we make it too English, too comfortable, too cosy. The words bias the argument in favour of the parliamentary republic. 'Parliamentary republic': two nice words and no mention of that alien thing – a president. Also 'parliamentary republic' emphasises that good thing – a parliament – while 'presidential republic' suggests there might not be a parliament at all. Yet in the classical presidential republic, the USA, the parliament – the Congress – performs most of the functions of a modern parliament more effectively than any parliament in a parliamentary republic. Just think of the various parliamentary enquiries on aspects of the war in Iraq that have emerged from the British House of Commons, the Australian Parliament, and the American Congress. I think there would be little doubt that the most hard-hitting and the most effective reports in challenging the executive and keeping it on its toes have emerged from the American Congress.

NEAL BLEWETT

The Hon. Neal Blewett AC has had a varied career as academic, politician, and diplomat. A Tasmanian Rhodes Scholar, he taught successively at the universities of Oxford and Adelaide and became Professor of Political Theory and Institutions at Flinders University. He has written books and articles on British and Australian history and politics. As Health Minister in the Hawke government he was responsible for the introduction of Medicare and Australia's AIDS policy. His diary of the Keating government was published in 1999. From 1994 to 1998 he was Australian High Commissioner in London as well as a member of the Executive Board of the World Health Organization. He now writes, gardens and walks in the Blue Mountains.

Thus, while from now on I will use the terms 'parliamentary republic' and 'presidential republic', one should always remember that parliamentary republics have presidents and that the classic presidential republic has a distinguished parliament.

Having for the moment disposed of terminology let me examine the state of the republican question in Australia in the aftermath of the referendum of 1999.

DEATH OF THE 'MINIMALIST' MODEL?

First I make an assumption that is debatable and will need to be argued through: that the defeat of the republican referendum in 1999 ended the possibility of a conservative or minimalist republic in Australia. This assumption derives much of its plausibility from a common political proposition that the longer the inevitable is denied or resisted the more radical the outcome is likely to be. There is a classic example from within the British political tradition. If any one of the Home Rule for Ireland bills of 1885, 1895 or 1912 – granting Ireland a degree of autonomy within the United Kingdom – had been passed then it is likely that today Ireland would still be part of a probably federal United Kingdom. Instead the essentially conservative proposals were each rejected and a more radical solution emerged – an Ireland independent from the United Kingdom.

I suggest that a similar move from conservative to more radical solutions is likely for the republic in Australia.

In 1999 the Australian people were offered by referendum the most minimal of parliamentary republican models. Well perhaps not quite the most minimal. There was floating around the so-called McGarvie model whereby nothing was changed except that the governor-general (McGarvie was not keen on the title 'president') would be appointed and dismissed by a Constitutional Council, in place of the Queen, acting on the advice of the prime minister. The Constitutional Council was to be composed of three distinguished and elderly Australians – maximum age of 79 – drawn from retired governors-general, retired governors and retired judges.

The model was virtually identical with the status quo. It could well be described as the republican model for those who did not want a republic. It is perhaps a commentary on late 20th century Australian democracy that this extraordinary proposal was not simply laughed out of court. Neville Wran did his best, suggesting that with so many septuagenarians on the Constitutional Council 'you would have to send the wagon around to all the nursing homes to get a complement'.[1] But the McGarvie model served various political purposes. It provided a refuge for faint-hearted republicans, mainly of Liberal persuasion; it was an instrument which could be used to compel mainstream republicans to minimise their own proposals; and in the end it was used as the vehicle at the Constitutional Convention to see off the radical and dangerously seductive model of a directly elected president.

The minimalist proposal ultimately put to the people was an advance on the McGarvie model but there was little else to be said for it. It was proposed to establish a president with powers identical to those of the governor-general, the president to be nominated by the prime minister, from a non-binding shortlist of three prepared by a broadly representative nominations committee, and confirmed by a two-thirds vote of the parliament. In essence the nomination was in the hands of the prime minister though he would need the prior agreement of the opposition leader in order to secure the two-thirds vote of the parliament, and in practice it would be difficult for the leaders to move away from the names on the shortlist. The power to dismiss the president lay unequivocally with the prime minister, requiring as it did simply the backing of a majority vote in the House of Representatives. Any codification of the undefined reserve powers in order to clarify the powers of the president and his relations with the prime minister was eschewed as too difficult and likely to arouse controversy.

Apart from the inclusion of the nominations committee – a sop to those who favoured direct popular election of the president – the minimalist model put at the referendum represented a retreat by the mainstream republican movement during the course of the 1990s. Originally they had favoured both appointment and dismissal by a two-thirds vote of the parliament, Malcolm Turnbull arguing impeccably in 1993 that 'establishing a two-thirds majority in a joint sitting as the pre-requisite for removal eliminates any prospect of the president being sacked simply because he or she has offended the government of the day'. However, as the defenders of the existing parliamentary order, particularly the McGarvyites, pointed out if a president breached the unwritten conventions in order to favour the opposition as against the government the prime minister would be unable to get the two-thirds majority to get rid of the president, given that in modern times no government has ever had a two-thirds majority in the parliament. The mainstream republicans acquiesced and so the power of dismissal rested with the prime minister backed simply by a majority vote in the House of Representatives.

The mainstream republicans had originally favoured codification of the reserve powers either through spelling them out in the Constitution or by empowering the parliament to define them in legislation. In the mid-90s Malcolm Turnbull had dismissed the refusal to codify calling it 'the ultra-minimalist solution' and advanced compelling reasons for codification: 'first, just as good fences make for good neighbours, so do clear ground rules make for stable and predictable government ... second ... it is quite wrong in a democracy such as ours to have fundamental elements in our democratic system left to so-called unwritten rules or conventions'.[2] Yet under the pressures of the Constitutional Convention he and his allies succumbed to 'the ultra-minimalist' solution – no codification.

On 6 November 1999 this minimalist proposal went down to resounding defeat, rejected in all states and territories except the ACT, and overall by 6.4 million votes to 5.3 million. And yet it was supported by the bulk of the media and probably by a majority of the great and the good. What went wrong?

It is easy in retrospect to see the flaws in the minimalist model. So easy in fact that a conspiracy theory has developed which posits that the Machiavellian Prime Minister, in cahoots with his monarchist allies, schemed to secure the emergence of this model from the Constitutional Convention as the one least likely to seduce monarchists on the one hand or arouse the enthusiasm of republicans on the other. The minimalist proposal certainly split the republicans with an embittered minority of direct electionists supporting the 'No' case. It certainly lent itself to easy caricature – damned as 'the politicians' republic', the president 'a prime minister's puppet', presidential selection left to 'the political deal-makers'. (These quotes are from the intellectually disreputable but emotively powerful official 'No' case on the referendum.)

The alienation of the populace from the political class was widespread in western democracies at the end of the 20th century, though Australia was probably unique in that leading members of the political class were at the forefront of the self-denigration. The minimalist proposal certainly mobilised little enthusiasm among the population at large, the nationalist appeal of 'an Australian as head of state' lacking the popular resonance possessed by the demonisation of the 'politicians' republic'.

This demonisation has made it very difficult, probably impossible, to resurrect the minimalist model. It is inevitable that the next proposal must represent an advance on minimalism and that almost certainly will involve a popularly elected president. But as noted earlier that will still offer us a choice of republics – between a parliamentary republic or a presidential republic, that is between a republic in which even though elected the president is essentially, as regards politics, a bit player, or a republic in which the president is the key figure in the political executive. And such are the variety of possibilities beyond our shores that these two systems – a parliamentary republic or a presidential republic – represent but each end of a continuum with many models in between, the most obvious of these hybrids being the quasi-presidential republic of France.

Yet if we are to explore these other options we need to understand why the intelligent and experienced leadership of the mainstream republican movement – and remember the model was as much Paul Keating's as it was Malcolm Turnbull's – chose a model which ended ultimately in the debacle of November 1999. Why did they turn away from other less minimalist models? There were indeed very powerful reasons for adopting the course that they did and anyone seeking to advance the republican cause needs to ponder them.

The mainstream republicans were haunted by the history of referendum failure in Australia. They drew from it three lessons. First, change had to be as simple as possible to minimise negative red herrings. This served a key tactical purpose as well. 'The Australian Republican Movement's platform had to be as simple and as short as possible', wrote Turnbull, 'so that our opponents would be left without anything to defend except the monarchy itself.' This was to underestimate the ingenuity of the monarchists. Secondly, anything that was not absolutely necessary to the change should be jettisoned. 'We could not afford', warned Turnbull, 'to encumber ourselves with radical baggage that would impede the achievement of our core objective.'[3] Ultimately that meant the jettisoning of nearly all baggage, radical or otherwise. Thirdly, from the few successes and the many failures in referendum history they drew the lesson that a referendum could only succeed if both major parties were behind the proposal or at least did not oppose it. Throughout the 1990s the Australian Republican Movement hoped that the Liberals could be brought on board and that this could be done by advancing the most modest and conservative of republics. That is why, although the divisive shadow of Paul Keating may have brooded over the Constitutional Convention, his name was scarcely mentioned. All three lessons pointed towards the most minimal of solutions.

I will suggest in a moment that we Australians have perhaps been too dominated by these so-called lessons. We have allowed our imaginations to become too cribbed and confined by referendum failure and that bolder, sweeping more imaginative change, particularly if it can galvanise and resonate with the public, may be the way to go. David Solomon has suggested that the 'widespread public discontent with politicians and the political process might be tapped and harnessed by proposals that make the governance and political system more open and accountable'.[4] Certainly there is an example that points in that direction from across the Tasman.

But it was not simply the lessons of referendum failure that influenced the minimalism of the republic proposal. There was in all the leading republican protagonists – from Keating perhaps above all – an unquestioned conviction that the Westminster system of an executive selected from and responsible to the parliament was the best of all possible political worlds. It was of course one which gives political supremacy to the prime minister provided he maintains the mastery of his party and through it the control of the parliament. Anything in the passage towards a republic that threatened the balance of that system, in other words the supremacy of the prime minister, was anathema. As Keating instructed the Republic Advisory Committee, they must devise a method of replacing the Queen and the governor-general but in so doing to examine no options 'which would otherwise change our structure of government'. This conservatism guaranteed that the republican proposal would be minimal. I will suggest later that this involves too rosy an evaluation of the Australian version of the Westminster model.

The republicans recognised that their minimalist, conservative project was hardly likely to galvanise the masses. Keating seems to have instinctively realised this, his radical nationalist tirades providing a camouflage for the very modesty of his proposal. Yet cooler heads around the Prime Minister and in the republican movement recognised that such tirades were counter-productive, for a conservative republic could come only through the support of the right and the prime ministerial remarks tended to alienate the very conservatives whose support the republicans would need. The Australian Republican Movement's hope all along was that if the Liberal leadership could be got into the republican cart then the fact that the minimalist proposals did not stir the people's imagination would not matter.

The symbolic issues of the republic, which stirred intellectuals, found little purchase with the broader population and the tepid nationalism of the republican cause seems to have had little resonance with the masses. Australian-born men had been governors-general for a generation while the Queen, a hard-working kindly old matron with a dysfunctional family, aroused sympathy rather than antipathy and anyhow didn't seem to have much to do with Australian governance. Perverse monarchists further confused the matter by claiming that the governor-general was really our head of state or, echoing Sir Henry Parkes, claimed that we were already 'a crowned republic'. Most importantly of all, anti-monarchical nationalist rhetoric was simply bypassed when the monarchists decided not to defend the monarchy as such but rather to concentrate their energies on demonising 'the politicians' republic'.

Minimalist republicans might not agree with me that the minimalist option is now dead, particularly in the light of the cogent reasons for adopting it in 1998–99. They would argue that its defeat in 1999 was due to peculiar and contingent political circumstances unlikely to be permanent. Above all they would argue that if John Hewson or Peter Costello had been Liberal leader rather than John Howard then there could well have been effective bipartisan support for the minimalist model. With Howard's eventual passing a new bipartisan alliance could be consummated around the minimalist model ensuring its triumph in a future referendum. Thus there would be no need to contemplate such dangerous options as popularly elected presidents.

These seem to me to be counsels of extraordinary optimism. They ignore the extent to which the republican movement itself has been radicalised by defeat, hesitant to advocate ever again a minimalist model. They ignore the extent to which the trend within the Labor Party, already apparent before the referendum, in favour of a popularly elected president has been accelerated by the referendum defeat. They ignore the extent to which the conservative community has been galvanised against anything that has the taint of 'a politicians' republic'. They ignore the extent to which the demonisation of the 'politicians' republic' has made the minimal option something from which most politicians would keep their distance. Above all they ignore the extent to which the notion of a popularly elected president has become rusted on in Australian public opinion, has become the indispensable condition for the people's acquiescence in a republic.

If we abandon minimalism there is probably no escaping the popular election of the president. Indeed probably the most minimal model that is now viable is Western Australian Premier Geoff Gallop's proposal that the parliament nominate three candidates on whom the electorate would vote. Given that the politicians would dominate the nomination process even this might no longer be acceptable. Whatever process we adopt, a directly elected president does not, of course, commit us to a presidential republic: we could still have a parliamentary republic like Ireland, Austria, Iceland or Portugal, in which most political powers lie with the prime minister and Cabinet, not with the directly elected president.

ELECTING THE PRESIDENT IN A PARLIAMENTARY REPUBLIC

I will examine the parliamentary republic option first. I will not propose any detailed model but simply canvass the major issues involved.

Three arguments are commonly advanced against popular election of the president. First that it would deter the great and the good from becoming our head of state for such figures would not submit themselves to popular election and possibly popular dismissal. This seems to me an argument that can be truly labelled elitist (I hesitate to use the term given its perverse use in recent debates but here I think it appropriate). Yet if we remove monarchical mystique as the basis of authority in the polity then in a democracy we can only rest authority on the people. If someone is too fastidious to submit him or herself to the rough and tumble of the popular arena, that would seem to disqualify such a person as a suitable head of state of a genuine democratic republic.

Dismissal of a president, as we have seen with the minimalist model, always raises difficulty. Obviously an elected president could not be summarily dismissed by the prime minister or the parliament. We can go a long way to obviate any need for dismissal on political grounds by carefully specifying and circumscribing presidential powers. In the case of other grounds for dismissal – misbehaviour, unfitness for office, bringing office into disrepute, incapacity – a judicial finding endorsed by a two-thirds majority of the parliament would probably be the way to go.

Secondly it is argued that popular election would inevitably guarantee that we would get a politician as president. To prevent a plethora of weird candidates we would need tight electoral rules specifying large numbers of voters for nomination and significant sums for deposits, which would favour the party organisations. Yet the parties themselves might well choose distinguished non-partisan figures in order to sway the undecided in the electorate. And anyhow if the parties did offer the electors only a choice between politicians I suspect people would themselves prefer to choose a politician as their president rather than leave it to the politicians to choose a non-politician as president without any reference to the people.

Thirdly it is argued that the popular election of the president would upset the delicate balance between the parliamentary executive and the head of state, between the prime minister, indirectly elected, and the president, directly elected. 'If a new Australian head of state were to be elected by popular mandate,' warned Paul Keating, 'he or she would inherit a basis of power that would prove to be fundamentally at odds with our own Westminster-style of government'.[5] For once John Howard agreed with him, putting the position more bluntly: 'Direct election of the president would inevitably create a rival power centre – and I mean a political power centre – to that of the prime minister'.[6] When Keating and Howard agree ordinary Australians should be on their guard.

On one point there is unanimity: to enhance the legitimacy and hence the authority of the president by direct election yet to leave the shadowy monarchical powers in our Constitution untouched would be to create a potential monster. There is also agreement on what follows from this: if we were to have an elected president then we would have to spell out in some way the reserve powers and the unwritten constitutional conventions that govern their use. To recognise the prime minister – at present not mentioned in the Constitution – and to spell out how the prime minister would be appointed by the president and possibly dismissed by the president, and the conditions under which the president would grant or deny a prime minister a dissolution of the House of Representatives or a double dissolution of both houses, would be invaluable in itself. There would be much to be said for presidents, prime ministers and school kids being provided in the Constitution with an outline of the mechanisms of executive authority. It would make the Constitution an instrument for understanding rather than, as it is at the moment, an impediment to understanding. It was a pity the Constitutional Convention ducked this issue in 1998. It cannot be ducked if we have an elected president.

Such codification is not, as has sometimes been suggested, beyond the wit of man. Every European parliamentary republic designed since World War II, and there have been a host of them, has with considerable success laid down the ground rules establishing the relationship between president and parliamentary executive. McGarvie himself, who instinctively disliked the idea of codification, nevertheless provided the philosophical basis for such codification: the essence of a convention is its constitutional rationale. Much work has already been done in Australia on the necessary codification by the Constitutional Conventions of the 1970s and 1980s, by the Advisory Committee on Executive Government (1987) and by the report of the Republic Advisory Committee in 1993. It would be foolish to pretend that there is as yet a complete consensus but there is a fair degree of agreement on how to spell out most of the ground rules.

There does remain one outstanding issue, which arises from a unique feature of the Australian system: the power of the Senate to reject supply – the source of the greatest gubernatorial crisis in our history. How is the president to respond if a Senate rejects or refuses to pass a budget backed by a majority of the House of Representatives? How do you codify that? The simplest solution would be to remove the power of veto over budgets from the Senate. But this is unlikely to win the support of the Coalition parties and would be resisted by the smaller states.

On the other hand, even today Labor would probably oppose any codification of presidential powers in this matter, which might be taken as endorsing Sir John Kerr's actions in 1975. The most elegant solution so far advanced is that if the Senate blocked supply and the government refused to compromise its position to meet Senate demands, then the government would remain in office until lawfully appropriated funds ran out and the government sought to spend monies not lawfully appropriated, which would be a clear breach of the Constitution. This has the great advantage of ruling out any pre-emptive strike by the president, which was the weightiest of the criticisms of Kerr in 1975. On the other hand it does so by risking the financial integrity of the government and possibly of the nation. However, if this position were clearly set out in constitutional rules then it is unlikely such an ultimate crisis point would be reached.

These are the major constitutional changes that would be required if we were to establish a parliamentary republic with a directly elected president. They would involve considerable re-writing of the Constitution. At this point we might ask ourselves should we go further? Given the constitutional changes required to accommodate a directly elected president, would this facilitate the contemplation of more ambitious changes? Should we seize the opportunity to move towards a presidential republic in which day-to-day political power rests with the president? This would involve borrowing from the American experience – the classical example of the presidential republic – and would entail not merely the reform but the reconstruction of Australian government.

CHALLENGES OF A PRESIDENTIAL REPUBLIC

I am encouraged in contemplating such ambitious questions by those doyens of republicanism Donald Horne and Malcolm Turnbull. In quite general terms Horne has argued that a republic should come 'only as part of one of those great unfolding processes in which the people of a nation discuss things among themselves, trying out this, trying out that, until one of those miracles of democratic society occurs: the people find a new way of seeing themselves, a new consensus.'[7] The more practical and pragmatic Turnbull, contemplating the wreckage of his hopes in late 1999, wrote that next time round 'it is very important that we have a proper debate on the issue of a directly elected president … my preference would be to include two direct-election models: one with a ceremonial president like the governor-general and the other a full-blooded United States-style system, with a president who is also the head of government.'[8] What follows is a modest contribution to that proper debate, to that national discussion.

We should note here that the founding fathers of the Australian nation were much more imaginative, much more ambitious, and much more ready to break with the Westminster model than any of their successors in the past century. They compromised the classic Westminster system by major borrowings from the great democracy across the Pacific. At the very time when conservatives in the United Kingdom were arguing that Westminster and federalism were incompatible, the Australian founding fathers set up a federal structure adapted from that of the USA. In imitation of the American system they established a High Court to interpret the Constitution. The enumeration of powers and the limitations on parliamentary sovereignty were more characteristic of the United States than they were of Westminster. Indeed a plausible case can be made out that a presidential executive of the American type was not seriously considered by the founding fathers chiefly because it was incompatible with Australia remaining a monarchy. A parliamentary executive broke with none of the monarchical traditions inherent in the British system; a presidential executive would have sundered them. Could you possibly have a presidential monarchy?

To make the case for a presidential republic we have first to take a more dispassionate, and thereby inevitably more jaundiced, view of the parliamentary system than usually prevails in this country, and second to stress the virtues of the presidential republic and distinguish them from a host of contingent factors that are not inherent in the system but are often adduced by reference to the United States. An example of the latter is the allegation that only a millionaire can be president of the United States. That may be true but it is not a necessary feature of a presidential republic, merely the result of the particular nominating and primary election processes that have developed in the United States and the prevailing cultural attitudes to the role of money in election financing in that country.

I do not intend to develop the case for a presidential republic as against a parliamentary republic in any detail, but rather to sketch out the major lineaments of the arguments involved. We have noted that the essential difference between a parliamentary republic and a presidential republic is that in the former the president is a ceremonial figure with a minimum political role, with executive power resting in a Cabinet led by a prime minister, while in the latter day-to-day executive powers are exercised by the president.

The essential structural difference in which this contrast is rooted is this: in the parliamentary republic, executive and legislature are fused in a single institution – the parliament – to which the executive, that is the prime minister and Cabinet, belong and to which they are responsible, and which itself has the power to elect and reject the political executive. By contrast in the presidential republic the political executive and the legislature are separate and neither institution can select or remove the other. The advantages and the disadvantages of the two systems flow from this central structural fact.

Paradoxically it is the very power of the parliaments to determine and to bring down governments that has been the source of the decay of parliaments in parliamentary systems with dominant two-party systems during the course of the 20th century. As one American observer has noted 'the parliamentary system formally assumes legislative supremacy, [but] in fact assures the almost unassailable dominance of the executive over the legislature'.[9] Given that parliaments have the formal power to bring governments down, governments have set out to ensure that this never happens.

Their instrument has been the modern tightly disciplined political party. Provided the party leadership can retain control of the party's MPs – and they have developed a fine array of sticks and carrots to do so – they need have no fear of parliament. Rather than parliaments bringing governments to account, parliaments, or at least their lower houses to which governments are usually responsible, have been turned into rubber stamps for the actions of the executive. The result is that in Australia we have between elections an elected or democratic dictatorship. I do not want to exaggerate this point. I mean simply that between elections citizens have little power to influence an executive determined to carry through its programs.

There are of course institutional constraints on the authoritarian inclinations of the executive government. Its great power is tempered by the Senate – over which, because of its electoral system, governments have had no control for a generation, though this may be about to change – by the states with their constitutionally allocated powers, by the High Court and its role in constitutional interpretation, and above all by the prospect of the next election.

By contrast, in presidential systems where neither executive nor legislature is responsible to the other, parliament has retained much of its authority. As one English observer noted a generation ago 'as a legislature the Congress ... has continued to exercise a degree of independent decision-making power far greater than that retained by the other legislatures of the Western democracies.'[10] It is still true today that despite the accretion of power to the modern presidency – the so-called imperial presidency – there remains a real tug of war between president and Congress, most striking when the party complexions of president and Congress are different, but continuing in more muted forms even when the same party has the presidency and dominates the Congress. Presidents have continually to bargain with the Congress for policies and funds. President Bush cannot assume the acquiescence of the Congress in his budgets or his legislation as can Tony Blair of the House of Commons and John Howard of the House of Representatives.

Of the three functions attributed to a modern parliament – remonstration of individual grievances, scrutiny of legislation, and rendering the executive responsible to parliament – only the first, remonstration of individual grievances, is performed with any distinction by the Australian House of Representatives.

There is no effective scrutiny of legislation in the lower house: the representatives simply rubber stamp the legislative wishes of the government. The principle that the executive has the right to use its majority to get its legislation through the house has made a farce of the subtle mechanisms of the committee and report stages of bills, increasingly simply truncated by the application of the guillotine. This is not true of the Senate where there has been effective scrutiny, particularly through committees, of the government's legislation. But this may be simply a function of an electoral system that has denied the government of the day a majority in the Senate over the course of the last generation. In the years ahead we are likely to discover whether this scrutiny power is inherent in the upper house or simple a function of the electoral system. For the Senate is as permeated by executive influence as the House of Representatives. It is simply that for some time past the executive has not had the numbers.

In the presidential republic, however, the legislature remains a significant legislative body, that is an important maker of legislation. Although the president inevitably initiates most legislation and retains an ultimate veto power over legislation, Congress is no rubber stamp. Both houses of the Congress contribute often significantly to the legislation that emerges and ultimately can override the presidential veto. Thus, unlike the parliamentary system, we have a reciprocal, give-and-take relationship in law-making between president and parliament in the presidential republic.

In Australia the House of Representatives plays little effective role in scrutinising the general operations of government, in asserting the control over the executive that is supposedly the essential characteristic of the Westminster system. In the parliamentary system the accountability of the government to the parliament – the principle that ministers are responsible to parliament for their actions – is a lofty idea with grand traditions but today it is little more than a hollow sham. Provided the Cabinet retains the loyalty of the majority party it cannot be made accountable nor its ministers made responsible.

The most authoritative text on the Australian Parliament concludes that ministerial responsibility is 'entirely a question of political judgement'. The notion that a minister must resign for failed actions or administration because he is accountable to the parliament has been junked in practice, as with so much else, although the rhetoric remains. A minister only resigns today if his Cabinet colleagues, or more particularly the prime minister, think it would not be in the political interests of the party to retain him. Much touted as another means of securing effective parliamentary oversight, 'Question time' often provides fine political theatre but rarely much substance. It is perhaps revealing to note that the only monograph to study question time in the Australian Parliament is entitled 'Questions without answers'.[11] The standing orders of the House are full of requirements as to what constitutes a question. They are almost totally silent on what constitutes a ministerial answer. That is because it is the executives of both parties which together write the rules for the House of Representatives.

In a presidential republic the president and his Cabinet ministers are not responsible to the legislature and cannot, except in the extraordinary case of a presidential impeachment, be dismissed by the parliament. While, as we have seen, the practical consequences of the responsibility principle have been neutered within Westminster systems, its absence in the presidential republic has paradoxically freed up the legislature to be much more energetic in its oversight and scrutiny of the executive. The powerful Congressional committees of inquiry in the United States have no equivalents in the Westminster system in terms of the energy and depth of their research, in the vigour of their inquisition of Cabinet ministers, and in the hard-hitting nature of their conclusions. This is in part because the Congress of the United States is its own master and not a creature of the executive and thus creates its own rules, determines its own research needs, finds the back-up staff required and allocates the funds that will be invested in Congressional inquiries.

The decay of parliamentary authority in one system and its survival in the other has had important consequences for the legislators themselves. Few in the Australian Parliament would place commitment to the parliament before commitment to the party. This is because status and authority within the parliament go overwhelmingly to ministers and shadow ministers and these positions are determined by the political parties. Virtually the only worthwhile career path in the parliament is to rise into and through the ranks of the executive or the shadow executive. The whole ethos of the parliament is permeated with the ambition to make one's way in this executive world. Committee chairmanships are but stepping stones to that ambition. Even the speakership of the lower house or the presidency of the Senate is rarely bestowed for distinguished parliamentary service but rather for services to one's party or as compensation for missing out on executive opportunities. A few among the minor parties and the independents do display the characteristics of parliamentarians but this is mostly by default – the executive route is closed to them.

In the parliament of the presidential republic it is very different. Few congressmen will seek and even fewer actually secure executive office. For most of them, including many of the most able, parliament will be their career. I am not suggesting party is not important to them, but that their ambitions through the party will be parliamentary ambitions. There are many parliamentary career pathways through the Congress: majority and minority leadership of the Senate and the House, the speakership of the House, chairmanships of the prestigious committees of the Senate and House – Appropriations, Budget, Rules, Ways and Means in the House of Representatives, Budget, Foreign Relations, Governmental Affairs, Judiciary in the Senate. All play critical parliamentary roles in the management of the Congress, the scrutiny of legislation, the oversight of the executive. Such men of course serve their parties and the achievement of their ambitions is secured through party support. But they also serve the parliament in its never ending struggle with the executive. They are not suborned by an all-powerful executive entrenched within the parliament itself.

One other important contrast arises from the fusion of executive and legislature within one system and their separation in the other. The Australian founding fathers made no formal decision about the executive being responsible to the legislature and there is no reference to such responsibility in the Constitution. What they did decide was that the members of the executive, the ministers, must of necessity be or become members of the parliament. This has meant that the executive has been drawn exclusively from members of parliament, from an extraordinarily limited pool of talent. Moreover with the increasing professionalisation of politics this pool – perhaps pond is more appropriate – has become in a sense more limited. Increasingly the bulk of the ministry and the shadow ministry are made up of men and women who have had no other significant work experience than that of politics.

By contrast the separation of powers by insisting that Cabinet members not be members of Congress opens up the heart of executive government to all the talent in the community. The president can choose his Cabinet from all walks of life. He usually does choose some from the Congress, who must give up their seats there, but otherwise he chooses businessmen, soldiers, lawyers, academics, state politicians – indeed the whole talent pool of the nation is open to him. A group of young Australians has recently advocated a similar flexibility for Australia arguing that it represents a way for Australia to ameliorate gender and racial imbalances in Australian public life.

These are the issues and choices which will confront us if we contemplate a presidential republic. Much will depend on the priorities we give to various key values. Those who value efficiency and clear accountability may well prefer the untrammelled executive authority of the parliamentary republic over the possibilities of deadlock and buckpassing inherent in the presidential republic; those who value liberty and participation may prefer the presidential republic over the elective dictatorship of the parliamentary republic. Or perhaps we should look at the halfway house of French quasi-presidentialism. It seems to get the best of both worlds. When the Elysée and the Matignon are in the same party hands it functions as a presidential republic; when those palaces are in the hands of opposing parties then it functions like a parliamentary republic.

Like the Australian founding fathers, we should be prepared to exercise our imaginations and range across the world for ideas.

LESSONS FROM THE NEW ZEALAND MODEL

If all this seems too difficult, if the challenges appear too great, and the weight of tradition and established forces too overwhelming, let me conclude on a tale of inspiration from across the Tasman. Proportional representation, particularly of the German kind known as MMP (mixed member proportional), is almost as alien to the Westminster tradition as an executive president. Proportional representation of a less foreign bent has turned up in a few odd Westminster places – in voting for European MPs and peripheral assemblies in the United Kingdom, in Tasmania and in the Australian Senate, but god forbid that it should ever be used for electing the house to which the executive is responsible. It is disliked by political elites in dominant two-party systems for exactly the same reason as directly elected presidents and executive presidents are disliked by the same elites – it threatens prime ministerial–Cabinet dominance of the system.

In the late 1970s and early 1980s there was considerable dissatisfaction with the workings of the first-past-the-post electoral system for the election of the single-chamber New Zealand Parliament. The Nationals won the 1978 and 1981 elections with less votes than their Labour opponents while minor parties were significantly underrepresented by the electoral system. In opposition – and these things are always easy and tempting in opposition – the Labour party committed itself to a royal commission on the electoral system including the possibility of proportional representation and when it came to power appointed such a commission. The commission reported in 1986 and to the shock of the political elite recommended the German MMP system as 'the best voting system for New Zealand's present and future needs'. Even worse the commission recommended that the decision on its adoption be taken out of the hands of the parliamentarians, with their vested interest in the existing voting system, and given to the people through the unusual procedure of a popular and binding referendum. In 1987 the Labour Prime Minister, David Lange, possessor of an endearing if naïve idealism, promised, without consulting his colleagues, a binding referendum on the electoral system in 1990.

But neither his ministerial colleagues nor the parliament were having any of this nonsense. The parliament set up an Electoral Law Committee which in 1988 enthusiastically endorsed the first-past-the-post electoral system, suggested a few minor amendments and questioned the wisdom of imposing an alien West German model on New Zealand. It did, however, recommend an indicative, not a binding, referendum on whether a few extra members could be elected by a different voting system. By 1989 the Labour government, in full revolt against the royal commission, introduced an electoral reform bill which 'in no way alters the fundamentals of our electoral system' and offered the people a referendum on the length of the parliamentary term as a substitute for Lange's promised referendum on the electoral system.

In their election manifesto in 1990 the Nationals promised a binding referendum on the electoral system. This did not signal the conservative party's conversion to proportional representation but was essentially a tactical device designed to highlight Lange's failure to honour his referendum promise. No sooner had they got in to office than the Nationals began watering this commitment down. The binding referendum became an indicative referendum in which the people were asked if they wanted change and if they did which of four reform options would they prefer. It has been suggested that four options were included in the hope of watering down support for any one option. The leadership of both major parties having too much to lose campaigned against any change. To the dismay of the politicians this exercise in bipartisanship was overwhelmingly rejected by the New Zealand people. On an admittedly low turnout 85 per cent voted to change the electoral system with 71 per cent preferring the German MMP option. With Labour now abandoning opposition and the Nationals reluctantly committed to a binding referendum the people got their way. In 1993, 54 per cent of the population voted for MMP.

There are many lessons in this for Australia but two stand out. If the people have got the bit between their teeth, then even a united stance by the political elite may be insufficient to prevent change, indeed in the present climate of opinion may even enhance its prospects. Secondly, creative proposals outside conventional boundaries should not necessarily be ruled out. Their advocacy may at least provide the space within which major changes may be achieved.

Notes:

1 Constitutional Convention, Transcript of Proceedings, Thursday 12 February 1998, *Hansard*, p. 865.
2 Turnbull, Malcolm, *The reluctant republic*, William Heinemann Australia, Port Melbourne, 1993, p. 166
3 Turnbull, Malcolm, *Fighting for the republic*, Hardie Grant Books, 1999, p. 4.
4 Solomon, David, *Coming of age: charter for a new Australia*, University of Queensland Press. 1998.
5 Paul Keating, speech in the House of Representatives, 7 June, 1995; http://australianpolitics.com/1995/06/07/an-australian-republic-the-way-forward.html
6 John Howard, statement in support of the 'No' case, 25 October 1999; http://australianpolitics.com/1999/10/25/john-howard-statement-against-a-republic.html
7 'Now there's a thought', *Sydney Morning Herald*, 18 May 2002 http://www.smh.com.au/articles/2002/05/17/1021544074455.html
8 Turnbull, Malcolm, *Fighting for the republic*, Hardie Grant Books, 1999.
9 Schlesinger, Arthur M. Jnr, 'Leave the Consitution alone' (1982) in William Lasser, *Perspectives on American politics*, 6th edition, Wadsworth Cengage Learning, Boston, 2012, p. 302.
10 Vile, A. J. C., *Politics in the USA*, Routledge, London & New York, 5th edition 1999, p. 102.
11 Uhr, John, *Questions without answers: an analysis of Question Time in the Australian House of Representatives*, Australasian Political Studies Association & Parliament of Australia, Canberra, 1982.

"Politics is a valuable activity, a way to bring about real change for the better, and a means of managing substantial disagreements within a society or a community. Cynicism about politicians and our motives corrodes faith in that process."

Apathy and anger: our modern Australian democracy

John Faulkner
22 October 2005

Sir Henry Parkes Memorial School of Arts, Tenterfield NSW.

IN AUSTRALIA TODAY there is a dangerous indifference to politics accompanied by a simmering resentment of politicians. Citizens who haven't enough interest in the democratic process to stay even vaguely informed of the issues of the day have only one profound political conviction: that politicians can't be trusted. Politicians show reciprocal cynicism in an electoral climate where a lie about mortgage rates has more impact than the truth about lies.

Our democracy is drowning in distrust. And at a time when our Australian democracy most needs an honest appraisal, we are instead being told to do nothing. On the one hand, a Prime Minister who invented the 'non-core' election promise is using tax-payer's money to fund advertisements telling us things are good and getting better. On the other, former Labor leader Mark Latham giving us '10 reasons why the idealistic should forget about organised politics' and telling us things are bad beyond repair.

We need better leadership than John Howard's self-serving soft-focus reassurance. And we need more thoughtful answers than the glib solution proposed by Mark in his recent lecture. He advised his listeners to turn their backs on organised politics because 'social problems require social solutions'.[1]

No wonder he found the political landscape a bleak and barren one.

Politics is one of the ways our large and diverse nation works out solutions to our problems – including our social problems. Politics without a social purpose is the empty pursuit of power, brutal and meaningless.

Not because politics prompts particular viciousness. Mark Latham's suggestion that we turn to 'local charities, sporting and community organisations' to escape the unpleasantness of factions and power struggles could only be made by someone who has never been to a meeting of the P&C, local progress association or cricket club! Politics is as it is, not because of the nature of politics, but because of the nature of people.

To expect the practice of politics to be somehow nobler than your own workplace or community organisation, to expect politicians to be better and more virtuous than you yourself are, is to guarantee disappointment. If these are your criteria for a healthy democracy, you will inevitably conclude that the system is mortally sick. How else to react, but with anger, or with apathy?

Too many in our community and our media have precisely these unrealistic standards, combined with the weary cynicism of having seen so many fall short.

Australians go to the ballot box with hopes too high, and fears too great.

By all means, let us be idealistic in what we hope to achieve. But let us be realistic in what we will be satisfied to get done. Let us be realistic in our expectations of our colleagues and our opponents. Let us be realistic about the distribution of altruism and selfishness in our fellow citizens.

Politics has never been easy. Reform is always slow. Compromise is always necessary. Bismarck famously said that politics is the art of the possible. It is popular in our anti-political culture to sneer at those who agree. They are that most despicable of creatures, a pragmatist. Well, politics requires pragmatism.

Politics also requires commitment and patience, and a sense of proportion. If you don't have those things, then yes, it will be a terrible job. And if you are unable to compromise with those who disagree with you, and unable to persist in your goals over a long period of time, then you may well find party politics, community politics, any politics, your own personal hell – a personal hell very much of your own making.

Unless we have mature and realistic expectations of the possibilities of politics and the capacity of politicians, we cannot as a society understand or resolve the real problems within the political system. If our analysis is as shallow as Mark Latham's complaints that people were mean to him, our solutions will be as self-defeating as his decision to take his bat and ball and go home.

JOHN FAULKNER

The Hon. John Faulkner has been one of the most high-profile and most highly respected figures in the Australian Parliament. A senator from 1989 to 2015, he was Leader of the Opposition in the Senate for eight years (1996–2004) and held a wide range of ministerial and shadow ministerial portfolios, but is best known to the public for his role in chairing a series of important Senate Inquiries. His probing and incisive chairmanship in pursuit of the truth about the activities of government and the bureaucracy made an invaluable contribution to improving the workings of democracy in the country.

And I believe that there are real problems with our modern Australian democracy and an urgent need for us all to address them.

Henry Parkes stood in Tenterfield in 1889 and called for the Australian colonies to work towards federation. Twelve years later, Australia became a nation.

I find it hard to imagine Australians today having enough faith in our political classes to bring the Commonwealth Government into existence. But then, Henry Parkes was not asking his contemporaries for that much faith. His appeal was for a government of limited powers compared to our government today, and by insisting on a directly democratic model, Parkes' model of federalism extended the power of the Australian people rather than the power of Australian politicians.

That was the genius of Parkes and our other democratic pioneers: they were designing institutions – federal democracy, universal suffrage, free state schooling – to operate in a climate that they hoped would be created by the institutions themselves.

But in the rapidly changing 20th century, our 19th century democracy developed in unexpected ways.

Our parliament was first imagined when modern political parties were only beginning to emerge, by men who assumed that the interests of a local community would be the most important factor in voting decisions. Universal voting, public education and an Australian government accelerated the development of an Australian identity. Voters went to the polls thinking of the nation as a whole. Importantly for the development of the political system we see today, Australian workers took their sense of class solidarity to the ballot box. For survival, non-Labor politicians banded together. The two-party system was born and from then on candidates' party allegiance, not their personal view or individual abilities, were the most important factor in their election.

Nineteenth century democrats saw the vote as a right to be fought for and prized. They did not anticipate voter turnout declining to less than 60 per cent, prompting the introduction of compulsory voting in 1924 to guarantee that all Australians would participate in our democracy.

Nor could they possibly have imagined the technological changes the 20th century brought, or the social transformations that resulted.

From telegraph to email, from horse and carriage to jet plane, from newspaper to television, technology has shrunk and accelerated our world. Today's media is far more immediate than ever before. Events are reported online moments after they happen. Rapid turnover leads to the constant search for the latest scoop – however flimsy the connection to the public interest. News now comes packaged, enhanced with manipulative sound and image. Stories that don't suit simplistic illustrations are dropped. Stories about scandals boost circulation, and take priority over complex discussions on policy. As British journalist and commentator Malcolm Muggeridge once said: 'Who sleeps with whom is intrinsically more interesting than who votes for whom.'

One wonders how Henry Parkes would have fared, forced to resign from public life for bankruptcy not once but twice – once with debts so huge he narrowly escaped fraud charges.

The short attention spans of today's media 'consumers' are trained by infotainment that seeks to reduce our political process to a more boring version of *Survivor*. There is little incentive for our citizens to dig deeper with increased demands on our time in the modern world. Work and family commitments grow ever greater as more families have two wage-earners, but the greatest increased demand on our time is from multiplying kinds of leisure, most prominently television.

Opinion pollsters report a lack of interest or understanding from the very same people racking up massive mobile bills trying to save or evict a *Big Brother* housemate or *Australian Idol* contestant. This disinterest breeds a vicious cycle, for those who don't speak up will find nothing so certain as that they won't be heard.

Our material prosperity has markedly improved since the 19th century. Although there are still many Australians living in real poverty and hardship, most of us are not; and the most direct interaction many people have with their government is in times of need.

Around the world political parties and community organisations of all kinds are suffering declining and ageing membership. As volunteer associations and community organisations fade, our society suffers. As mass political parties wither, our democracy suffers. My own party, the Labor Party, feels this most keenly. We are the oldest Australian political party and the only one in existence today that was founded in Henry Parkes' lifetime.

Like Henry Parkes' democracy, the Australian Labor Party was conceived in the 19th century and endured throughout the 20th. As the only Australian political party to see the whole of that 20th century, Labor has a great tradition of support and respect for the institutions and conventions that underpin our democracy.

Now at the beginning of the 21st century, Labor is not the only party facing new challenges and new struggles but as Australia's best example of a mass democratic party, the decline in political activity among Australians affects not only Labor's strategies but also Labor's soul. The last decades of the 20th century saw the introduction of public funding for election campaigns, an effort by the ALP to combat massive corporate donations to the non-Labor parties. It didn't work. Campaigns have merely become more expensive, and parties have spent even more time chasing corporate donations to pay for them. Shrinking membership means a greater need for big donors, but the pursuit of big donors alienates the remaining members. Instead of a broad political movement, Labor has become a party of parliamentarians with a machine element dedicated to funding campaigns and influencing the composition and often behaviour of the parliamentarians elected. Grassroots members are an afterthought and for many in the machine, an inconvenience. They shouldn't worry. If things keep going as they are, they won't have to worry about party members at all.

Another substantial change since the time of Henry Parkes is the decline of the power of the nation-state in the face of multinational corporations and international organisations. In the past, economic policy has been the main ground of debate between politicians. Australia's first political parties were called 'Protectionist', 'Free Trader' and 'Labor'. Now there is a general agreement between political parties and public commentators that there is only one real way to run the economy: by 'free market' precepts. National sovereignty is diminished as global markets, multinational corporations and international institutions play a major role in shaping Australia's economy.

For most people, the strength and the structure of the economy is the single greatest contribution the government can make to their well-being. It is little wonder that Australians lose interest in politics when the economy so often seems beyond the reach of their democratic power.

Our society, our technology and the institutions that govern our lives have changed radically since Henry Parkes called for a federal and a democratic government of the Commonwealth of Australia. The environment we do politics in has changed dramatically, but the way we do politics has hardly changed at all.

All these are convincing reasons for the indifference of many Australians to our political processes.

But partly, politicians must take responsibility for the pervasive sense of political impotence. Low-content, high-colour campaigning, slogans as vague as they are reassuring and the deliberate downplaying of ideals, vision and hopes for the country leave Australians with the impression that there's little politicians can do, and less they'd try. Australian politicians sometimes seem to believe that Australian voters have all taken to heart Bernard Baruch's advice to 'Vote for the man who promises least; he'll be the least disappointing'.

Baruch's cynical joke is popular among political aficionados who compete to seem the most jaded and disillusioned. Few know or care that Baruch left a more lasting legacy as Franklin Delano Roosevelt's economic advisor. He voted – and worked – for the man who promised the most – and delivered.

In the modern climate of ever-lowering expectations, apathy and disengagement are self-protective reactions to an equally powerful and dangerous current: anger. You never hear someone say as they refuse a how-to-vote on the way into a polling booth: 'It doesn't matter who I vote for, someone good will get in.'

Politics is a valuable activity, a way to bring about real change for the better, and a means of managing substantial disagreements within a society or a community. Cynicism about politicians and our motives corrodes faith in that process. And if the pervasive belief is that politicians have nothing but self-interest at heart, then their allowances, their pay, their very existence is the subject of resentment.

From time to time, simmering resentment flashes over into populist campaigns with hostility to politics and politicians as a defining feature. The brief success of One Nation and Pauline Hanson is perhaps the best example: Hanson was wildly popular because of, not despite, her economic ignorance, political naiveté and nervous, unprepared media persona. The Democrats were never so popular as when promising to 'Keep the bastards honest'. The Greens have expanded their base from environmentalists to protest votes, campaigning as the 'anti-political' political party.

Such posturing makes for fleeting popularity as voters seek an outlet for their frustration, but does nothing to address the causes of that frustration.

I would like to recommend three main areas of reform.

The first is in Australia's political parties. In our two-party system, with state and federal governments changing back and forth, the selection of candidates and the setting of policies within the political parties has as great an influence on Australia's governance as general elections. It is therefore essential that Australia's political parties are open, transparent and democratic – no code-words, no cabals, no secret handshakes.

This applies most acutely to the Australian Labor Party – not because we are the party most in need of change or least democratic as things stand, but because as Australia's progressive political party dedicated to principles of inclusiveness, democracy, and merit, we have to practice what we preach.

A hundred years ago, the difficulty of travel and communication around our huge continent made party members' direct participation in the ALP's organisation impractical. The solution was for local members to delegate their democratic rights. Today, the problem and the solution are out-of-date.

A hundred years ago, the ALP's structures provided for the greatest possible participatory democracy under the circumstances. Today, the abuse of those structures too often smothers party democracy. Today, we can do better.

Undemocratic practices are often blamed on factions and factionalism. There is nothing inherently wrong or undemocratic about like-minded people voting together to maximise their chances of success. It is, after all, the principle of party politics. When such groupings are based not on shared beliefs but on shared venality, factionalism goes bad. When factional interests are put ahead of the party's interests, the party rots.

As party membership declines, the influence of factional warriors increases. They maximise their influence by excluding those who disagree, not through leadership and persuasion. Those who defer to the powerbrokers are rewarded with positions in the party and with employment.

This is not factionalism. It is feudalism, and it is killing the ALP.

Mark Latham, having benefited from this system throughout his career, ultimately turned on it. His conclusion was that since he could see no way to reform the ALP, it was unreformable. I have a higher opinion of Labor's capacity for renewal.

Democracy and transparency must be the watchwords of our reform. Under Simon Crean's leadership, some reforms were made, and they have been moderately successful. Our national party president is directly elected by the membership. And delegates representing unions at conference have to actually be members of the union they represent – a long overdue change.

The sky did not fall, as was prophesied when Simon introduced these reforms. I think it's time we went further.

If our national president can be popularly elected, then why not our state presidents? I believe it is time for the state and territory branches to follow the lead of the national ALP and introduce direct democracy in electing their branch presidents. Indeed, I believe as many as possible party officials, executives, committees and for that matter Senators, ought to be directly elected or preselected by the party membership.

Those are some reforms that would enable Labor's supporters to have confidence in the party's commitment to democracy.

The next area of reform I think is important is media reform. Our ideas of press freedoms and rights are based very much in the 19th century. When Henry Parkes ran *The Empire* newspaper, the 'professional' model of peer regulation seemed adequate protection for the public interest, particularly given the narrow influence of the 19th century newspaper and the diverse range of newspapers published.

Today, we deal with massive media corporations that pursue their business interests on a multinational scale. In many of Australia's media markets, one single company dominates. Accurate reporting and the public interest struggle to compete with the imperative for advertising sales and pursuing the corporate agenda. Media proprietors use the best marketing techniques to shape public opinion in the guise of news.

For 30 years, no government of any political persuasion has done enough to ensure diversity, although media diversity is the greatest protection of the media's vital role in scrutinising and informing our democracy. Neither the Press Council in its present form nor industry watchdogs like the ABC's *MediaWatch* can force our media outlets to be honest and accurate, and neither provide remedies strong enough to discourage huge corporations from putting their own interests ahead of the public interest.

The media's freedom to publish was once a safeguard for our democracy. Today, as trash tabloids and opinion-for-hire commentators destroy any semblance of a debate of ideas, the principle of informed decision-making at the heart of the ideal of democracy drowns beneath racy headlines and print-now, retract-later coverage. Radio shock-jocks and shallow television infotainment do the same.

If our Australian democracy is to recover its health, one essential step is for standards of accuracy and responsibility to be set for all media outlets – print, radio and television – and enforced with meaningful remedies. For one thing, retractions ought to receive the same coverage and the same emphasis as the original incorrect reporting. Putting the lie on page one and burying the retraction inside makes a mockery of press responsibility.

Extending the role of the Press Council to cover all forms of media and ensuring it has adequate staff and resources would be steps in the right direction. We are entitled to insist that the media's self-regulation mechanisms are strong and effective, and that any self-regulatory body is vigorous and independent.

The third area of reform I would like to deal with is perhaps the closest to Henry Parkes' original purpose at Tenterfield in 1889.

The reason we remember the speech Parkes made there is that he set out the argument for the nation of Australia, and in advocating a Constitutional Convention he recommended the machinery to establish that nation.

In the 19th century colonial environment, the main preoccupation for our pioneer national democrats was to preserve the rights of the residents of the colonies while creating a new democratic institution. To do so, they adopted the model of a federal parliament, not a national one. Our Senate, and our mechanisms for constitutional reform, are designed to protect the rights of the states against the power of the Commonwealth.

Australia has been a nation for more than a hundred years, I believe it is time our machinery of government recognised that fact. We are all first and foremost Australian citizens.

But part of the difficulty in changing our Constitution has been the federalist requirement for a referendum to be passed in a majority of states, as well as receive a majority of votes nationally.

There are many important constitutional reforms that would vastly improve our national democracy. Fixed simultaneous four-year terms for both houses and the removal of the Senate's power to block supply are two overdue Parliamentary reforms. An Australian Republic is a more substantial constitutional change, but one I strongly support.

Existing federalist requirements for constitutional reform, for state as well as national majorities, remain a roadblock.

In Henry Parkes' time, the federal system protected democratic rights. Today, I'm sure we can do better. We need our Constitution and our mechanisms of constitutional change to reflect the reality that Australia is today 'a nation for a continent'.

I believe we need, as a starting point, a commission into constitutional reform. Its task should be to explore the best ways to maximise democratic participation in the constitutional reform process. This is of course only a beginning: as our nation continually grows, so the suitability of our Constitution ought to be under constant review.

I began by talking about the apathy and anger that characterise modern Australian democracy. I believe both are symptoms of the widening gap between the Australian people and the Australian polity. Without both an understanding of the practicalities of political change, and the confidence that the citizen can shape the state, Australians will drift further and further into disengagement and resentment. It is a dangerous moment for our democracy.

I hope it will be the impetus for renewal.

Notes:

1 Latham, Mark, 'Ten reasons why young idealistic people should forget about organised politics', public lecture at the University of Melbourne, 27 September 2005.

"We have the opportunity for unity. We must see this despite our fears of disunity. We need the opportunities, and the freedoms to take part in public activities at all levels. The framework for such freedom lies in our commitment to democracy and the public good. ... It is here that the crimson thread still runs."

The crimson thread: what unites Australians today?

Helen Irving
28 October 2006

Coventry Room, Parkes Shire Council, Parkes, NSW.

SPEAKING IN MELBOURNE in 1890 at the dinner for representatives of the Australasian colonies attending the first Federation Conference, Henry Parkes, Premier of New South Wales, responded to a pessimistic speech that had just been delivered by a former Victorian prime minister. The Victorian, James Service, had painted a worrying picture for advocates of federation, emphasising the barriers, especially those created by the differing tariff regimes across the six Australian colonies.

Any barriers to federation, said Parkes in response, could be overcome. Australians were united: 'The crimson thread of kinship runs through us all.'

These words were to become a rallying cry for the federationists, a beacon of hope for those who feared that disunity would keep Australians apart forever. And Parkes, it turned out, was right. Although he did not live to see it, the unity – the kinship – he identified among Australians was eventually given shape in a nation, the Commonwealth of Australia.

PARKES' VISION

Parkes meant two things by the 'crimson thread'. First, a common British ancestry – what we might call a common 'ethnic' identity today. He also meant the 'crimson thread' of shared commitments: commitments to British institutions, to British law and forms of government, and to a New World version of these institutions. What bound all Australians together, Parkes believed, was both a common origin and common vision of a future Australian nation. The British heritage would be built upon, developed and *Australianised*.

Those, like Parkes, who dedicated themselves to building the Australian Commonwealth, had a vision of Australia as a great and powerful nation in the Southern Hemisphere. Among other things, they imagined that the Australian population would be greatly expanded both by birth and by immigration. Ideally the immigrants would come from Britain, drawn from among those who also shared the crimson thread of ancestry.

The federationists confidently predicted a population outpacing Britain's within less than one hundred years, numbering at the least around 40 million and possibly by the end of the 20th century as many as 100 million. Today's small population would be one of the biggest surprises confronting the founders of the Commonwealth were they to return in 2006.

But while the population hasn't grown as was forecast, it has diversified. And just as much, it has *Australianised*. We no longer think of ourselves as *British*. We are diverse, but we also have a shared and common culture that is distinctively Australian. Those who built the Commonwealth of Australia welcomed this: they anticipated it; they helped foster it.

Henry Parkes was English. He was born in Warwickshire in 1815, and he came to New South Wales already an adult, already educated, married and the father of the first of his children. But Parkes quickly became a New South Welshman, and he also saw himself as a future Australian.

Parkes was a democrat, an advocate of the expansion of democratic rights for working men *and* women; he advocated and promoted public institutions – most notably, public schools and hospitals. He was a proponent of immigration. Certainly, his ideal was British immigration, but his vision of what could be achieved did not depend upon this.

In 1881 and 1882 Parkes travelled to the United States. What he saw there had a profound impact on him. In my view it was here that Parkes made a decisive shift in thinking, adopting an all-or-nothing vision of a full Australian nation, where previously he had anticipated incremental steps to a distant, as

HELEN IRVING

Helen Irving is Professor in Law at the University of Sydney, where she teaches and researches in constitutional law and history. She is the author of a number of works, including *To constitute a nation: a cultural history of Australia's Constitution* (1999) and *Five things to know about the Australian Constitution* (2004). She was active for many years in Centenary of Federation initiatives and in the campaign for an Australian republic. In 2003 she was awarded the Centenary Medal, and in 2005–06, she held the Chair of Australian Studies at Harvard.

yet unachievable, goal of federation. From this came a commitment to federating the Australian colonies, if possible, within his lifetime.

Within a few years, back in power, he followed this through, and remained committed to the goal to the end of his life. He almost saw the end of the process. He died in April 1896, less than five years before the Commonwealth of Australia was inaugurated.

In his memoir, *Fifty years in the making of Australia*, Parkes wrote of his travels in America, and of the impressions he formed there of industry and energy and growth. He also saw the 'crimson thread' – common ancestry – among Americans, and, being Parkes, he was not reluctant to lecture them on this.

At another dinner, this time in New York, Parkes responded to the toast, as he later recounted, by

> *tak[ing] up a bold position. After dwelling upon the vast strides which the great Commonwealth [of America] was taking in wealth, science, and material prosperity, I ventured to warn Americans against the danger of losing sight of the stern maxims of the founders of [their] Union. I then passed on to the ties between England and her noble offspring, and expressed the hope, amidst loud cheering, that they might grow stronger and closer, under the nurturing influence of justice and peace and kindred aspirations.*[1]

It was 'abundantly clear', he concluded, 'how these American hearts beat towards England and their scattered kin in England's colonies.'

I recently spent a year in America, living and working in Boston, Massachusetts, where the American War of Independence began, where the oldest written constitution in the world still operates, and where the Supreme Judicial Court that upholds this constitution was [at the time of my stay] presided over by a female Chief Justice.

Like Parkes in the 1880s, I am intrigued by the contrasts between the two countries and, like Parkes, I think that we can learn much from America. It's probably not a fashionable thing to say these days, but I think there's something in it.

ETHNIC DIVERSITY AS A GIVEN

Among other things, it was the great American openness to immigration in the post–Civil War years that contributed to the vitality Parkes found there in the 1880s. In the famous words on the Statue of Liberty, America had held its arms out to the tired, the poor, the huddled masses yearning to breath free.

But let's not exaggerate. Soon after – in the time when the Australian colonies were coming together – America began to restrict its immigration program, much as the Australian colonies were doing, and as the Commonwealth of Australia was to do after Federation, refusing entry to persons considered undesirable on the grounds of race. In Australia's 'sister colony', Canada, the same thing was happening. Those who claim that the 'White Australia Policy' is specifically, even uniquely Australian, are simply ignorant of these shared histories.

But, even with restrictions in American immigration, vast numbers of immigrants had already gone to America, and they would continue to do so. In the 1890s, Australians compared themselves with the American population at the time of American union in the 1780s. Its population then was 4 million – close to Australia's population of just under 4 million on the eve of Australian federation. In the century that followed America's federation, its population had grown to 60 million. The Australians imagined that their own would follow a similar rate of growth.

The demographic impact of immigration in America was not only in larger numbers. Certainly the growth was phenomenal, and the United States now has the third highest population in the world, but the impact was also in the enormous cultural and ethnic diversity that marks its population. Multiculturalism and diversity continue to challenge Australians. It has long been a simple fact of life in the United States.

One of the lessons we can learn from the United States is to accept ethnic diversity as a given. It is the demographic character of all comparable countries in the world; it is a product of globalisation, of changes in policy, in economics and technologies that cannot be reversed, even if we wanted to.

We need to think more creatively now about ways other than common ancestry in which we may be united.

We should also not exaggerate the difference between the past and the present. Australia has always had diversity in its population. Even one hundred years ago, it was much less ethnically and culturally uniform than many imagine. There were, for example, sufficient immigrant communities from Italy, Scandinavia, France, Germany and China, to support regular newspapers in their national languages at the turn of the century. There were major divisions, both religious and cultural, between those of Irish origin and those of English origin. There were, of course, tremendous differences between the indigenous and non-indigenous peoples.

What has changed are the scale and range of diversity. We encounter, interact with, and do business with people from non-Australian backgrounds, from non-English-speaking backgrounds, now more than ever. But this is in itself not necessarily disuniting. Australians are good at adapting. We have always known how to make the best of things. We are great improvisers, and good at experimenting with what is at hand. We are an adaptable people. While we see each new wave of immigrants as strange and sometimes disturbing, we – and they – soon adapt. We do not require the 'crimson thread' that unites us to be a common ancestry or single ethnicity.

IS THERE AN AUSTRALIAN IDENTITY?

What, then, unites Australia today? We often talk of an Australian *identity*. If this is what unites us, what does it mean? Does it refer to a particular physical *type* – the freckled, sun-bleached 'cornstalk'? The Paul Hogans of the world, the modern-day counterpart to Henry Lawson's bushman? Or do we mean a particular model of physical prowess – the sporting hero, the Don Bradmans of the world? That cannot be right. The vast majority of Australians would fail the test, and our own indigenous people would not qualify – a very strange thing – if this was what we really had in mind in talking of Australian identity.

Probably, what we mean by 'identity' are Australian ways of doing things, more than Australian features. Here we are on safer ground. There *are* characteristically Australian ways of doing things, and we recognise these particularly when we travel. Indeed, our willingness to travel long distances is itself characteristic of the Australian way. Many times, when overseas, I have heard people comment that Australians are great travellers. And many times during my recent year in America, I was surprised to hear Americans say that while they would love to visit Australia, it was simply too far away. The irony of saying this to an Australian who had, somehow, got herself to America, almost always went unnoticed.

There are other Australian characteristics, or cultural habits: our friendliness, for example. Australians are known – quite rightly – as a friendly people. We are outdoors people; we are hedonistic. At the same time, we are tough and resilient. Our sense of irony, and our scepticism are also recognisably Australian.

There are Australian symbols, in which these cultural characteristics can be captured; there are events or institutions that sum up or stand for Australian ways of doing things: the Sydney 2000 Olympics; the Socceroos' victories and defeats in Germany; our taste for Vegemite (and outrage at learning that Vegemite has been banned in the United States); our institution of compulsory voting, and our willingness to defend it – something that amazes other people – especially Americans.

These characteristics are not always positive, of course. Our scepticism can disguise a mistrust of innovation and ambition. It was revealing to hear people in America speak openly and without inhibitions, about their ambitions, their ideas and their dreams. I was also surprised to find that Americans are as polite and courteous in stressful situations as Australians like to imagine themselves to be – that ambition and assertiveness do not necessarily mean aggressiveness or pushiness. We Australians could probably do with a little less scepticism when it comes to new ideas, or stories of success.

The particular ways we do things will change and evolve, necessarily adapting to economic and technological changes, to the contribution of immigrants, and to the influences that come from globalisation. New symbols – new ways of capturing what is distinctively Australian – will emerge.

But I'm convinced that the culture – the characteristics themselves – will remain much more constant than many people fear.

Many overseas writers visited the Australian colonies in the 19th century, and some left accounts of what they observed to be the Australian character. More than one hundred years later, these still read as familiar. Australians, they reported, were friendly, hedonistic, egalitarian, sports-loving, sceptical and a little defensive.

Cultural change happens very slowly. New waves of immigrants make an impact, but they themselves adapt and take on the characteristics of the national culture much more quickly than the culture itself changes. Their children and their grandchildren, if given the opportunity, are no different from the children of non-immigrants in their ways of doing things. That is to say, they quickly come to share Australian characteristics and mannerism. They are also just as varied as everyone else in their appearance, their interests, and their aspirations.

I say, *if given the opportunity*. And I mean this in a particular way. I mean this for all Australians. Our opportunities to be part of a common culture, our opportunities to experience those things that genuinely do unite us, cannot be taken for granted.

What I am saying here is that the Australian identity is not a physical or an ethnic identity, but a bundle of characteristics – we can share these, and still be very different from each other in many other ways, like members of families often are.

We can also share these characteristics, and hold different personal *values*. Our identity, our characteristics, and our values are not the same thing. We cannot demand that all Australians hold the same values. Not only is this an intrusion into our freedom of conscience – a freedom that is at the heart of our democracy – but we cannot demand it and at the same time be true to what is characteristically Australian. We can't insist that all Australians hold a single set of 'Australian' values, but still remain a friendly, ironical and sceptical people.

We often hear it said, in response to clashes of values, that we should be tolerant of other points of view. We often hear *tolerance* included among the core values – perhaps even as the most significant value – that all Australians should share. Tolerance sounds good. Who could argue against it? But tolerance is a poor substitute for unity.

We cannot be united by mutual tolerance. That is merely a recipe for mutual indifference, or shared apathy. Tolerance, in this sense, can even *erode* unity. We can, and we should, attempt to see each other's point of view, and have – I would hope – compassion for the weaknesses and even the stupidity that we see in others, hoping that they will do the same for us. But we cannot be asked to tolerate anything or everything.

What can unite us is neither tolerance nor values, but *commitment* to the legal and political system that permits and encourages mutual engagement, and that requires us at least to hear the other person's point of view – a legal system of equality and a political system where debate, open information, and transparency in government, are its foundations. *Democracy*, in other words.

We can, certainly – and we should – ask of all Australians (whether citizens or residents) to hold in common democratic *commitments*.

AUSTRALIAN COMMITMENTS RATHER THAN VALUES

In an address on 25 January 2006, Prime Minister John Howard said of Australian citizenship: 'The truth is that people come to this country because they want to be Australians. … [But] the irony is that no institution or code lays down a test of Australian-ness. Such is the nature of our free society.'

'[E]thnic diversity,' he continued, 'is one of the enduring strengths of our nation. Yet our celebration of diversity must not be at the expense of the common values that bind us together as one people – respect for the freedom and dignity of the individual, a commitment to the rule of law, the equality of men and women, and a spirit of egalitarianism that embraces tolerance, fair play and compassion for those in need.'

Despite the recognised difficulty or 'irony' that a free society cannot set down a test for its own membership, the idea of some sort of *test* of values has recently been supported by many on both sides of politics. Last month the Commonwealth Government prepared a discussion paper on the merits of introducing a formal citizenship test for prospective new citizens. The introduction to this paper re-states the Prime Minister's ideas:

> *Citizenship provides an opportunity for people to maximise their participation in society and to make a commitment to Australia's common values – which include the respect for the freedom and dignity of the individual, our support for democracy, our commitment to the rule of law, our commitment to the equality of men and women and the spirit of a fair go, of mutual respect and compassion to those in need.*

This is a worthy and important list. But, these are not exclusively *Australian* qualities. All liberal democratic countries in the world would support such a statement, even though they might use different words to describe what we mean by the 'fair go' – equality of opportunity, for example.

British Prime Minister Tony Blair said something similar in his speech to the Australian Parliament, on 27 March 2006:

> *We know the values we believe in – democracy and the rule of law, but also justice, the simple conviction that given a fair go human beings can better themselves and the world around them. … We are open societies. We feel enriched by diversity. We welcome dynamism and are tolerant of difference.*

The problem here is not the worthiness of those institutions and practices that both the Australian and British Prime Minister have endorsed. It is the language of values. 'Values' are personal. They may underpin our support for public institutions and practices, but it is to reach too far into the individual conscience to ask us to have the same set of 'values'.

When we try to find what unites *Australians*, we should at least distinguish between personal and public values. But I think we should talk less about values and emphasise the idea of public *commitments*.

People's values will always vary, and democracy must allow for differences in values – indeed it is essential for debate over values to take place, if democracy is to be genuine, and democratic progress is to occur. Democracies like Australia's *require* debate and contestation. Our parliamentary institutions are built around these: this is why we have an official Opposition, why we have political parties, and why freedom of the media and freedom of expression are an essential part of our political system.

And it is a commitment to these public institutions and these freedoms that can genuinely unite us.

THE AUSTRALIAN PUBLIC AND PUBLIC AUSTRALIA

To have common public commitments, we need opportunities to experience ourselves as part of the Australian public. If governments want to facilitate a sense of public community – one that rises above the separate sub-communities that are common in all societies, especially in cities – then governments must be committed to maintaining and fostering public institutions.

No test of a person's 'values' can substitute for the public resources and the opportunities that give people a sense of being part of the public, and with it a commitment to the shared public good. The recent calls for tests of citizenship values and declarations of adherence to these values, in the belief that this will make new immigrants more *Australian*, put the cart before the horse.

A declaration of adherence to a set of values made on a single occasion is not going to make people behave differently, especially if they don't already share those values; it won't stop people thinking or saying outrageous things; it would not have stopped the Cronulla riots, and it won't prevent terrorist acts in the future, if this is what we are afraid of.

For one thing, those who commit acts of violence are not always non-citizens. Probably the majority among those involved in the Cronulla riots – nearly all of them youths – were already Australian citizens. In Britain, the test of history and knowledge about British institutions for naturalisation would not have stopped the terrorist attacks in London in July last year. The majority of those who committed those acts were already citizens *by birth*. It would have had no impact either on them, or on those who were naturalised.

A test of 'values' or a test of historical knowledge for naturalisation won't harm anyone, but it's unlikely to do much good for the unity of Australians as a whole.

Immigrants, just like Australian citizens, will have different values. People have different religious values, different ideas about the importance of family, different views about friendship, different ideas about how money should be spent, different views about how we should prepare for death, and many more.

Ethnic diversity means an added layer of diversity in values, and practices, but it is not incompatible with shared commitments. It is possible to have different values, and still have a commitment to the public good, which rests upon democracy, equality, freedom of expression, and the rule of law.

But commitment will not come about by testing people, or by lecturing them. It will come through *practice*, through experiencing the benefits of the public. And these will require support for the public – for public institutions, public spaces and opportunities to participate in public life.

The public good, as we understand it in Australia, and in respect of which it makes sense to require – and to *foster* – commitment, involves local, state and Commonwealth government initiatives, as it should do in a federal system like Australia's. It includes three elements that, notwithstanding all the changes that have occurred in Australia in the one hundred and ten years since Henry Parkes died, are the same elements Parkes himself defended and fostered throughout his life and in his work.

These are: public education; public spaces; and public institutions. The most important of the public institutions are the institutions of democracy.

Public education: Henry Parkes was one of the prime movers behind the introduction of free, secular public education in New South Wales in the mid-19th century. His *Public Instruction Act* of 1880 laid the foundation for the state's modern education system. Parkes believed that education created opportunities for children to take part in society. This principle still holds true.

Today, public education is under threat. Parents, sometimes reluctantly, turn to private schools because local public schools are under-resourced or overcrowded. In inner Sydney, many have been closed down, or amalgamated.

Today, we need a revitalised public education system, both for schools and for adult education. If we are serious about encouraging our children to share a commitment to Australian institutions and to each other, we need to foster a sense that public education is valuable, that it is not a second-rate alternative to private education. We need to be proud of our schools, and proud of being a country that values and supports public education.

Good public education will go a long way towards fostering a sense of shared public commitment in a diverse society.

It is reasonable to hope that people will speak a common national language, although it is a mistake to think that failure to do so indicates unsuitability for integrating into the Australian community. But if we want our immigrants to have a knowledge of English, we need to offer English classes in ways that make it possible for people who work and support families to take advantage of them. English language programs were a familiar feature on the radio when I was a child, and free English classes were available in other forms. The current Adult Migrant English Program offers free classes for recent immigrants, between around 500 and 900 hours, depending on the type of immigrant; we need to support this form of public education, and we need to expand it, including in flexible ways, using a variety of media.

Public space: A commitment to the public also depends upon the availability of public spaces. Parkes was a visionary on this principle too. In 1888, on the Centenary of British settlement in New South Wales, Premier Parkes set in train the creation of Centennial Park in central Sydney – more than 600 acres of land re-claimed from the Lachlan Swamps, which was landscaped and planted with lawns and trees, with lakes, and paths and playing fields integrated into native bushland and small pine forests. It is the place where, five years after his death, the Commonwealth of Australia was inaugurated, and where more than 200,000 people sat comfortably on grassy slopes to watch the ceremony.

Now, on any day of the week, and especially on a sunny weekend, one sees the benefits of Centennial Park in a multitude of ways: people of all national origins using the space, walking dogs, running, strolling, riding horses or bicycles, playing games, enjoying picnics, and parties – there is always at least one children's party, with balloons tied to a tree, near the dedicated bicycle track where children can learn to ride safely, clear of the traffic. This park is one of my favourite places in Sydney. I think of it as 'Henry's Park,' and I bless his memory, and think it should be a model for all towns and cities.

There are, of course, public parks in most towns and most city suburbs, but how often are these attractive? How often, however, are they surrounded with so many rules and regulations that to do anything other than sit on a bench – if, indeed, there is a bench – is forbidden? How often are the following things prohibited: playing ball games, riding bicycles, lighting fires, drinking alcohol, allowing dogs off leads except, perhaps, after hours?

I am, of course, a law-abiding, indeed legally trained, individual, but I love to come across the event where all of these rules are broken at the same time – a Saturday afternoon children's birthday party in a local park, where the child's new bicycle is shown off, where the parents have a glass of champagne or a beer together while kicking around a ball with their children and cooking fish or sausages on a portable barbecue. And, of course, with the family dog joining in.

All of these activities, it seems to me, are characteristically Australian and, if we want commitment to the public good, as Australians, we should be encouraging them, instead of prohibiting them, just as we should be supporting other free, open and accessible public spaces, where people can mix safely, and where we can see each other, out of our sub-communities, as ordinary people with common commitments, as members of the Australian public, even if our values and ethnic origins are varied and divers.

Public institutions: A common commitment to democracy, equality, and compassion for others, also requires the fostering of our institutions of government. The Australian colonies, along with New Zealand, were the democratic innovators of the 19th century. It was here in the Southern Hemisphere that the secret ballot, payment for members of parliament, votes for women, permanent electoral rolls, direct election of both houses of parliament, were first introduced. For more than a century, the institutions of Australian democracy have, with the occasional setback, continued to innovate and thrive. The Australian Electoral Commission, for example, has been a model for other countries; as has public funding for election campaigns.

We are often cynical about politics and even more so about politicians – this is, indeed, characteristically Australian – but we are surprisingly united in defending the type of political institutions we have in this country. I mentioned compulsory voting and public funding for election campaigns; others, like our federal system, the referendum for changing the constitution, our particular electoral systems, are also core parts of our national commitments.

But recent initiatives have begun to wind back some of these avenues of participation. Amendments to the Commonwealth Electoral Act in 2006 now mean an early closing of the electoral rolls, so that persons turning 18 will have three days, and others only one day to enrol. Previously, tens of thousands of new voters were able to enrol in time for the election in a seven-day period, and many more could update their enrolment details. All prisoners are now denied the Commonwealth vote, where previously only prisoners serving sentences of five years or more were disenfranchised.

The Australian Constitution provides for representative government and the direct choice by the voters of their representatives. Enrolling to vote and participating in elections are among the most fundamental of the public activities in a democracy, and yet – for reasons that are not at all clear – the new laws are discouraging, rather than encouraging participation.[2]

In making it harder to vote, we are becoming more like Americans, treating voting less as a right and more as privilege. This, I think, is regrettable. Democratic rights should not be at the whim of governments. To exercise such rights is a central part of our identity as Australians, and experience of democratic practices is a central part of creating a sense of membership of the public.

But there are still some things we can learn about American commitments. While Americans are much less committed to public education and to public spaces than we are in Australia, Americans have, overwhelmingly, a shared commitment to the public institutions of American democracy. Their democratic institutions are a little different from ours, and their sentiments sound sometimes corny to sceptical Australian ears. But they have public commitments that hold them together and that allow diversity to flourish.

They believe in the presidency, although they have very divergent views on the merits of individual presidents; they are committed to the ideas expressed in the Declaration of Independence, and to the US Constitution, both as a symbol and as an institution; they have, indeed, a 'constitutional identity' that is quite unfamiliar to us here in Australia. It is this that still unites Americans today, as it did in the past. It is this that allows Americans to feel united, despite cultural and ethnic diversity on a scale far greater than in Australia; despite great differences in values and lifestyles among its population. It was this that Parkes experienced firsthand on his visits to the United States in the 1880s, and saw as a model for a future Australian nation.

CONCLUSION

Without government support for, and the development of public institutions, we cannot expect a shared sense of the public good among all Australians, whether immigrants or citizens by birth. Without an active public sphere, we will inevitably experience ourselves as separate, as members of sub-communities, as people who have little in common with each other.

We have the opportunity for unity. We must see this despite our fears of disunity. We need the opportunities, and the freedoms to take part in public activities at all levels. The framework for such freedom lies in our commitment to democracy and the public good. It is this that unites us, as it did when the Commonwealth started. It is here that the crimson thread still runs.

Notes:

1 Parkes, Henry, *Fifty years in the making of Australian history,* Longmans, Green and Co., London 1892, pp. 69–70.

2 The early closing of the electoral rolls was held unconstitutional by the High Court of Australia in *Rowe v Electoral Commissioner* (2010).The disenfranchisement of prisoners serving sentences of less than three years was held unconstitutional by the High Court of Australia in *Roach v Electoral Commissioner* (2007).

"Many of the people who founded Australian democracy may have been self-taught, but they were good philosophers who were unafraid to think in terms of first principles and ideals ... We, by contrast, have allowed ourselves to become utilitarians and technocrats, dominated to the exclusion of almost all else by economics and accountancy."

Whatever happened to Australian radicalism?

Geoff Gallop

20 October 2007

*Sir Henry Parkes Memorial School of Arts, Tenterfield NSW.**

LIKE ALL GREAT speeches, Parkes' Tenterfield Oration is a call to action, a call to the Australian people to achieve by peace what the Americans had achieved by war. The time had come, he said, to have 'an uprising in this fair land of a goodly fabric of free government' with 'all great national questions of magnitude affecting the welfare of the colonies' disposed of by 'a distinct executive and a distinct parliamentary power'.[1]

In saying these things Parkes was pointing to the need not just for any national system of government but one that embodied freedom. He was drawing upon the theories, insights and arguments of the British radical tradition, albeit modified by his experience of hard-edged parliamentary politics. This is the tradition of parliamentary and electoral reform, freedom of association and

* Following the presentation of this speech for the Henry Parkes Foundation in 2007, a version was subsequently published in *Griffith REVIEW 19: Re-Imagining Australia* as 'A Radical Legacy', https://griffithreview.com/articles/a-radical-legacy; and in the anthology *Best Political Writing 2009*, Melbourne University Press, edited by Eric Beecher.

expression, national self-determination and social equality. From this tradition also emerged the argument for popular sovereignty, democracy and republic. At a deeper level the radicals recognised that good political systems weren't just important as means to an end but were ends-in-themselves.

To put it in contemporary terms they saw people as 'citizens' rather than as 'customers' or 'consumers'. It would seem most appropriate, then, that my lecture should deal with this subject of radicalism and more particularly with the question: 'whatever happened to Australian radicalism?'

AUSTRALIA'S RADICAL INHERITANCE

We know where radicalism came from: people like Sir Henry Parkes and John Dunmore Lang – two of our most important intellectual founding fathers, who laid the base on which men like Barton, Deakin and Reid later built the nation.

Funny that, because when we think of founding fathers we think of grey-haired, conservative old men who believe that the old ways are always best. Little do most Australians realise, though, that our founding fathers were followers of and sometimes proselytisers for ideas that many of their contemporaries considered to be positively dangerous.

Take Parkes, especially in his early years, and the even more radical figure, Lang. More than half a century before Federation, they were calling for, among other things, the following:

- an end to transportation and the creation of a free society;
- federation;
- responsible parliamentary government, with a bicameral legislature, equality of electoral districts and short, regular parliamentary terms;
- universal manhood suffrage;
- a society without either a privileged aristocracy or an impoverished, starving working class;
- public education for all;
- and, at various times, an Australian republic.

Now, I want to ask you: does this sound familiar? It should, because with the addition of votes for women, it's the Australia we gained in 1901, and still live in today – enhanced, of course, by innovative social legislation and occasionally radical interpretations of the Constitution by the High Court.

It's important to remind ourselves that the time in which the radical social, political and constitutional demands were being formed – the 1840s and early 1850s – was a time of European revolution and political ferment in England.

GEOFF GALLOP

The Hon. Geoff Gallop AC is Professor and Director of the Graduate School of Government at the University of Sydney. After attending school in Geraldton, Professor Gallop studied at the University of Western Australia, and at Oxford and Murdoch universities. From 1986 to 2006 he represented the Australian Labor Party in the Western Australian State Parliament and was Premier from 2001 to 2006. He was Deputy Chair of the COAG Reform Council from 2007 to 2011 and Chair of the Australia Awards Board 2011–2013. He is currently Chair of the Australian Republican Movement. As Opposition Leader in Western Australia he published *A state of reform: essays for a better future* (Helm Wood 1998) and in 2012 he published *Politics, society, self: occasional writings* (UWA Publishing).

Parkes, Lang and others got their ideas from their own egalitarian interpretations of the Bible, to writings of the American revolutionaries, radical liberals like Jeremy Bentham and, most remarkably of all, from the British radicals and Chartists – whose ideas conservatives considered nothing short of seditious and revolutionary, and for the supporting of which men were often transported to the colonies.

Obviously, there were many other important intellectual, social and economic influences on the establishment of Australian democracy, but here's my first key point, one which Australians too often overlook: the founding principles of our democracy were laid in a time of European revolution by men soaked in radical political ideas.

Of course, while sharing many constitutional principles, men like Lang and Parkes were chalk and cheese when it came to their visions of the future. Lang wanted a radical revolution. Parkes, at least in his later years, wanted radical reform to head off even more radical revolution. But the practical effect of their agitation was the same: the establishment of a liberal democracy in the former colony of New South Wales.

Ideas, though, come and go. What seems radical at one time can seem conservative at another, and vice versa. This alerts us to the fact that radicalism is more than a set of ideas; it's a way of thinking that puts the thinker at a critical angle to society.

And this brings me to my second major point: many of the people who founded Australian democracy may have been self-taught, but they were good philosophers who were unafraid to think in terms of first principles and ideals as they confronted the challenges of creating a nation in a time of change. We, by contrast, have allowed ourselves to become utilitarians and technocrats, dominated to the exclusion of almost all else by economics and accountancy.

THE NEW NATION

These radical ideas and ways of thinking made the Australian colonies and nation from the 1850s to World War I perhaps the most advanced and envied democracy in the world. Before we turn our minds to how we can improve it, make it more relevant to the challenges we face, and gain that envied status once again, let's examine what these ideas gave us.

Firstly, they gave us nationhood. Now it's true they never gave us a republic in the form in which most now conceive it – with an Australian head of state. But republicanism had a number of connotations in the 19th century. For many, the establishment of an independent democratic nation, free from tyranny and the control of an overbearing aristocracy, constituted a republic – 'a republic in disguise', as the historian Mark McKenna has called us.[2] In fact the title which Parkes first dreamt up for our nation – the *Commonwealth* of Australia – was an early modern translation of the Latin term *res publica*.

Secondly, our founding ideas gave us popular sovereignty. The significance of this achievement isn't always fully appreciated. At Federation, never mind the 1850s, responsible government elected through universal suffrage was far from the norm. Universal manhood suffrage wasn't fully achieved in Britain until 1918 and unrestricted female suffrage wasn't passed until 1928. In Germany, the government was responsible not to the parliament but to the Kaiser. Responsible government there came only after World War I. Russia was still an autocracy. Of course while in 1901 we included women in the franchise, we omitted our original inhabitants, so the term 'universal' must be highly qualified.

We also added the concept of the referendum. Our federation itself had been created through a series of democratic acts that had been drawn up by the elected federal convention and accepted by a popular referendum. And, of course, one of our first great national controversies – the conscription issue – was settled by not just one, but two plebiscites. Try imagining today a national government putting such a contentious issue relating to matters of war, peace and foreign alliances to the people. It's almost inconceivable.

Radicals had a significant influence over this quite remarkable achievement of nationhood, and it's not surprising that many chose to work within the contours of the newly established system. This allowed them to achieve many important reforms, some sooner than others, which have never quite been accepted by conservatives and are still being fought over today:

- conciliation and arbitration;
- a comprehensive opportunity and welfare state;
- and recognition of aboriginals, followed by land rights.

This was despite the serious reservations some radicals had about the limitations of the 1901 constitutional settlement. Many radicals had wanted full constitutional independence from Britain – which they later attained through the Balfour Declaration (1926), the Statute of Westminster (1931) and, much later, the Australia Act (1986).

A 20TH CENTURY RADICAL TRADITION

It is to the broader question of the limitations of the 1901 Constitutional settlement that I would now like to turn, particularly for those on the left of the political spectrum who believed in the need for comprehensive social and economic change.

Not surprisingly they opposed many of the liberal elements designed to prevent 'the tyranny of the majority'. Some too resented the monarchical elements which tied the system together and kept alive the reserve powers of the Crown. From within the labour movement there emerged a critique of the federal system itself and all those elements which constrained the will of the majority as expressed in the composition of the lower houses of parliament.

Radicalism stayed alive as a critique of the constitution and for some as a movement for an Australian republic with a strong and centralised national government. The concept of national development and full employment with social justice featured prominently in the thinking of Labor leaders John Curtin, Ben Chifley and Dr Evatt. Their attitudes were also influenced by the economic impotence of state governments in the face of the Great Depression and the need for national economic direction during and after World War II.

As far as state governments were concerned there were many achievements but generally radicals baulked at the lack of one-vote one-value, the gerrymandering of electoral boundaries and property franchises for second chambers. For those radicals keen to build a nation from a continent, the states were seen as barren ground. If change was to come it would have to be led by the Commonwealth.

Add to this the growing belief in radical circles in the 1930s and beyond that the Constitution was being used opportunistically by reactionaries to block mandated reform:

- The sacking of the Lang Labor government by New South Wales Governor Sir Philip Game in 1932 convinced many that the continued existence of the reserve powers of state and Commonwealth governors and governors-general pointed to the need for a republic.
- The obstructionism of state upper houses elected with a restrictive property franchise – such as the blocking of supply by the Victorian Legislative Council, which led to the defeat of the government of John Cain Senior in 1947 – convinced radicals that upper houses themselves were the problem and that electoral reform was needed. In some states it was Labor policy to abolish upper houses altogether.
- The blocking of attempts to control and nationalise banking in the late 1940s by the High Court and the Privy Council, using sometimes contentious legal reasoning, convinced others that judicial reform was also needed and that new constitutional ways had to be found to facilitate a new era of national development.

Undoubtedly the greatest Australian radical of the 20th century, Gough Whitlam, gave a particularly modern flavour to his mix of democratic socialism and nationalism by adding many of the issues associated with the social and political movements of the 1960s. He took an activist view of the Commonwealth's constitutional and political position. Whitlam's radical constitutional innovation was to find new constitutional means to extend Commonwealth involvement in social and economic development – mainly through his use of tied grants to the states under section 96 of the Constitution and the creation of new bodies like Medibank and the Schools Commission to raise and disperse funds and lead national policy.

However, it was the circumstances of Whitlam's dismissal and defeat in 1975 that was to be most controversial. The combination of state and Senate obstruction and the exercise of reserve powers put the focus back onto the Constitution and what it meant for those seeking reform. It also raised a question mark against the Whitlam strategy and the assumptions behind it.

CHANGE FROM BELOW

Ironically, while the Whitlamite majoritarian and centralising version of radicalism was stealing the limelight, a new radicalism was being created, slowly and without fanfare, at the state level.

The governments of Don Dunstan in particular (1967–68 and 1970–79) demonstrated what could be done by using the powers available to a state government. As the Labor Party's premier historian, Ross McMullin, has written:

> *... after being renowned during the Playford era for its conservatism, South Australia became an enlightened pace setter under Dunstan in many spheres, including electoral fairness, community welfare, consumer protection, planning and environment, education, equal opportunities, Aboriginal affairs, public administration and the arts.*[3]

Dunstan was truly a pioneer and similar changes were to follow in other states, mainly but not wholly from the efforts of modernising Labor administrations. Indeed, in more recent times this tradition has been further developed with innovations in democratic engagement and human rights protection coming from state Labor. These governments have proved that significant state-based progress could be made even under federal governments with more conservative priorities.

Perhaps more enduringly, through ambitious democratic experimentation, the states set out to solve one of the problems the radicals of the 1850s and federation hadn't been able to adequately address – the capacity of state institutions to frustrate radical social reforms. One-by-one the systems of state constitutional checks and balances were rid of their conservative biases:

- gerrymanders were negated;
- upper houses were given new proportional representation electoral systems; and
- anti-corruption commissions and other monitoring agencies were set up to make state institutions more accountable.

The end result is that it's much rarer these days to hear state Labor governments making serious complaints about the in-built, *Yes Minister* conservative biases of the public service and the judiciary. In fact, the complaints about these bodies are more likely to come from conservatives, who claim they are dominated by radical elites. The result is that purposeful but practical reform has allowed Labor to dominate the last decade at the state level, even with one of the most right wing federal governments the country has ever known.

Proportional representation and the rise of stronger third parties like the Greens have likewise reduced the likelihood that the Senate and other upper houses will be able to frustrate radical reform in the future. Despite the setbacks of the 2001 and 2004 Senate races, the upper house is still more likely to be a defender of existing rights and a generator of pressure for more radical reform than the reverse.

In my view, the idea of a centralised national system as the necessary basis for radical change in Australia only made sense if there was electoral malapportionment and inbuilt conservative constitutional and institutional biases at the state level.

So there's my third key point: radical progressives should embrace democratic checks and balances as the means to further their agenda. This means a more positive embrace of the American elements of our Constitution such as federalism and divided power more generally considered.

LEFT AND RIGHT

While these radical constitutional reforms were occurring at the state level, other changes were occurring in Australian politics.

One of the most remarkable features of contemporary Australian politics has been the Left's embrace of market economics and economic rationalism generally, particularly at the federal level. This focus on market economics has been coupled with a more conservative and less populist political disposition. This was clearly demonstrated during the debate over the republic in the 1990s when the Left failed to support a direct election model for the election of an Australian head of state. Ultimately Australia's leading republicans just couldn't contemplate sharing power with the people.

However, at the same time it opened Labor's ranks to arguments about choice in politics, diversity in society and innovation in public policy – all small 'l' liberal values. It was an era of substantial revisionism, not just in respect of means but also in respect of the ends of power. Increasingly evidence-based public policy rather than a more narrowly based ideology became the basis for thought and action.

At the same time, the Right has become radical in the social and economic spheres. The Right now regards the checks and balances created at Federation – like the Senate, the delineated responsibilities of the states, and the idea of balance on the High Court – as impediments to the will of the people expressed through elections to the House of Representatives, and as standing in the way of its radical right-wing reforming ambitions. Take the following statements on state–federal relations by Prime Minister John Howard in keynote speeches in April 2005 and August 2007, outlining his vision of 'aspirational nationalism':

> *...fears of centralism rest on a complete misunderstanding of the government's thinking and reform direction. Where we seek a change in the federal-state balance, our goal is to expand individual choice, freedom and opportunity, not to expand the reach of central government.*
>
> *I am, first and last, an Australian nationalist. When I think about all this country is and everything it can become, I have little time for state parochialism.*
>
> *Sometimes [aspirational nationalism] will involve leaving things entirely to the states. Sometimes it will involve cooperative federalism. On other occasions it will require the Commonwealth bypassing the states altogether and dealing directly with local communities.*[4]

He's re-writing the Constitution through political fiat. You don't have to read between the lines to get the Prime Minister's vibe: that centralisation isn't just the most direct way to maximise the electoral benefit of pork barrelling, it's the best way to remove the impediments to his version of our national values and the free market posed by the Australian constitutional and political inheritance.

So here's my fourth major point: the radicals' old dream of centralised national governmental power has been taken over by the Right in the interests of electoral pork barrelling, unchecked economic rationalism and populist cultural politics.

UPDATING OUR RADICALISM

I mentioned earlier how radicalism is as much a way of thinking as a program for government. One of the problems for Australian progressives over the years is that they have been too locked into a centralising bureaucratic view of Australia's future and are too often unable to think in clear and decisive ways when it comes to non-economic issues. Progressive 'once-radicals' have lost the intellectual ascendancy. We need to get it back by noting the space that now exists for a new and more liberal and participatory version of politics that supports social diversity and civil society.

First a warning. Regaining the ascendancy won't be achieved through a risky lunge to the left, forgetting economics and responsible government and joining doomed crusades like the anti-globalisation movement.

Perhaps the answer lies in the example of the people I discussed at the start of my lecture – in recapturing the radical democratic potential of federation and federalism.

Huge challenges face us today, just as they faced Henry Parkes and John Dunmore Lang. For them the challenges were national development, organising national defence and freeing interstate trade (as well, of course, of implementing a White Australia policy). For us, the challenges are to become environmentally sustainable, develop our human capital and succeed in a globalised world economy without sacrificing the concept of equality. Addressing these issues gives progressives the opportunity to revive our sense of purpose and to reassert ourselves as a major intellectual and practical force for radical change. Pragmatism is a necessary and usually honorable reality of politics, but to regain the ascendancy, movements need more – they need a sense of purpose and direction. How do we conquer these challenges through an appeal to our federal past? The concept of 'balance' provides a compelling answer.

I believe the dramatic decline in the Howard government's popularity over the last 12 months doesn't represent a rejection of strong leadership, but a rejection of arrogant, centralised power. It's a rejection of the trampling of state power; the over-riding of checks and balances; and the abuse of the resources of the state. People want continuing economic reform, but not at the price of social progress and environmental irresponsibility. They don't want a swing to the left; they want balance.

Before you object that calling for balance is hardly radical, let me repeat what I said earlier: ideas that at one time seem conservative can at other times seem radical. In the mid 19th century and at Federation, the idea of individual rights, popular sovereignty and a balanced federal constitution were radical democratic beliefs. They can be again today.

So here's my fifth and final main point: we need a new radicalism that moves away from majoritarianism and centralism to one that emphasises the balance between individual rights and state and federal power.

To guarantee individual rights, I believe progressives should once again push for the enshrining of a national Charter of Rights to constrain any government from using various pretexts to slowly and unnecessarily chip away at our freedoms. We need a more sophisticated and proactive approach to the whole issue of rights protection that requires questions to be asked from the earliest to the last stages in the decision-making process. The fact that it has proved all too easy to change the electoral laws to intentionally keep young or itinerant voters off the electoral rolls because they're likely to vote for another party, to deport citizens like Vivian Solon because they're unable to speak up for themselves, or to take away a person's right to bargain collectively with an employer should be a cause for concern. The Charters established by the ACT and Victorian governments show the way forward. As the Hon. Justice Michael Kirby said of such Charters earlier this month:

> *In effect, it provides a stimulus to the democratic process, it encourages us to think in terms respectful of the basic rights of one another. It promotes a culture of mutual respect of basic rights. But it leaves the last word to elected parliaments, whilst rendering them and their processes transparent and promoting vigorous debate on such matters.*[5]

To build a modern Australian economy and society, we need a new commitment to federal–state cooperation. Instead of 'aspirational nationalism' we need 'cooperative federalism'. The proof of what can be achieved through cooperative federalism is already before us. Over the last two to three years the Labor state governments led by Victoria have worked together to create a new federal agenda that encompasses economic reform; human capital investment; infrastructure development; sorting out the hospital, health, dental and aged care systems; and addressing sustainability. This agenda is designed to work without undermining the subsidiarity principle and the multiple centres of power required to promote innovation. Indeed, the 'Third Wave of National Reform' is a worthy successor to similar initiatives from the past and like them will succeed or fail depending on the level and depth of Commonwealth/state co-operation and appropriate mechanisms for sharing the costs of reform.

And, finally, to symbolise this new era of reform, we need a new movement to establish an Australian republic – one which demonstrates that reformers once again trust the people by providing for our head of state to be directly elected and with clearly enumerated powers. Australia not just as a republic, but as a pluralist, federal, progressive republic under popular sovereignty. In other words we should aspire to a system that embodies the highest ideals of our liberal and democratic inheritance.

CONCLUSION

What I've tried to demonstrate here is that, contrary to the prevailing view, radicalism has played and should continue to play a big role in the Australian story.

It's true that Australia is incredibly fortunate and prosperous, for most of our people at least. But we didn't get there by taking the easy way out, relying on utilitarianism and pragmatism alone. And we didn't get there by focusing on economics alone and ignoring the insights of political philosophy into the relationship between citizenship, community-building and economic progress.

So my challenge to you is not to reject involvement in mainstream electoral politics – as many disillusioned radicals have done in the past – but to recognise the radical reforming potentialities that still exist within our federal system of government. It's a bit like our personal computers – we're only using a fraction of their potential. As reformers past and present have found, we can find new ways of bringing about quite radical change within the open boundaries set for us by the founding fathers, who truly did take their political philosophy seriously.

Notes:

1 The Tenterfield Oration was delivered on 24 October 1889 and reported in the *Sydney Morning Herald* the next day. See page 185 of this volume.

2 See Mark McKenna, *The traditions of Australian republicanism*, Parliament of Australia, Parliament Library, Research Paper 31 (1995–1996)

3 Ross McMullin, *Light on the hill: the Australian Labor Party 1891–1991,* Oxford University Press, Melbourne, 1991, p. 393.

4 Howard, John, 'Reflections on Australian federalism', address to the Menzies Research Centre, 11 April 2005; and address to the Millennium Forum, Sydney, 20 August 2007.

5 Hon. Justice Michael Kirby, 'Consent and dissent in Australia', 10th Annual Hawke Lecture, Adelaide Town Hall, 10 October 2007.

"Our Australian tapestry is fascinating, strengthened by the weaving together of many threads and colours. The last 220 years make up a small section compared to the 60,000 years or more of Aboriginal life that preceded it. ... I don't believe democracy has 'had it'. But it needs our attention: more responsibility on the part of leaders and the citizenry, more truth-telling."

Weaving the Australian tapestry:

creating a society 'of beauty rich and rare' from threads of harmony and contradiction

---

Linda Burney
17 October 2008

National Library of Australia, Canberra ACT.

MAY I BEGIN by formally recognising the traditional owners of the land on which we meet: Ballumb ambol Ngunnawal yindimarra ngudu-yirra bang marang. I pay my respects to the ancient Ngunnawal nation.

These few words are from my language – Wiradjuri – one of more than 250 languages that were spoken in Australia when the British arrived in 1788. Whether it was 'settlement' or 'invasion' depends on whether you were standing on the shore, or on the deck.

Wiradjuri country spans the fertile plains that stretch from Nyngan to Albury, from Bathurst to Hay. It's one of the largest tribal areas in Australia and includes the Murrumbidgee, Lachlan and Macquarie Rivers. In Wiradjuri these rivers are the Galari, Wambuul and Marrambidya. I am of the Marrambidya Wiradjuri. My children are:

Binni Dironbirong. Strength like the shaft of a spear and
the red colours in the setting sun.
Willurai Ngurumbi Karramarra. Sweet like bush honey, winter water.

I named my children in the Wiradjuri language as a means of reclaiming some of my lost culture.

As an Aboriginal Australian I proudly continue the ancient custom of seeking permission before entering someone else's country. Isn't it extraordinary to think that a custom so ancient has survived, albeit in different forms, over so many thousands of years?

I am conscious of the standing of those who have given this address in previous years: the Honourable Gordon Samuels, Dr Neal Blewett, Professor Helen Irving, the Honourable Dr Geoff Gallop, the Honourable Senator John Faulkner. All these individuals have played a part in creating the Australian story ... weaving the Australian tapestry. And I am honoured to be in their company.

Thank you all for coming. Our democracy can't be in too bad shape when people are willing to come out on a Friday night to listen to an oration. Mind you, 84,000 Americans crammed into a Denver football stadium to hear Barack Obama. We might get a crowd like that at the MCG for an AFL match but hardly for a speech from a politician about the political process.

Americans love their politics. And their leaders are masters of political rhetoric. Australians are more likely to have their political conversations with the local greengrocer, or over a few drinks with friends. But wherever we meet, it's always good to see Australians talking about politics and exchanging ideas, whether it's in the pub, at work, or at a formal oration such as this.

I applaud the mission of the Henry Parkes Foundation to encourage Australians to understand their nation's political history.

And what a history it is: the creation of a new nation at the ballot box by a vote of the people. As former Premier Bob Carr said in a speech at Centennial Park, 1 January, 2001, to mark the centenary of Federation: 'Australian democracy is not a gift, it's not a fluke. It's at the heart of our very being. A hundred years of democracy – that's not an accident. It reflects the genius of a free people.'

But let me make an important point about the founding of our nation. It is often said that Australia has differed from so many other nations in that no blood was shed: there was no civil war, no outbursts of violence. But this statement denies the historical fact of the bloody conflicts that occurred as Aboriginal people fought to defend their land. And I will speak more of that later.

The first theme of my speech this evening is **responsibility**. Both our political leaders *and* the citizenry are responsible for the health of our democracy. A strong democracy needs both parties, and I will make some comments about this.

The other theme is **truth**. In Australia I do not believe we have embraced the concept of truth-telling to the extent necessary if we are to consider ourselves

LINDA BURNEY

The Hon. Linda Burney MP is a proud member of the Wiradjuri nation, and the first Aboriginal Australian to be elected to the New South Wales Parliament – for the seat of Canterbury in 2003. She took on the role of Parliamentary Secretary for Education and Training in 2005 and joined Cabinet as Minister for Fair Trading, Youth and Volunteering in 2007. In September 2008 she was promoted to Minister for Community Services and in December 2009 was appointed Minister for the State Plan. She was President of the Australian Labor Party in 2008. Linda became Deputy Leader of the Opposition in April 2011, and is also the Shadow Minister for: Family & Community Services; Early Childhood Education; Aboriginal Affairs and the Central Coast. A former teacher, she was awarded an Honorary Doctorate in Education from Charles Sturt University in 2002.

a mature and healthy democracy. We're certainly not a nation that has reached the point of reconciliation.

Australians have struggled with the historical fact that our development as a nation came at the cost of the original inhabitants. For years we avoided discussing the 'Australian stain' of our convict history; and behind the happy image of tolerance and diversity we project to the world, there is still fear, misunderstanding, ethnocentrism and intolerance – think Cronulla, December 2005, Pauline Hanson, the hatred unleashed over 'asylum seekers', people we used to call 'refugees'.

I believe in the power of truth-telling. It's not comfortable or easy. You have to dig deep. But truth-telling helps us grow, as individuals, and as a nation.

It helped bring about peace in Northern Ireland.

It was part of the healing in post-apartheid South Africa. Handing over the final report of the Truth and Reconciliation Commission, Archbishop Desmond Tutu said:

> *It is up to all of us South Africans to say 'this is our land'; we are committed to it. We are concerned about the welfare of all South Africans, not just of my particular section or group.*

But before I get to the heart of that discussion, I want to tell you something of my own story. That is one of the wonderful things about Aboriginal culture – the practice of storytelling. If you've been lucky enough to spend time with Indigenous people – whether in Canberra, or Mount Druitt, or a remote community in the Kimberley – you will have experienced some of our most talented storytellers. Funny, descriptive, engaging tales that may concern important matters of culture and law but are just as likely to be a hilarious account of a simple mishap a person has experienced the day before. That's not to say blackfellas have a monopoly on storytelling! Think about Henry Lawson, Banjo Paterson ... about nights you've spent in country pubs listening to the locals spinning yarns.

So tonight I'll begin with a little of my own story. I'll tell some of Sir Henry Parkes' story. And I'll speak of two other Australians from around the same era – Louisa Lawson and Jack Marsh. While Sir Henry Parkes was building a fledging democracy, Louisa Lawson was agitating to change the system, and Jack Marsh, a name you may not recognise, was fighting to be included and, ultimately, for his own survival.

First, a few things about me.

I was born in a small town called Whitton near Leeton, New South Wales. My mother was of Scottish descent, my father Aboriginal. In 1957 it was a disgrace to have a child out of wedlock; to have a child with an Aboriginal man was scandalous. I was raised by my mother's aunt and uncle, Nina and Billy Laing, a drover and a station hand, a brother and sister, both unmarried, who taught me my core values of honesty, loyalty and respect, the gift of compassion and the importance of humility. They taught me manners, too, and I think a few more of those wouldn't go astray in a healthy democracy, either!

It was a typical country kid's childhood – riding horses, cooling off on hot days with a swim in the irrigation ditches, building forts in the rice stubble after the harvest. Of course, being Aboriginal in a conservative country town had its challenges. I'll never forget sitting in class in my first year in high school listening to the teacher describe the Australian Aborigines. They were savages, she explained, with no culture and no technology, the closest thing to Stone Age man in existence. I wished I could turn into a piece of paper and quietly slip through a crack in the floor.

At the age of 27 I met my father. What a day that was. I learned I had 10 brothers and sisters and discovered that during all those years of growing up and wondering, my father lived only 40 minutes away. Such was the power of racial segregation and denial in those dark days.

During my career I've held many roles – teacher, executive director, social activist, board member, mother, politician, Cabinet Minister and volunteer. But my core purpose has remained constant: driving change, working for social justice.

To me, Sir Henry Parkes – that grand old man of Australian politics – is both inspirational and intriguing. He arrived from England as a young man from a poor background with very little formal education. Just like the waves of migrants who followed him, he saw the possibilities of creating a new life and dedicated himself to his new homeland. His love affair with Australia began as soon as the ship sailed into Sydney Harbour, a waterway that his forebear, Governor Arthur Phillip – founder of the first British colony in Australia – described as the 'finest harbour in the world'. Arriving in Sydney in 1839, Sir Henry was inspired to immortalise his impressions in verse:

The wild bush stretching far o'er ridge and creek
The homesteads scattered o'er the smiling land,
The expanse of quiet water, and the gleam
Of the fair city in the summer beam.

I'd have to say Sir Henry was more successful in politics than poetry!

As a political leader, his skills were legendary: five times premier of New South Wales, architect of public education, champion of universal suffrage, advocate for federation. He was also married three times, hopeless with money and as premier imposed a tax of 100 pounds on Chinese immigrants, which represented around 50 weeks pay.

As a member of the same parliament where Sir Henry spent much of his working life, I can assure you his presence is still felt. One of the most stately and elegant rooms in the building is named after him and a portrait painted by Tom Roberts hangs in the foyer: the serious face, the full white beard, and the thoughtful eyes, watching members come and go.

Sir Henry Parkes devoted his life to developing a fair and democratic society through the institution of parliament. As a woman, Louisa Lawson was excluded from society's institutions. So she fought and won her battles in other spheres. In 1888 she set up the ground-breaking feminist magazine *Dawn: A Journal for Australian Women.* At one point she employed 10 staff, all female, defying the New South Wales Typographers Union which refused to accept women as members and tried to close her down.

Louisa Lawson campaigned for marriage and divorce reform, for women's right to work, and for women to take their rightful place in public life. Most significantly, she fought for women's right to vote. If Sir Henry Parkes is the

Father of Federation, then Louisa Lawson is the Mother of Women's Suffrage. She was also the mother, of course, of one of our best loved poets, Henry Lawson.

She is every bit as much a towering figure as Sir Henry Parkes and other political figures of the past century. For me, she is a huge inspiration.

Finally, Jack Marsh. Jack Marsh was a Bundjalung man. He was born in about 1874 on a station called Yulgilbar on the Clarence River in New South Wales. This was the era of missions and reserves, of government-sanctioned policies of child removal, of paternalism, control, racism, and exclusion from mainstream society.

Jack's passion was sport. In 1894 he ran the hundred yards in 9.8 seconds, equalling the world record and becoming the fastest man in Australia. His achievement received little coverage and soon disappeared from the public record. Three years later a cricket official saw him throwing a boomerang at La Perouse and recruited him as a fast bowler. For a while he was the fastest in Australia – until falling victim to a raging controversy about bowlers being accused of 'throwing'.

Despite his talent, calls for Jack to represent Australia were ignored. One selector said he didn't have 'enough class'. In 1902, a visiting English team refused to play a tour match if he was in the side. Warren Bardsley, who later captained the Australian team, said the reason he was 'kept out of big cricket was his colour'.

Jack died in 1916, aged about 40. He was beaten to death in a brawl outside a hotel in Orange. Two men were tried for manslaughter but acquitted. A judge is recorded as saying, and I quote: 'Marsh may have deserved it.'

Let's think about what was happening in other parts of the country at around the same time.

In 1928,12 years after Jack Marsh died, between 60 and 100 Aboriginal people were killed in Central Australia in retribution for the death of a white dingo hunter. That was the Coniston massacre. A board of enquiry laid the blame on Aboriginal people, concluding the shootings were justified on the grounds of self defence. The son of one of the men killed recently sang at a ceremony to mark the 80-year anniversary – and finally, there is a memorial at Baxters Well, 180 kilometres south of Tennant Creek.

Louisa Lawson and Jack Marsh speak to us clearly from history, reminding us that as much as we honour Sir Henry Parkes for the role he played in building a nation, as much as we honour the achievements of our governors and prime ministers, our businessmen and architects and surveyors, our engineers and explorers, we also honour the radicals and activists who championed the cause of women – and we honour the First Australians, whose land, language and children were stolen, and who were kept outside the boundaries of the new nation that was being built on the land they and their forebears had lived in and nurtured for more than 60,000 years.

When I look at these three stories, I realise that despite the massive change that has occurred over the last century, some things never change. Let me offer you a classic Louisa Lawson quote from the October 1890 editorial of *Dawn* magazine: 'Men govern the world, and the schemes upon which all our institutions are founded show men's thoughts only.'

Women are still fighting to take their place on equal terms with men – in the parliament, the board room, in local government and the professions. But imagine Louisa popping into the 21st century and meeting our first female Governor-General...our first female Deputy Prime Minister...and, as of six weeks ago, in New South Wales, our first female Deputy Premier.

I wonder how Henry Parkes would rate our nation's progress against his ideals? The Henry Parkes Foundation's website defines his vision as: 'To build a just, fair, egalitarian society through a democratically elected government with everyone educated and aware of their rights and responsibilities with equal opportunity to participate.'

I think he'd say there's plenty of room for improvement. Three years ago my colleague Senator John Faulkner delivered the Parkes oration at the Tenterfield School of Arts. His title was: 'Apathy and anger: our modern Australian democracy'. It was a powerful speech in which he argued that our democracy is 'drowning in mistrust ... with a dangerous indifference to politics accompanied by a simmering resentment of politicians'.

Three years after that speech, I'd have to say that in my home state of New South Wales, that sentiment recently reached boiling point. In fact, just last weekend I heard someone say, lamenting the recent state of affairs: 'Democracy's had it.'

There is public cynicism about politics and politicians. But despite its many failings, let's all agree that democracy remains our best and only option. As Winston Churchill famously said: 'Democracy is the worst form of government except all those other forms that have been tried.'

The election of the Rudd government 12 months ago did much to restore public confidence. And we are now setting about the task of regaining the trust of the electorate in New South Wales under the leadership of new Premier Nathan Rees.

I believe confidence can and will be restored – by creating and implementing sound policies, managing the state's finances responsibly, and changing the *way* in which we operate. And I think our new Premier has already demonstrated a significant change in approach. He's a straight-talker and someone who understands social justice.

The electorate wants to see vision, intellect and passion in their political leaders. They want to see sensible, successful administration, *and* they want to see fundamental change for the benefit of society.

At the very least they expect absolute honesty and integrity from their elected representatives.

But let me make a point here. As a politician I can tell you the public does sometimes have an unrealistic view of politics. Most of us put up our hand because we want to make a difference. As John Faulkner said in his address: 'Politics is as it is, not because of the nature of politics but because of the nature of people. To expect the practice of politics to be somehow nobler than your own workplace or community organisation, to expect politicians to be better and more virtuous than you yourself are, is to guarantee disappointment.'

Having said that, people do expect a higher standard of their leaders, and rightly so. It is, after all, an immense privilege to hold public office and to serve the community. As Faulkner also said: 'Politics without a social purpose is the empty pursuit of power, brutal and meaningless.'

Every time I talk to a constituent, take part in a Cabinet decision or vote on a bill in parliament, I am reminded of the enormous trust that the people of New South Wales have placed in me. I must also admit that when I have attended a function seven nights in a row and been button-holed by everyone in attendance I am also reminded of the people's sometimes unrealistic expectations!

I'll make a confession to you tonight – just between you and me: I didn't vote until the age of 26. While Aboriginal people have been eligible to vote since 1962, voting was not made compulsory until 1984. The message I took out of that was: you don't have to vote so you're not really accepted as part of society, and that society had let Aboriginal people down. So, like many of my peers, I felt an outsider; alienated. I remember thinking about the Aboriginal Diggers who returned from the war to find they were barred from the RSL clubs, and their wives not eligible for benefits.

In time, I realised I wasn't exercising the most important right of a citizen in a democratic society – the right to vote. And I came to the realisation that being an 'outsider' was in part my own creation. Today I challenge young

Aboriginal men and women: stand up, I tell them, take your place! You never know where you might end up.

For me to become the first Aboriginal Australian to serve in the New South Wales Parliament and to become National President of the Australian Labor Party is something I would never have dreamt of when I was a child running through the rice stubble after the harvest.

I am passionate about working within the party to make our processes more open and democratic. It's the only way we will succeed in growing our membership base. The ALP is the oldest political party in Australia – it is a tough and resilient institution that has demonstrated its ability to evolve.

As National President, I will seek to start a conversation within the party. Currently, the term of National President is one year, with a president, vice president and junior vice president elected to serve on a rotational basis, with 12-month terms. As a colleague recently suggested, it is a kind of rotisserie arrangement. Perhaps a new method needs to be cooked up. The party needs to ask itself – is this the best model? Or should we end the rotisserie and allow the president to establish themselves and serve a three-year term...*and* have a vote on the National Executive.

One strength of the current model is that the president is elected by the rank and file. And perhaps this approach could be extended to the state branches.

I'd also like to look at ways to improve the quality and diversity of people entering politics. For a start, the men and women who stand in local government elections should be those who have worked hard to win the support of their fellow residents by advocating change and solving local problems. Their election to council, therefore, should be based on merit, not just affiliation, not just on their rise through the local branch of the Labor Party, or, for that matter, the Liberal or any other party.

And, another issue that is close to my heart: I will seek to build and strengthen the Indigenous Labor Network – with a view to getting Aboriginal people voting, active in the party, and standing for Parliament.

But what about the responsibility of the broader community? I fear that some Australians may see their job as done once their vote is cast. Their job is then simply to stand back, watch the drama unfold, commentate and criticise. When anything goes wrong – and I mean *anything* – it's the government's fault and the government's role to fix it.

Perhaps politicians have fed the culture of blame and complaint with their grand promises and commitments. But let me tell you right here, right now: government cannot solve every problem. Society's expertise, money and resources and energy are by no means confined to our elected leaders and our permanent public service.

As citizens in a democratic state we all have responsibilities – not only to obey the law, vote and pay taxes, but to contribute to the health and well-being of that society in whatever way we can. That might mean volunteering with the local sports club or hospital, as millions of Australians do. It might mean big business making an effort to employ people with disabilities, or going beyond mere compliance to actively contribute to environmental protection and rehabilitation. It might mean calling on an elderly neighbour to see if they're ok. And it certainly means taking part in the conversations, the public contest of ideas, and the political processes that are the cornerstones of a democratic society.

Throughout my career I have always taken opportunities to mentor young people, especially young women. One of the things I say to them is: get active in your community, look for opportunities to show leadership.

Now let me come to my final theme this evening.

Eight months ago in this city of Canberra, just a short walk from where we meet this evening, a momentous event occurred. Our Prime Minister, less than three months into the job, offered a solemn and genuine apology to the Indigenous people. It is a day that I will never forget.

When I left the Chamber, an elder from South Western Sydney, Aunty May Robinson, came up to me carrying an old black and white photo in a frame. It was of a young Aboriginal girl at Cootamundra Girls' Home. 'Linda,' she said, 'I've brought Mummy with me.'

This was a day that will be recorded in the stories of Aboriginal people to be passed down through the generations. A great hurt had been inflicted. And the truth of what happened needed to be told. Finally, after years of needless prevarication, it was. In the grand, colourful, complicated tapestry that is Australia, that moment in history will stand out as a pivotal event.

I encourage you to learn more about the truth about Australia's history by watching the current series on SBS, *The First Australians*. The first episode told the story of the resistance leader and warrior Windradyne, a Wiradjuri man who fought against the encroachment of settlers in his country, my country. In 1824, after an outbreak of violence that resulted in the deaths of several stockmen and the indiscriminate killing of Aboriginal women and children, Governor Brisbane placed the western district of New South Wales under martial law. The Wiradjuri became legal targets and the results were devastating. It was my people who first drank from those poisoned water holes.

These are important historical facts. This is part of the truth we need to face and accept as a nation. I pay tribute to historians such as Henry Reynolds, Marcia Langton, C. D. Rowley and Inga Clendinnen who have brought these truths to light.

Of course, an apology, no matter how heartfelt, doesn't translate into better health, clean water, adequate housing, a longer life expectancy or an end to welfare. As the Zen proverb says: 'Before enlightenment, chop wood, carry water. After enlightenment, chop wood, carry water.' A huge amount of work needs to be done and I acknowledge the Prime Minister's genuine commitment to 'closing the gap'.

But do not underestimate the importance of that moment of truth in the history of Aboriginal and non-Aboriginal relations.

Let me come to another example. Part of truth-telling is plain speaking. So let me speak plainly on the subject of Australia's ethnic diversity.

We are a culturally diverse society – nearly a quarter of Australians were born overseas and over 30 per cent speak another language at home. The evolution of our country's physical landscape over millions of years is evident in the layers of rock and sediment. To see the evolution of our population you need only walk the streets of my electorate of Canterbury: you will see every wave of immigration represented – layer upon layer of migrants who arrive and, in time, settle.

My experience as local member in one of the country's most culturally diverse areas is overwhelmingly positive. Of course, there are many examples where this is not the case. I think we need more plain speaking. More truth-telling. More conversations between different groups at the kids' netball club or the local community centre.

One positive to come out of the Cronulla riots was the initiative 'On the same wave' that set out to break down the Anglo-Saxon dominance of surf lifesaving. Go down the beach this summer and you will find Abduls, Mohameds and Habibs on patrol. As a newspaper recorded a father from Bankstown saying as he watched his son train in the local pool: 'I want him to be a part of Australian life.'

What a great quote – an immigrant father's wish for his young son: to be a part of Australian life. Think of the hope and optimism contained in that simple sentence!

When I think about Australia, I think first about the land – our great continent, the driest on earth, with its wet tropical wilderness, arid centre, and snow covered mountains. I think about the original inhabitants, from whom I am descended. And that momentous day in January, 1788, when the 11 ships of the First Fleet sailed into Sydney Harbour; the Gadigal people standing on the shore, watching, unaware of the dramatic upheaval that was about to occur.

I think of the millions who have fled here to escape terror and violence, or those who came looking for jobs and a better life.

And of the individuals like Henry Parkes, Louisa Lawson and Jack Marsh who have been part of the Australian story.

When I think of Australia I cannot help but contemplate her contradictions: Dorothea Mackellar's drought and flooding rains; our belief in the fair go that is being tested as wealth becomes concentrated in certain strata of society; and where poverty is entrenched in many of our postcodes. I think of how an Aboriginal painting will sell at auction for a million dollars; yet on the news that night we see another story about Aboriginal children with lower health standards than their counterparts in third world countries.

Yet it works.

Our Australian tapestry is fascinating, strengthened by the weaving together of many threads and colours. The last 220 years make up a small section compared to the 60,000 years or more of Aboriginal life that preceded it. But think of what is crammed in to those two centuries! And of what is yet to come.

I don't believe democracy has 'had it'. But it needs our attention: more responsibility on the part of leaders and the citizenry, more truth-telling.

Tapestries tell a story. They can take a long time, and many hands, to make … and they can be repaired.

"There are strong arguments for the federal system, strong when Henry Parkes and the colonial statesmen of the 1890s devised the Constitution, and strong in today's complex and globalised world."

Great national questions and local matters: Australia's Federation then and now

John Bannon
24 October 2009

Sir Henry Parkes Memorial School of Arts, Tenterfield NSW.

IN THE 1890s Parkes and his colleagues, with the endorsement of the people, brought together six self-governing colonies of very different size, population and wealth into a federal partnership. Respect from the federal authorities for the nature and equality of that partnership has been under threat for the past 100 years, but it remains fundamental to the strength and coherence of the Commonwealth of Australia.

It is exactly 120 years ago that at a banquet in Tenterfield Sir Henry Parkes, then Premier of New South Wales, delivered a speech, remarked on by those present but not widely noticed or reported at the time, that is now seen as a key moment in the making of the our nation, the Commonwealth of Australia. Sir Henry died seven years later, less than five years before the Commonwealth he had prophesied was inaugurated. That Commonwealth and its constitution has proved to be very resilient and over a hundred years after Sir Henry's death Australia now takes its place as a middle-ranked nation, dominant in its region and among the most prosperous 20 nations in the world.

My theme is taken from the words of Sir Henry himself.[1] He asked his audience to consider:

> *whether the time has not now arisen for the creation on this Australian continent of an Australian Government, as distinct from the local Governments, and an Australian Parliament.*

His answer to the question was unequivocal:

> *I believe that the time has come, and if two Governments set an example, the others must soon of necessity follow ... This means a distinct executive and a distinct parliamentary power, a government for the whole of Australia, and it means a Parliament of two houses, a house of commons and a senate, which will legislate on these great subjects. The Government and Parliament of New South Wales will be just as effective as now in all local matters, and so will the Parliament of Queensland. All great questions will be dealt with in a broad manner, just as Congress deals with the national affairs of the United States, and as the Parliament of the Dominion of Canada deals with similar questions.*

And he was not content just to talk about it – he had a clear idea of how it should be brought about:

> *... we must appoint a convention of leading men from all the colonies, delegates appointed by the authority of Parliament, who will fully represent the opinion of the different Parliaments of the colonies. This convention will have to devise the constitution which would be necessary for bringing into existence a federal government with a federal parliament for the conduct of national undertakings.*

In his formulation of the question Parkes defines the essence of federalism: that it exists to allow the big national questions to be dealt with while preserving local matters to the level of government nearest the people. If only Sir Henry knew it, he was describing the concept of 'subsidiarity'. This rather clumsy term is defined as the means by which government is brought as close to the people as possible. To put it more formally: responsibility for regulation and for allocation of public goods and services should be devolved to the maximum extent possible consistent with the national interest, so that government is accessible and accountable to those affected by its decisions.

The concept also recognises that while local interests are reasonably subsumed by larger matters in certain situations, nevertheless the case must be made before

JOHN BANNON

The Hon. John Bannon AO is an Adjunct Professor at the University of Adelaide Law School, a Visiting Research Fellow at Flinders University, and immediate past Chairman of the National Archives Advisory Council. He is a member of the Prime Minister's Expert Advisory Panel for the White Paper on Reform of the Federation. He specialises in Federation History and state/federal relations. Among his publications is *Supreme Federalist: the political life of Sir John Downer*, a primary founder of the Commonwealth. A former parliamentarian (1977–1993), he served as a Minister in the Dunstan and Corcoran governments (1978–79), as Leader of the Opposition (1979–1982), and Premier and Treasurer of South Australia 1982–1992. He was National President of the Australian Labor Party 1988–1992.

taking something to higher and necessarily more remote levels of government. It also acknowledges the culture and background of the components that make up a polity. In the case of Australia, what we know as the Commonwealth would not have been possible without a compact or agreement – in effect a treaty between separate self-governing colonies all of which looked individually to Britain to protect their interests and territorial integrity.

Each of the colonies, founded at different times under different circumstances from each other, had by the 1890s developed a different history and culture as well as robust institutions which allowed them to see themselves not unreasonably as 'nations' albeit under the aegis of the British Empire. The language they used mimicked that of the United Kingdom. Politicians would go to 'the country' to get a mandate for their policies; they talked of 'national interest', the term 'the people of New South Wales' (or wherever) was used to describe their populations. The head of government was more usually called the prime minister; the two colonial houses of parliament represented the Commons and the Lords and followed their procedural precedents and standing orders; the judiciary was protected from political interference. From the 1870s each colony had developed its own military and militia structure. For instance, a relatively small colony like South Australia even had a navy – admittedly of only one vessel, the torpedo-carrying *HMCS Protector*.

Each colony's origin was separate – and it's worth briefly noting this in each case from the 1890's perspective:

- Tasmania, established in 1804, was an island state like New Zealand. One of its first acts on attaining self-government was to change its name from Van Dieman's Land to remove the convict taint which still bedevilled its social relations in order to establish its national credentials.
- In the west, the Swan River settlement of 1829 had struggled to survive, even introducing convict transportation to assist that survival after the eastern colonies had prohibited it, which persisted until 1868. By the 1890s it had finally achieved self-government and in the midst of east coast depression Western Australia boomed following the discovery of gold. It would be the hardest colony to convince of the merits of federation.
- South Australia, established as a Province by Act of Parliament, the convict-free 'paradise of dissent' settled since 1836 and from 1863 with the added responsibility to administer the Northern Territory, was feeling its economic vulnerability. Its vast hinterland had proved to be too arid and dry for productive settlement.
- Queensland had its hands full, governed from Brisbane in its far south-eastern corner with tropical and subtropical centres springing up along its extensive coast. Just across the Torres Strait lay New Guinea, seen as a plaything of the European powers, which caused Queensland to make a unilateral declaration of accession on behalf of the British crown to protect its security.
- Victoria, small and compact in area but with a population and prosperity unprecedentedly increased by the gold rush, was now finding times a little hard as the boom collapsed; and finally
- New South Wales, the convict settlement of 1788, now an established free self-governing polity, was the key to any kind of united nation or federation. Its strategic location, its population and its economic importance would have made it impossible for Australia to unite or federate without it. It saw itself as the progenitor of European settlements – all the rest, except the remote New Holland in the west, had been carved out of its original territory, most recently for the establishment of Queensland in 1859. When the first major attempt at a statutory forum, the Federal Council of Australasia, was established in 1886, it had refused to join (as did South Australia for all but two years) seriously jeopardising the effectiveness of that body.

This made Parkes' intervention in 1889 more significant. The senior colony (or the mother colony as many preferred to call it) was also in recession but not suffering to the same degree as its southern rival. In any case if there was to be any talk of unification it was always with New South Wales as its centre. The only serious proposal for a United Australia, as opposed to a United States of Australia, came from New South Wales Premier George Dibbs in 1894. He was attempting to define his difference from Parkes and others by suggesting a unification of New South Wales and Victoria. This was taken seriously by his Victorian counterpart James Patterson and the two premiers began to negotiate. The scheme would have seen the other colonies initially isolated and compelled to apply to join the new entity on terms set by the big two colonies in their unified form. It failed to take off because both governments fell within months of it being explored.

The proposal was very much bound up in the belief that Australia needed New South Wales more than New South Wales needed Australia. Its most blatant manifestation was in the context of the centenary of the first fleet in 1888. Among other measures of celebration the Parkes government proposed to re-name the colony. Sir Henry introduced a bill to change the name of New South Wales to 'Australia'.[2] The elder statesman Sir John Robertson supported him with the comment that 'If this colony is not Australia I would like to know what is'. The other colonies all objected and there was what is described as a 'prickly' correspondence between Parkes and the Victorian Premier, Duncan Gillies. Representatives of the colonies gathering in England for the Imperial Conference were 'vehement in their denunciations' and there was even a protest from the Colonial Office.

The Governor, Lord Carrington, subtly intervened by securing the superior knighthood, GCMG, for Parkes in honour of the centennial occasion on one condition. Carrington wrote: 'He accepted with pleasure, promising to send me a letter abandoning the change of name'. Parkes claimed later:

> *Though I could easily have carried the Bill I think it had best be dropped... [although] the hasty hectoring spirit in which the other colonies have interfered has set my back up a little.*

It is interesting to reflect that it could well be partly the reaction to his bill changing the name that made Parkes think more positively about federation as an inclusive process.

The big centenary celebrations in New South Wales included the dedication of Centennial Park and a grand banquet for leading citizens paid for by the government. Asked what he would do for the poor and needy Sir Henry offered to distribute food parcels on the day. A radical, Thomas Walker, interjected 'Then we ought to do something for the aborigines', to which Parkes replied: 'And remind them that we have robbed them'. Although abandoning the name change, Sir Henry was unrepentant about the significance of New South Wales. At the banquet, his toast was not to his colony but 'To Australia: her trials and triumphs, her union and progress for the future'. Later while proposing a toast to the visiting colonial governors at a regatta Sir Henry remarked, 'This city of Sydney at the present time must be the capital of Australia.'[3] This New South Wales attitude showed itself again later in its insistence that the federal capital must be within its borders if it was to enter the Commonwealth. Canberra is the result. Even today New South Wales is usually confident of its prime place in the Federation and confident it can get its way.

So we must put aside thoughts that federation was easily accomplished. All the colonies had reason to be happy with and fiercely protective of their status powers and sovereignty. Factors such as population size, geographical area, wealth, or time and manner of founding did not create circumstances that led to an affinity to federate.

We have an accurate way of validating that statement by examining the voting for the referendums on the Constitution. Four colonies voted in the first referendum in 1898, five in the second in 1899, and Western Australia voted at the last minute in 1900 to qualify as an original state:

- In the first, both Victoria and Tasmania gave a substantial endorsement of over 80 per cent. South Australia was less enthusiastic with a 67 per cent approval. Although the 'yes' vote narrowly won in New South Wales, with 52 per cent, it did not gain the number of votes in favour required by the legislation and failed. There was a belief by many that federation was dead.
- After negotiation and some concessions made to New South Wales, another referendum was held in 1899, and this time Queensland also voted. Every one of the four increased the 'yes' vote. Victoria and Tasmania again led the way, this time with an astonishing 94 per cent in favour. South Australia was nearly 80 per cent in favour. New South Wales and Queensland just managed over 50 per cent. In the case of Queensland, Brisbane and the south voted 'no' and it was only the four to one majority in Far North Queensland that got it over the line.
- The Western Australian poll was forced on the government by a threat of secession by the goldfields. It voted in 1900 after the bill had been proclaimed, achieving a majority because 80 per cent of the goldfields voted 'yes'.

The conclusion is that Victoria and Tasmania were enthusiastic for federation, South Australia very committed, but in New South Wales, Queensland and Western Australia support was lukewarm, and in their capitals broadly hostile. This underlines the fact that federation was the only real possibility to unite Australia. If this was the case, what were the 'great national questions' and are they the same today?

For Parkes at Tenterfield it was primarily about defence. A British general had reported on the state of military arrangements in the Australian colonies. He had advised, Parkes told his audience in Tenterfield, 'that the forces of the various colonies should be federated together for operation in union in the event of war ...'

> *If we are to carry out these recommendations it will be absolutely necessary for us to have a central authority, which can bring all the forces of the different colonies into one army. ... I would like to know what is to become of an army without a central executive power to guide its movements? ... Believing as I do that it is essential to preserve the security and integrity of these colonies that the whole of our forces should be amalgamated into one great federal army ... and seeing no other means of attaining the end, it seems to me that the time is close at hand when we ought to set about creating this great national government for all Australia. ...*
>
> *... One great thing to be accomplished is the massing together of their military forces, and this can not be controlled by any other power than one representing all the colonies.*

The only other 'great national question' he mentioned was also linked to defence: the coordination of transport by the conversion of the railway system to standard gauge.

> *This subject brings us face to face with another subject. We have now, from South Australia to Queensland, a stretch of about 2,000 miles of railway, and if the four colonies can only combine to adopt a uniform gauge, it will be an immense benefit in the movement of troops. These, he said, are the two great national questions which I wish to lay before you.*

This did not mean, however, that there were no other questions that should be 'laid before' the electorate.

Free trade between the colonies, the elimination of inter-colonial customs barriers, was high on the list – as important for 'free trade' New South Wales as it was for 'protectionist' Victoria. There would need to be replacement of the revenue lost to colonial governments, which were, except for New South Wales, very heavily dependent on tariffs as a revenue source.

Postal and telegraph communication would be nationally administered.

Immigration was not stressed by Parkes, as he was fresh from Queensland where it was a bitterly divisive issue. His government had taken part in an 1888 Premiers' conference on the topic that resulted in the enactment of the Chinese Exclusion Bill. Queensland's policies on indentured labour from the Pacific islands were undermining a national approach to the question and a cause of their reluctance to federate. It became one of the first laws enacted by the new Commonwealth Parliament.

Foreign Affairs equally did not loom large but for different reasons. It was of course bound up with defence, but was still seen (and remained so until World War II, primarily for Britain to take the lead).

The final Constitution listed a number of other powers (mostly contained in what is now Section 51). They were specifically enumerated in an attempt to make clear what the 'national questions' were. Anything not so listed was to remain in the jurisdiction of the states. That is still the situation today.

And this indicates the nature of the relationship.

We tend to be bedazzled by the British system of government, and ill-informed about other models such as the United States and Canada. The supposed unfettered supremacy of Westminster is an aspiration of any government and parliament at the national level. Because our forms and procedures, our conventions and customs so closely follow the UK we tend to extrapolate and see our federal parliament and Commonwealth Government in the same all-powerful light. We tend to equate our House of Representatives with the British House of Commons and the Senate with upper houses of review like the House of Lords or Legislative Councils.

In fact they are modelled and structured like the United States Congress. The Senate is not simply a 'Westminster' house of review but a states house, with equal representation for the states irrespective of their population. It is a vital component of the federal system. And unlike Britain, our parliaments at both national and state level can only exercise their respective powers in accordance with the Constitution. The Constitution in turn cannot be changed by the parliaments but only by vote of the people.

While this erroneous view of parliamentary supremacy might have had some currency for most of the 20th century there is little excuse for it now as the United Kingdom grapples with the reality of recognising regionalism, both within Britain and in Europe. Under the heading of 'devolution' there are massive internal changes taking place. The Scottish Parliament is now 10 years old and generally regarded as a major success. The Welsh Assembly has had greater difficulty defining its functions and powers but is equally well established. The peace process in Northern Ireland has resulted in the restoration of its parliament and domestic autonomy. The supremacy of parliament has been modified and the clock will not be turned back. Meanwhile externally the once supreme Westminster parliament is having to deal with the implications and constraints of federalism in the form of the European Union.

We should have come to terms with these issues of shared power a century ago in Australia. Equally we should be looking more closely at the examples of the two great federations, the United States and Canada, on which our own was modelled. They have the same vigorous debate about what should be the appropriate powers for the levels of government that should inform our own, and similar disputes about tax sharing. But neither of them has replaced federation or seen a state leave the federal system despite, in the case of the USA, a bloody civil war, and in Canada the French separatist movement. The story of Canada has been one of new states joining it since the original confederation of 1867, including Newfoundland, which until 1947 was a Dominion in its own right. The federal system clearly has a lot going for it.

The centralising tendency of most federal governments cuts across the parties despite Labor's traditional commitment to centralism and Liberal's supposed commitment to states' rights. The unremitting propaganda of the press gallery in Canberra and the powerful and remote federal bureaucracy sets an agenda that says our problems could be solved by running our system centrally. Is this the case? Are there not significant matters that Parkes would call 'local' that could best be handled near the coalface?

My answer is 'yes' and I regret the tendency to assume that any controversial or difficult problem of the day needs central administration to overcome it. The Commonwealth Government rightly has the dominant financial role and collects most of the tax to fund government programs. But it collects that tax on a uniform basis on behalf of all governments not just for its own purposes, and state and local government should not have to go cap-in-hand as mendicants to get an adequate share to carry out their functions. The mechanism of the Grants Commission, and agreements on special payments, should ensure that the tax income is fairly distributed and applied to programs which match broad national priorities with local needs. Fortunately we have come a long way from the appalling annual haggle of the Premiers' Conference and Loan Council but agreement will always be hard to reach if the states are required to simply beg for funds.

There are strong arguments for the federal system, strong when Henry Parkes and the colonial statesmen of the 1890s devised the Constitution, and strong in today's complex and globalised world. They include the way in which government can be made more participatory and accessible; the healthy competition between the states which helps achieve best practice and ensure that development takes place throughout the continent and not just in corners of it; the diversity and flexibility which encourages experiments and allows their success or failure to be judged and adopted or avoided by other governments. Electoral reform, public health initiatives, minority rights, environmental protection, consumer protection, and many other reforms are achieved because of opportunities provided by federalism. The concerns of local communities can be addressed more readily.

I suggest there are three great fallacies which need to confronted before we can make the federal system function better:

- Firstly, that the 'national interest' is the same as federal government policy: In a federation all governments have a role in defining and pursuing national goals. The whole community can benefit if all are involved, rather than Canberra attempting to enforce an outcome by edict without consultation or regard for the limits of its power.
- Secondly, that centralised service delivery is by definition the most efficient: Large bureaucracies can be very wasteful and ineffective, slow to respond, and inflexible in a country the size of Australia.
- Thirdly, that 'uniformity' equals effectiveness: It is often only by trying different approaches, local variations and pilot experiments that the best outcomes can be achieved. We must also recognise that communities have different requirements and priorities.

But even if all those arguments were rejected, there is a practical reason to ensure federalism is working: there are no real alternatives.

- Referendums to change the Constitution are rarely successful – people like what they have better than any alternatives that are proposed. These alternatives can only be generated from the federal parliament and usually involve extending federal power and they are not supported.

- Referral of powers by the states can work in some limited cases, but this is not going to occur in any wholesale manner.
- The idea of re-drawing state boundaries or replacing states with a network of regions is not going to get off the ground. It has been tried a number of times without success (even here in New England).

I came across a formulation of federalism the other day from a source that surprised me – it was a quote by Harold Holt, Sir Robert Menzies successor as prime minister, who died in office in 1967. He spoke of:

> *a co-operating democracy ... not trying to make Federation work by imposing authority from the centre or by so construing the federal powers that the states were reduced to nothingness, but a true Federation based upon a spirit of cooperation rather than the strict definition of powers.*[4]

This is a long way from the practice of the Liberal Party of Prime Minister Howard in government, but strangely close to the approach taken by the Labor government of Prime Minister Rudd so far. I hope we are moving to revive the concepts envisaged by Henry Parkes and the founders. The key I believe is to think less of 'levels of government' – a hierarchy – and more of the concept of power-sharing, a rational division of powers between partners which have a respect for each other. This will certainly match the vision articulated so eloquently at Tenterfield by Sir Henry Parkes 120 years ago.

Notes:

1 Quotations from the Tenterfield Oration are taken from the report in the *Sydney Morning Herald* of 26 October 1889. See facsimile with an introduction by John Williams in *The New Federalist: the Journal of Australian Federation History*, No. 1, June 1998, pp. 71–73. Quotes have been rendered in direct speech for this address. Also available through the National Library of Australia's Trove database: http://trove.nla.gov.au/ndp/del/article/13746899. See also page 185 of this volume.

2 The following account is based on Martin, A. W., *Henry Parkes*, Melbourne University Press, 1980, pp. 368–370.

3 See Martin, op. cit., pp. 369–371.

4 Quoted in Frame, Tom, *The life and death of Harold Holt*, Allen & Unwin, Sydney, 2005, p. 145.

"By all means, let us feel free to celebrate our cultural diversity – our religious and ethnic and other social traditions and loyalties. But let us agree this should not mean aspiring to a class-stratified school system where choice and competition are driven by gross resource disparities among schools. Let us agree not to confuse disparity with diversity."

Public education and the common wealth: towards sustainable democracy

Lyndsay Connors
29 October 2010

National Library of Australia, Canberra ACT.

THE SIGNIFICANCE of Sir Henry Parkes in the history of Australia is not a matter that lies settled in the past. It will be affected by decisions of this and future generations.

Parkes is known as the 'Father of Federation'. But his reputation as a reformer in the colony of New South Wales pre-dated Federation. His vision of nationhood was inextricable from the action needed to cultivate the capacity of citizens to think freely for themselves.

In 1879, he had introduced the bill that became the New South Wales *Public Instruction Act* of 1880. This established a minimum period of compulsory schooling and a Department of Public Instruction under a Minister of the Crown.

I am a direct beneficiary of that system of schooling in what was soon to become the state of New South Wales in the new Commonwealth. Under the Australian Constitution, the responsibility for ensuring that every child received a minimum period of formal education was left to the states. Their primary obligation, in meeting that responsibility, became the provision of free, public, secular schooling.

The New South Wales *Public Instruction Act* went beyond the provision of universal elementary or primary education. High schools were also provided, to fit those girls and boys who were 'so disposed' to proceed to University, and '...to take their place, if they should be fitted for it, amongst the first persons in the land'.[1] By contrast, across Australia as a whole, it was not until the 1950s that public schools became the main providers of secondary schooling. The high school I attended in the 50s, named after the St. George district in which it was located, owed its existence not to the vision of any saint but to that of Henry Parkes.

Schooling in New South Wales was then compulsory between the ages of six and fifteen. The vast majority of students received only three years of secondary school education.

But I had three years more schooling than most of my peers. I had the benefits of a full secondary schooling despite the fact that by the time I left school I had lost both my natural parents. I entered school before, and I left it after, the compulsory period defined in law. I was enrolled at my local public school at the age of four by my widowed, working mother, who had no other form of child care. I then repeated the fifth year of primary schooling to catch up in age with my peers before high school. And I had a full five years of high schooling instead of the typical three that corresponded with the legal minimum. This was because I had gained entry to an academically selective high school.

I was born into that common wealth that exists in a society that commits itself to the principle of providing education for its children in their own right, regardless of what privileges or burdens they may have inherited from their parents, or even whether they have parents. In adult life, I have felt keenly aware that the circumstances of my own early life have placed upon me a particular obligation to Sir Henry Parkes and to the public school system of New South Wales; and, in particular, to the teachers that saw me through to finish my schooling.

How remarkable it now seems that this self-educated man understood that 'there can be no good school anywhere without a good teacher'. In recent times, we have seen the corporate world investing heavily in research to reach precisely the same conclusion; and to advocate greater public investment in teaching. Parkes spoke at length to an audience at Dundas in 1869 of the need for 'a body of men and women trained for the profession of teaching, admitted to the several grades of the service by their merits alone ... There will be no royal road to the

LYNDSAY CONNORS

Lyndsay Connors AM FACE is an Adjunct Professor in the Faculty of Education and Social Work at the University of Sydney, where she chairs the Teacher Education Advisory Board. She has long been a forthright advocate for the equal entitlement of all Australians to high quality education and for a system of strong and socially representative public schooling that is open freely to all.

school service. No man – from the Prime Minister downward – will be able to get a boy or girl made a teacher unless he or she is qualified for the calling'.[2]

Public schools had existed in the colony prior to the 1880 Act. Parkes was speaking at Dundas in 1869 at the opening ceremony of such a school. In his role as President of the then Council of Public Education, he told the gathering that what they were doing on that day was '...one of the most important things that can at any time be done in a state of civilised society'.

> *... We are endeavouring to supply the means of sound instruction to those who, in a very few years, are to constitute the strength of the country ... a Public school system in any country is an essential part of its institutions in the large sense of politics. It is part of the policy of the country. It is part of the intention and action of the Government; part of the very life of constituted authority.*

In his closing remarks, he drew the links between public education and the act of federation to come:

> *Whatever may be our form of Government ... Let us by every means in our power take care that the children of the country grow up under such a sound and enlightened system of instruction, that they will consider the dearest of all possessions the free exercise of their own judgment in the secular affairs of life, and that each man will shrink from being subservient to any other man or earthly power.*

Our obligation to Henry Parkes does not require us to defend the realities of the organisation and delivery of public schooling, past or present, or to deny the scope for ongoing reform. It does not require us to accept the proposition that the fact of schools being funded and operated by governments and open freely to all makes them good schools.

History shows that it has been a long and sometimes painful process to grow into what one of our finest education thinkers, Jean Blackburn, once called 'the great idea of public education'. Henry Parkes had referred, that day at Dundas, to the 'children of the country'. But when I started school in outer Sydney in the 1940s, 'children of the country' did not include all the children of the country. Indigenous children were largely excluded from the educational largesse I enjoyed. So were many children with disabilities.

We are not required to accept that compulsory, free and secular education should have pride of place in our nation simply by dint of its having provided many of us with direct and material advantages. For many have profited personally from enterprises that are far from right and proper. The obligation that is placed upon all Australians who have benefited personally from their public schooling is simply this – to use that education to think rationally about the significance of public education and its place in our society.

My theme is that this is a shared obligation we have neglected in recent years. This is partly because the relationship between Henry Parkes' two great legacies – the nation's public schools and its federal system of government – has become unduly complex and dysfunctional.

One indicator of malaise is Australia's persistently poor completion rates for secondary schooling or the vocational equivalent. After sliding in international rankings compared with other OECD countries, Australia's position is now close to the bottom third in this regard. Those leaving school prematurely are concentrated in schools serving the poorest communities – the great majority in public schools. The recent report of the Bradley Review of Higher Education warned that the costs of failing to deal with this persistent problem go well beyond those directly disadvantaged. They put at risk Australia's capacity to sustain its much vaunted economic performance.

In making schooling compulsory, governments had to make it universally affordable by parents, including those who could not meet even a nominal fee.

Perhaps such wide acceptance of compulsory schooling has blinded us to the need to think seriously about the responsibilities that governments embrace by making it so. These extend well beyond universal affordability. Access to schooling entails more than attendance, vital as this is. It raises the question of access to what?

Compelling children to attend school obliges governments, at the very least, to do all in their power to ensure that this will not expose them to risk or harm. In any decent democracy, it obliges governments to provide in school for all our children what could be called 'conditions of flourishing'. In this country, we have the capacity to equip all our public schools with the resources they need to assist students to learn about the world they share, to expand their capacity to consider how things came to be the way they are and what action they might take to improve their own lives and those of others. This was what Henry Parkes saw as the essential objective of public education – to confer 'the dearest of all possessions – the capacity for informed judgment in the secular affairs of life'.[3]

As Henry Parkes told his audience at the Dundas school opening in 1869, it is the compulsory nature of schooling that obliges governments to provide secular schooling – 'so that all children can be partakers of it. What right would the state have to direct the religious instruction of children? But it has a right, and it is its solemn duty, to see that the children of the country are instructed so as to understand the laws, and be competent to take an intelligent part in the work of civil society'.

There were, in Parkes' day, those prepared to argue that their secular nature meant that public schools were operating in some morally empty space, or were by definition hostile to religion. Over recent years, we heard this line of argument revived by some politicians and lobbyists seeking to justify mounting public expenditure on non-government, largely religious, schools by portraying public schools as lacking in values.

Schools provide secular education outside the public sector. At least one such school in Sydney is, moreover, proud to advertise that it is an equal opportunity employer and selects its teachers on the basis of teaching ability, which Henry Parkes would have approved. But that school charges fees well beyond the financial reach of most families with school age children.

There are schools outside the public sector that are affordable, if not by the poor, then by many other families. These are mainly religious in character. Most can claim to assist their students to think rationally for themselves. But their prime reason for existence is religious formation.

The school place provided for me when I sat the New South Wales Leaving Certificate all those years ago, like the primary schools I attended before it, was not in a charitable institution for those with careless or absent parents; it was not a place provided by the grace and favour of a private fee waiver. It was a place provided for me in my own right, as for all my classmates, as citizens of the nation – the Commonwealth. The school was not where we met the children with whom our parents decided we should mix socially, and it was not there to save our souls. Its teachers had one primary mission – to assist its students to gain the knowledge, understanding, skills and values to learn to think for themselves. And, because Parkes and his colleagues had a canny grasp of the practical benefits for society of economies of scale, it was a school within a large system

In my experience, the legal obligation upon schools to accept students from all walks of life produces in teachers a capacity for invention that is bred by necessity. And that necessity tends to create a disposition towards broadmindedness, liberalism and a tolerance of diversity. Such virtues, however hard to sustain, are the lifeblood of a democracy. The requirements on public schools are conducive to keeping them 'right for the times'. They cannot easily retreat into nostalgia for a real or imagined past or advance too far ahead of the understandings and expectations of the public they serve.

To distinguish public, secular and free schooling from privately owned and operated, fee-for-service schooling, religious and other, does not imply an attack on the legitimacy of either, and does not deny the necessity for their co-existence or their potential for reciprocity.

How can any democratic government ask us to believe, however, when it distributes the public funding that now covers the salaries of teachers in around 95 per cent of all Australian schools,[4] that the difference between public and non-government schools does not matter; or that it can simply be airbrushed away for political purposes, however bi-partisan? How can there be no difference between placing those publicly funded teachers in a system of public schools where their services are freely available to children without fees or religious tests, and placing them in schools where their services are available only to those that meet such tests, set privately by non-government authorities?

To fail to understand such differences, or to wilfully claim that there are none in order to silence public debate, is to put the future of our democracy at risk. The fact that there may be a coalition of those willing to engage in collective dementia should not be confused with consensus.

We should neither deny, nor exaggerate, the differences. There are vast differences among schools within the public and the private school sectors. There are many public schools, serving well-off localities, with a higher socio-economic profile than some non-government schools in poorer localities. These realities also need to be understood by those responsible for education policy.

David Malouf has recently written of Australia's having achieved nationhood in a rather 'offhand' way. He argues that our Federation did not come about through the flowering of a great utopian ideal, or the coming together after a long period of yearning by people who had known the anguish of division or that harboured any sense of manifest destiny.[5] But Parkes and his colleagues had inherited long traditions of freedom and social equality; and through their reforms they positioned Australia by the early 20th century as one of the world's most advanced democracies.

Over the years, the central government's powers have evolved well beyond its initial spheres of defence and trade. Key factors in this evolution were the states' ceding of their income taxing powers to the Commonwealth in World War II; and the increasing need for national economic policy and for national responses to various international pressures.

There are strengths in federal systems of government, but Australia has succumbed to a range of the recognised pitfalls. We have developed a bad case of 'vertical fiscal imbalance'. The Commonwealth has taken over collection of the bulk of taxation revenue, while the responsibility for much of the expenditure on essential services remains with the states. Where the Commonwealth has become a partner with states in key spheres, such as health and education, roles and responsibilities are often poorly delineated, irrational and conducive to cost and blame shifting and to substitution. The effects are poorly co-ordinated services with waste and duplication or, alternatively, gaps. Ambiguities tend to produce artificial and contrived forms of accountability for the achievement of policy goals; as well as countervailing policies.

The convergence of these factors has produced a fog over schooling in Australia. This has provided cover for policy moves that are radical by international standards. It has reduced schools funding to a policy imbroglio.

Few Australians understand, for example, that the recurrent grants from both levels of government to non-government schools now exceed the total salary bill for teachers for that sector.[6]

If a fair share and a fair go matter in relation to schooling, then they matter most in relation to access to quality teaching. But through the discontinuities of our federal system and in a context where the public school share of total enrolments has been contracting, governments have been progressively ceding to private authorities their responsibility for allocating publicly funded teachers among students and schools. With few questions asked, a growing proportion of the publicly funded teachers in Australia now works in schools where the price for access to their services is set privately according to what private authorities judge their target market will bear.

It has proven more possible to achieve highly controversial shifts of public resources in Australia than it would be under a unitary system of government, or a system where the roles of the state and Commonwealth in education were clearly delineated. The complexities of our federal system work against public scrutiny and understanding. It would be very difficult, for example, to sustain an argument that Australians knowingly voted for the shift of public funding that has effectively occurred – from universities to non-government schools. And it is the more extraordinary that this happened in a federal system where the Commonwealth has taken on formal responsibility for funding the provision of higher education, while the responsibility for schooling rests with the states. It has been able to happen because of the split-level arrangements that make it hard to track the effects, for example, of contradictory changes to the Commonwealth's indexation of schools and universities introduced by the Keating Labor government in the 1990s. This was an unorthodox, if not inappropriate, use of indexation as a political and policy tool.

Over the decade 1997 to 2007, the cumulative effect of indexation was to reduce public funding of universities by the Commonwealth by well over $5 billion. This was because indexation did not keep pace with salaries and other inflationary effects in universities. But indexation at a rate higher than the movements in such costs delivered the schools sector as a whole a windfall gain closer to $6 billion – of which around 60 per cent went to schools in the private sector.[7]

This was because of the imbalance that had developed in Commonwealth funding for public and non-government schools. Through basing indexation of its own funding for schools on movements in states' funding of public schools, the Commonwealth has been able to deliver real funding increases for even those non-government schools operating at resource levels, from their private fees alone, well in excess of what could be justified purely on grounds of educational need.

History has shown that when such issues are raised in an election context, those with power and influence have been able to focus media attention on the interests of this small minority of schools, at the expense of the schools that serve the vast majority of students. One unfortunate by-product of Australia's federal system is that Commonwealth and state elections are held at different times, with the result that the country is, in a sense, permanently in election mode. This makes it difficult to find the political space within which to deal with politically complex and sensitive issues. The future of our public school system has become one of those issues.

We have a federal system conducive to political opportunism. There are many examples where the Commonwealth, with no responsibility for the direct provision of schooling, is reduced to opportunism to create avenues for influence. This explains a tendency for the Commonwealth to provide funding in the form of special purpose payments, with little understanding of or respect for state priorities. The practical effect is that even when public funds are properly directed towards the most hard-pressed public schools, they arrive in the shape of an ever-changing array of re-badged programs each with its set of hoops to be jumped through. An over-reliance on such programs – especially where the scale of their funding and their timelines are inadequate to achievement of their grand objectives – leads to fragmentation of funding and effort.

At worst, the deficit view of public schooling adopted by numbers of leaders at the national level on a bi-partisan basis has, in the words of one of our most distinguished education researchers, Richard Teese,[8] subjected them to the indignity of 'scavenging on the scrapheap' of failed educational reform – flagpoles one year, league tables the next.

Flaws in our federal system of government are not, of course, the only factors that have affected the standing of our public school system.

Over recent decades, broad social, political and economic trends have taken us in the direction of a two-tiered education system, within which public schools are being positioned as the poor relation. The divides created by social geography within and beyond our cities have intensified social stratification among schools. Neo-liberal politics and economics have fuelled these trends in Australia, as well as in many other countries. They are characterised by arguments for reducing the role of governments, and increasing reliance on market-based competition and the commodification of services to achieve policy outcomes.

In this climate, however, spending public funds to expand private services and strengthen market forces can be justified as a means of achieving overall reductions in public spending. The Howard government claimed that increased Commonwealth funding to non-government schools would produce a shift in enrolments to the private sector with overall savings to the public purse. It achieved the first but not the second result, as confirmed by a 'before and after' snapshot of the financial effect of increasing enrolments in non-government schools over the decade 1996 to 2006. This shows that, had public schools been used to accommodate the extra 200,000 students who enrolled in non-government schools over that decade, the additional cost to the public purse would have been around $2 billion. But the actual public funding increase for non-government schools over this period was more than $3 billion. This was because the rate of public funding increase to non-government schools over this period significantly outstripped the rate of enrolment increase; as well as the rate of public funding increase to government schools. This was a longstanding pattern that gathered momentum during the years of the Howard government.[9]

Many countries have adopted neo-liberal policy approaches. But no other country has split responsibility for public funding of public and non-government schools between the national government and states in a federal system in a way so inimical to the health of public education. Australia sits around the middle of OECD countries ranked in terms of per capita investment in schooling. It now ranks third-lowest, however, in the developed world in terms of the public funding it allocates to public schools; and fourth highest in terms of the share it allocates to non-government schools.[10]

This is no counsel of despair. The fact is that the Australia's schools generally perform consistently well by international standards. This suggests that our teachers know what they are doing, and that a higher public investment in the supply of quality teaching and greater equality of access to it would be well justified.[11] But our system is heading in dangerous directions. The effects of inequalities now built into our school system are most damaging for those young people who most need the sustained and mindful support of government. And they threaten social mobility and feed a situation where too many young people are leaving school prematurely or without useful credentials – while the country faces a mounting skills shortage.

Australia's federal system has evolved in ways that are making it a toxic environment for public schooling.

But talk of public education becoming a 'residualised' system in Australia, with a declining share of overall enrolments and of those from better-off families, is misleading. It masks the reality. In Australia's hybrid school system, the public school system is, to borrow a biological metaphor, the host organism. Public schools could exist, though they never have, in the absence of non-government schools. But non-government schooling as currently operated is only viable because of the existence of public schools. In biological terms, non-government schools exist in a parasitical relationship with the host. This can be a mutually beneficial relationship in nature; or it can be a relationship that damages the host. It does not serve the interests of parasites for damage to occur to the organism on which their own existence relies.

I use this biological metaphor to illustrate that the future health of the public school system is the key to the health of the school system as a whole.

By all means, let us feel free to celebrate our cultural diversity – our religious and ethnic and other social traditions and loyalties. But let us agree this should not mean aspiring to a class-stratified school system where choice and competition are driven by gross resource disparities among schools. Let us agree not to confuse disparity with diversity.

Following the 1866 *Public Schools Act,* the galvanised iron buildings at Sydney's Cleveland Street School were demolished and replaced by substantial buildings in the Gothic Revival style.

Henry Parkes was there for the laying of the foundation stone of the school described by the press at the time as a 'palace'.

Parkes dreamed of a country in which 'each man will shrink from being subservient to any other man or earthly power'. But around the country, in their churches and Sunday schools, our colonial forebears were giving voice to this verse in their hymnals.

The rich man in his castle
The poor man at his gate
He made them, high or lowly,
And ordered their estate.

Rarely sung today, it always sat oddly among the other verses of 'All things bright and beautiful', which were devoted to the wonders of nature.

And in the very year – 1879 – when Henry Parkes was introducing his Public Instruction Bill and provision for high schools in New South Wales, a certain Mr Downer was striking a very different note in South Australia. A lawyer and one of that state's largest landowners, Mr Downer pronounced that to provide high schooling for people who had no business with it was interfering with the very laws of nature.[12]

It is time to ask which of our many traditions we want to honour, to sustain and to advance.

We can afford to think about whether or not the interests of a modern democracy are best served by sustaining our commitment to a federal system of government. But I do not believe we can sustain a democracy without a commitment to a high-quality, public school system that provides a framework of equal opportunity for all our children and young people to learn.

Urgent action is needed to put to right the relationship between the two great legacies of Henry Parkes, public schooling and our national system of democratic government. For both are critical to our common wealth. Such action cannot wait for the general Constitutional reform that is widely agreed to be needed.

A great great grandson of Sir Henry Parkes remarked drily in a recent conversation that one form of homage to his forebear that was not needed was another statue.

So let me propose here that, rather than statuary, we now need statutory action.

The Commonwealth's use of the powers it has gained through Section 96 of the Constitution has evolved to the point where it now provides almost 40 per cent of the nation's public investment in its schools.[13] Yet this has occurred through a dysfunctional and irrational sharing of responsibility with the states and territories in our federation. Statements such as the National Goals of Schooling read more like mission statements than genuine commitments to democratic ideals of schooling.

The time is right for a Henry Parkes Act.

What is needed now is legislation which provides that, in all its dealings with schooling, the primary obligation of the Commonwealth is to maintain and safeguard strong and socially representative public school systems that are of the highest standard and are open, without fees or religious tests, to all children and young people.

The problem is that the recent splitting by the Rudd government of the legislative framework for Commonwealth funding of government and non-government schools has complicated and arguably made even less transparent the Commonwealth's financial effort across both sectors of schooling. Ironically, the *Schools Assistance Act*, itself enabled under Section 96 of the Constitution for the granting of funds to the states has now become the vehicle for the payment of funds directly to non-government school authorities only. Commonwealth funding for public schools is now provided through the broader *Federal Financial Relations Act 2009* (Cwlth).

In these circumstances, and in the absence of an Australian Bill of Rights, a fine solution would be to use a stand-alone statute – a Henry Parkes Act – to set down the clear legal standard to be followed by the Commonwealth in all its actions relating to schooling, making explicit its primary obligation to public schools.

State and territory governments would also need to incorporate this principle, either in their current Acts covering responsibilities for schooling, or by bringing in a stand-alone Act such as proposed for the Commonwealth.

Complementary legislation of this kind could follow from discussion and agreement between governments in national forums, especially the Council of Australian Governments (COAG). Perhaps it is time to put the idea to that forum, possibly through the COAG Reform Council.

The enactment of such complementary legislation across the nation would be an important step towards restoring the vital connection between public education and the democratic federation envisioned by Henry Parkes.

Notes:

1 *Public instruction: speech delivered on the opening of the public school, Blayney, May 25 1880*, Sydney, reprinted, with corrections, from the special report of the *Sydney Morning Herald*, George Robertson, Sydney, 1880.

2 *The Public Schools Act: speech of Henry Parkes, President of the Council of Education, on opening the public school at Dundas on Thursday September 4 1869*, J. Ferguson, Sydney, 1870.

3 ibid.

4 Governments cover the costs of teaching in all public schools, in all Catholic systemic schools and in at least half all independent schools. Taken together, this means that governments are providing teachers, or the public funding equivalent, in around 95 per cent of all Australian schools.

5 Malouf, D. 'The states of the nation', *The Monthly*, August 2010.

6 The *National report on schooling 2008* reveals that governments, Commonwealth and state together, provided around $8.3 billion in public funding for non-government schools. That same report sets out the total expenditure of $6.6 billion for teaching staff salaries in those schools.

7 Teese, R. 'Suffer the children left behind', *The Age*, 16/8/2010.

8 When significant Commonwealth funding started to flow to schools in 1974, about 70 per cent went to public and 30 per cent to non-government schools, approximating their respective share of enrolments. By the end of the Howard years in 2007, this situation was completely reversed, with only 30 per cent of Commonwealth funding flowing to public schools. This was, in effect, a turnaround in Commonwealth funding of schools of 40 percentage points away from public schools, while the shift of enrolments away had changed over that period by only 12 percentage points.

9 These are both conservative estimates. They relate to real increases arising from indexation only. They take no account of increases arising from explicit policy changes in either sector or from enrolment growth.

10 Patty, A. 'Bad mark on school funding', *Sydney Morning Herald*, 9 September, 2010.

11 Rorris, A. in Bonnor, C. (ed) 'Investment in Australian schools – somewhere between the virtuous and the vicious', *2020 School Education Summit – the public good and the education of children*, 2008.

12 Miller, P. *Long division: state schooling in South Australian society*, 1986.

13 Leaving aside the large, but temporary, Building the Education Revolution program.

"Although Federation has conferred many benefits, the failure during the 1890s to include railways along with defence and communications as a federal responsibility has been costly to the nation. The railway gauge question, resolved in the late 19th century in Britain, Canada, the United States and New Zealand, still awaits resolution in Australia."

Railways in Australia: Federation unfulfilled

Philip Laird
22 October 2011

Sir Henry Parkes Memorial School of Arts, Tenterfield NSW.

ONE HUNDRED and twenty two years ago, Sir Henry Parkes as the Premier of New South Wales delivered a speech that gave real direction to federation of the Australian colonies.[1]

In this speech, Parkes had a clear vision of an Australian federation that included an efficient rail system to increase both the nation's defence capability and its prosperity.

If Sir Henry were to return today to Australia, he would be impressed with advances in railway engineering along with some world class operations. However, he would be greatly disappointed and quite angry at the substandard nature of rail in New South Wales. He would also demand to know why, 110 years after Federation, the nation's railway gauges had not been standardised; and why successive federal governments have failed to give Australia a fit-for-purpose rail system.

THE LATE 19TH CENTURY

To answer these questions, we need to go back to the late 19th century. On the first day of May 1889, a major rail bridge across the Hawkesbury River was officially opened by the New South Wales Governor, Lord Carrington. As well as joining the northern and southern sections of the New South Wales railways, the bridge completed a continuous railway link between Brisbane, Tenterfield and Sydney, and on to Albury, Melbourne and Adelaide. At a banquet with over 300 present, including from Queensland and Victoria, Parkes observed that the grand trunk line linking the four colonies had a length of nearly 1800 miles – or over 2800 kilometres. Parkes gave many examples of overseas railways that were shorter than the new trunk line, and stated that the New South Wales Government, in completing not only the Great Western Line with its Zig Zag, and now this great bridge over the Hawkesbury River, demonstrated taking on 'formidable obstacles' and that 'we have neither been sparing of our capital nor stinted in our public spirit in trying to give ... the people of Australia fair railway enterprise.'[2]

In short, Parkes was then able to say that New South Wales had a world class railway system.

Parkes went on to say that 'We have formed a communication by railway which may be said to bind the whole population of Australia in one chain … and … that the time has arrived for the political federation of these colonies.'

His speech concluded with a rousing call for a 'United Australia'.

However, the linking by rail of the four capitals of the eastern colonies involved no fewer than three different railway gauges. The opening of the Hawkesbury River bridge provided support for gauge unification and prompted the Chief Commissioner of the New South Wales Railways, E.M.G. Eddy, to stress the need for the colonies to affirm the adoption of a uniform gauge and to prepare for the ultimate conversion of other railway gauges to the uniform gauge. He asked that Parkes '… give this matter most careful consideration'.[3]

Further support for both federation and a uniform railway gauge was to follow with an official visit to each of the Australian colonies by an Imperial officer, Major-General Bevan Edwards. Edwards arrived from Hong Kong in July 1889 at Brisbane, inspecting defence facilities and troops in each Australian colony. He also travelled between Brisbane, Sydney, Melbourne and Adelaide by rail. This gave him a first-hand experience of the problems caused by break of gauge.

In October 1889, Edwards provided official reports to each of the colonies on not only defence matters but also railways. Here, if '… full benefit is to be

PHILIP LAIRD

Philip Laird is an Honorary Principal Fellow at the University of Wollongong and a graduate of Victoria University of Wellington, the Australian National University and the University of Calgary in Canada. He is a Fellow of the Chartered Institute of Logistics and Transport, a Companion of the Institution of Engineers Australia, and a Life Member of the Railway Technical Society of Australasia.

derived from the railways, a uniform gauge must be established – at all events on the through lines.' [4]

These themes were echoed by Parkes in his October 1889 speech at Tenterfield in his historic call for federation.[5]

However, it then took 106 years for all mainland state capitals to be directly linked by a uniform gauge. This occurred in 1995 when track from Melbourne to Adelaide was finally converted to standard gauge.

What went wrong? How could it have taken so long?

The answer, for the most part, is that under Federation, railways were left under state control. This was in contrast to the Commonwealth being given express powers to control defence, and services such as post and telegraphs.

Leaving railways with the states was also in contrast to the Canadian federation of 1867 that made their railways a federal responsibility. It was also in contrast to the decisions of the United States Supreme Court during the late 19th century that removed many state laws restricting interstate rail operations.

Here, the national approach to railways in both Canada and the United States went hand in hand with major progress in gauge standardisation during the late 19th century.[6]

In 1891, a National Australasian Convention was held in Sydney with Parkes as president. The convention adopted a draft constitution for a new Commonwealth.[7] This listed powers of a federal parliament that included defence and customs along with post and telegraphs. Plus the '… control of the railways for the purposes of the Commonwealth.'

At the 1897 Australasian Federal Convention in Adelaide, strong objections from South Australia to federal control of post and telegraphs were overcome with the help of 'the powerful and persuasive figures of Barton, Deakin and Reid.'[8] This federal control was then expanded to include 'telephonic, and other like services'. This was helpful during the 20th century with the national development of radio, television and internet.

Railways then went somewhat backwards at the 1897 convention. One delegate, Bernhard Wise from New South Wales, noted that, 'the telegraphs and the post offices are to be handed over to the Federal Government' and asked why not the railways? Here, a proposal of James Walker of New South Wales to include railways 'among the departments to be taken over at the outset'[9] was voted down 18 to 12. Instead, three clauses were inserted into the Constitution that limited Commonwealth powers to control railways for military purposes and only allowed conditional acquisition of any state railway and railway construction by the Commonwealth.[10]

A further vexing question at the conventions of the late 1890s was that of railway rates and charges. Here, the strong competition between Sydney and Melbourne interests to secure Riverina trade 'caused a series of long and critical debates'. This issue was in part addressed by further clauses allowing for the establishment of an Inter-State Commission, and Section 92 of the Constitution requiring trade between the states to be 'absolutely free'.

You can see that the situation in 1897 for rail had changed from what Parkes had envisaged in 1891 that control of railways was to be for Commonwealth purposes.

The end result was not a good one. As seen 100 years later by former prime minister Paul Keating, 'The state-centric nature of the Australian Federation ... gave Australia a rail system which failed to meet the continental needs of the country.'[11]

INTO THE 20TH CENTURY

Federation did confer some benefits to rail.

The first and foremost achievement was the completion in 1917 of a standard gauge railway from Port Augusta to Kalgoorlie. This work was noted by Burke[12] not only as 'the first great work of Australia's Federation' but for rail '... an exhausting effort which successive governments could not improve on ...'

The new transcontinental railway had been spurred on in 1910 by another British military officer, Lord Kitchener.[13] However, despite a recommendation made in 1921 by a Commonwealth royal commission into gauge standardisation, Kalgoorlie–Perth conversion had to wait until 1968.

This royal commission made many recommendations. Only two were taken up: new standard-gauge links being built firstly between Kyogle and South Brisbane by 1930, and between Port Augusta and Port Pirie in 1937.

The stern lessons learned during World War II[14] of the cost of multiple gauges led to a further rail inquiry. Here, Sir Harold Clapp's 1945 ambitious report had three main elements:[15]

- firstly, gauge standardisation of all Victorian and South Australian broad gauge lines as well as standard gauge access to Perth and from Port Pirie to Broken Hill;
- secondly, construction of a railway linking Bourke in New South Wales to near Mt Isa in Queensland and on to Darwin; and
- thirdly, based on good North American practice, modernisation of the railways.

His recommendations on all three fronts were thwarted by narrow state interests.

Following a Privy Council decision in 1954 that boosted interstate trucking at the expense of the railways, two federal parliamentary committees were formed in 1956. One, of government members, was called the Wentworth committee after its Chairman, Bill Wentworth; the second was of opposition members.[16] Both committees strongly supported three gauge standardisation projects: Albury to Melbourne, Kalgoorlie to Perth, and Broken Hill to Port Pirie. They were completed during the 1960s.

Since then, progress in further gauge standardisation has been slow.

Notable efforts to improve the rail situation were made during the 1970s by the Whitlam government. One initiative was an offer by the Commonwealth to each of the states to take over their non-metropolitan railways. This offer was made under the Constitution and was only taken up by South Australia and Tasmania. This led to the formation of the Australian National Railways Commission. The relevant legislation was signed into law on 10 November 1975, just one day before the dismissal of the Whitlam government.

Australian National worked hard to improve the efficiency of its rail freight operations. Denied federal funds, Australian National then raised its own loan funds to convert Adelaide–Port Pirie to standard gauge in the early 1980s. This gave interstate rail freight a chance to survive in Australia.

Further Whitlam initiatives included legislation for the construction of the Tarcoola–Alice Springs line and the allocation of federal funds to improve urban public transport. There was also a move to establish an Inter-State Commission.

When operating during the 1980s, this commission did much to set the scene for improved interstate rail freight operations, and led to inter-governmental agreements to establish a National Rail Corporation in 1992. Later, Australian Rail Track Corporation or ARTC was formed.

The ARTC has worked to allow rail freight to grow on the east-west corridor linking Melbourne to Perth. In 2004, after protracted negotiations with the New South Wales Government, the ARTC took a long-term lease of the New South Wales Hunter Valley track and the New South Wales interstate mainlines. The ARTC has worked hard to try and improve the New South Wales Main South and North Coast track and signal systems.

However, it was only in 2008 that an outmoded signalling system between Casino and Brisbane was replaced by modern Centralised Traffic Control, or CTC. This was long overdue and in fact by 1966, CTC had been installed between Auckland and Wellington in New Zealand.[17] Up to 2008, the extra costs imposed on Sydney Brisbane rail operations by this failure of federation to install CTC during the 20th century amounted to about $2 million per annum.

ROLE OF THE STATES

Under the Constitution, the states were left with the major role in rail development. Urban rail achievements during the 20th century include electrification of Melbourne's trains in 1919 followed by Sydney in 1926, and, over 50 years later, Brisbane in 1979.

Perth's urban rail system,[18] which was destined for closure 30 years ago was retained, expanded almost four-fold, upgraded and electrified. The result has been outstanding, with patronage since the early 1980s having grown nine-fold to nearly 59 million passengers last financial year.

For intercity rail, notable achievements include the introduction in 1937 of the Melbourne–Albury Spirit of Progress as the finest and fastest train in the Southern Hemisphere. Also of note is the Queensland tilt train with speeds up to 160 kilometres per hour starting in 1998 on tracks straightened for faster freight trains. This was followed by Victoria's Regional Fast Rail, also with trains moving up to 160 kilometres per hour, over upgraded track.

For freight, world best practice in rail operations is demonstrated by the iron ore railways in the Pilbara region of Western Australia. These railways go back to the 1960s and have since been upgraded to handle escalating exports. They now move over one million tonnes of iron ore each day and support export earnings amounting to $1 billion per week – keeping Australia prosperous at a time of global recession!

The movement of this iron by rail can take place in trains with over 300 wagons, with world record energy efficiency. Here it takes just three-quarters of a litre of diesel fuel to move one tonne of iron ore 426 kilometres from Mt Newman to Port Headland and bring the empty wagons back.

As it happens, Pilbara iron ore railways are built and operated by the private sector. In addition, the electrification of the Central Queensland railway in the late 1980s by the Queensland Government led to further world class operations, albeit on narrow gauge. At its time, it was the largest electrification project in the Western world. Today, it saves over 200 million litres of diesel a year and supports one of the world's great coal export supply chains.

More recently, in 2003, the Northern Territory completed the Alice Springs to Darwin rail link, with the support of the Government of South Australia, the Commonwealth and the private sector.[19] Over 1400 kilometres in length, the line was constructed in a record 29 months at less than $1 million per kilometre – again demonstrating that Australia is up to the task of building good railways in a cost-effective manner. As noted by former Deputy Prime Minister Tim Fischer,[20] freight traffic on the line has increased five-fold since it opened. Despite some gains, the states have set back rail development in Australia. Two of many examples will have to suffice:[21]

- firstly, South Australia's aversion to standard gauge over many decades leading to delays and extra costs; and
- secondly, the failure of the New South Wales and Victorian governments in 1980 to take up an offer of the Fraser government to electrify the Sydney–Melbourne railway.

SOME WARNING SIGNS

By the late 20th century there was ample evidence that all was not well with railways – particularly in New South Wales.

As seen in 1989 by a House of Representatives Committee 'The plain fact is that a greatly increased amount of freight could be carried across the continent by rail more efficiently and with greater safety than it ever could be by road. ... If rail were more efficient and carried the amount of freight it should, lives would be saved, less non-renewable resources would be used and less pollution would be generated.'[22]

As seen in the year 2000 by the Deputy Chairman of the same committee, Mr Colin Hollis MP (on 1 June in Parliament), there was a need for a national transport policy 'instead of this piecemeal state-centric nonsense that passes for transport policy in this country.'

In 2007, with yet another inquiry[23] the then chairman of the committee, Mr Paul Neville MP said (on ABC Radio 4 February): 'We know that the freight task is going to double in the next 20 years, and because of that, our roads will become totally and utterly congested if we don't do something serious about rail in that time.'

The committee also found that '... the greatest need for Australia is the reconstruction and realignment of the main freight networks'.

The track between Australia's two largest cities of Sydney and Melbourne is at least 60 kilometres longer than it needs to be, and has excessive curvature. In fact, between Campbelltown and Junee, trains twist to the left some 31 circles and have to twist to the right another 31 circles.[24] The 260 kilometres of track with substandard alignment and sharp curves could be replaced by construction of some 200 kilometres of new track at five locations to modern engineering standards. This would speed up all trains and save fuel.

Between Sydney and Brisbane, through Grafton, the curvature is even worse. This reflects the original branch line nature of over 600 kilometres of this track. Excessive length could again be reduced with track straightening. Quite simply, the tracks linking Australia's three largest cities '... are inadequate for current and future needs.'[25]

The substandard nature of this interstate track reflects decades of neglect. Such neglect was also suffered by the interstate road system until the National Highway System was put in place by the Whitlam government. In the 30 years from 1974 to 2004, in 2004 dollars, some $24.6 billion of federal funds was used to upgrade the interstate highways. However, the net federal interstate rail allocation over these 30 years was about $2.2 billion; a ratio of some 11 to one in favour of interstate highways.[26]

THE COSTS OF A SUBSTANDARD RAIL SYSTEM

At Federation, in 1901, except for the break of gauge, Australia had a good rail system for a large country of less than 4 million people. However, Australia's state-centric rail system is no longer fit for purpose.

For the first half of the 20th century, trains and trams were the dominant ways of moving people within our larger cities. Since 1950, the use of cars has grown almost ten-fold. As a result, Australia is now excessively dependent on road transport, while Sydney is choked by cars and buses.

In addition, Australia now has the highest amount of road freight per capita in the world.

A lot of this road freight is moving interstate. Each day, there are over 3000 trucks on the Hume Highway moving freight. These trucks move over 10 million tonnes of freight each year between Sydney and Melbourne, while rail moves less than a million tonnes of intermodal freight between Australia's two largest cities. Between Sydney and Brisbane, over six million tonnes per year is moved along the Pacific Highway, with less than one million tonnes per year by rail.

Branch line closures and deficiencies are putting more freight on road. One current example is with New South Wales grain transport. Here, as recently seen by *The Land*,[27] 'Third world' branch lines are driving freight on to the roads.

Our road vehicle use comes at a high cost. Firstly, over $15 billion a year is now expended by Australia's three levels of government on road construction and maintenance.[28]

Secondly, putting over one million new vehicles on the roads each year costs over $20 billion a year.

Thirdly, over 1300 lives are lost each year from road crashes in Australia. Coupled with other road injuries, the cost of road crashes has been conservatively estimated at $18 billion a year.

The total cost of road vehicle operations, including the fuel they use, buying and maintaining the vehicles, road works and road crashes, is broadly estimated at about $150 billion a year.[29]

There are numerous other hidden costs of road vehicle use, including health impairment from motor vehicle emissions, estimated at over $4 billion a year. In regards to hidden costs, Professor John Stanley has estimated, after taking into account fuel excise and annual registration charges, but not including road congestion, a 'road deficit' of $14 billion a year.[30] This compares with an older estimate of a road deficit of Professor Peter Newman and myself of $8 billion a year of hidden subsidies.[31] Under current road pricing, road deficits are increasing.

Road congestion costs are now in the order of $10 billion a year.

These road deficits include a 'road freight deficit' of at least $3 billion per year.[32] About half of this amount is unrecovered road system costs from the operation of articulated trucks. The other half is due to the involvement of such heavy trucks in road crashes coupled with other environmental and social costs.

OIL VULNERABILITY

A major input into road vehicle use is that of liquid fuel. During 2010, cars, buses and trucks used about 31 billion litres of petrol, diesel and LPG. By way of contrast, rail used less than one billion litres of diesel a year for a smaller passenger task but a larger freight task than road.[33] Rail also uses electricity, produced mostly from domestic coal, with an oil equivalent of about 1.2 billion litres per year.

In 1998, the Chartered Institute of Transport issued a sternly worded warning that cheap oil would not last forever and that 'more of the same' in our current transport plans is no longer tenable. The next year, the Institution of Engineers Australia issued a well researched call for transport reform.[34]

In 2002, the Secretary of the Australian Treasury, Dr Ken Henry, noted that projected increases in urban traffic and interstate road freight raised 'important issues'; also that 'not dealing with these issues now amounts to passing a very challenging set of problems to future generations'.[35]

Despite these warnings, the growing use of oil in road transport and the cost of oil imports was of little apparent concern to government. In 2004, oil prices were rising, yet there were government forecasts that oil could be expected to drop back to $20 a barrel. However, by mid 2008, oil prices had peaked at about $146 per barrel. With the global recession, oil prices have since receded to now about $80 a barrel and a case can be made 'that petrol prices are likely to be restrained in this decade'.[36]

On the other hand, as the current global recession lifts, oil prices could really escalate. Two recent books from Canada give information on oil vulnerability and suggest a need for rethinking transport policy.[37]

A further concern to oil vulnerability is climate change. The diversion of passengers and freight from road to rail would not only reduce the use of imported oil but also reduce greenhouse gas emissions.

In this regard, the 2008 Garnaut Climate Change Review observed that 'Governments have a major role in lowering the economic costs of adjustment to higher oil prices, an emissions price and population growth ... Mode shift may account for a quarter of emissions reductions in urban public transport ...'[38]

This could mean a reduction of fuel use by at least two billion litres per year.[39]

Mode shifting 20 per cent of Australia's road freight to rail would reduce diesel fuel use by over half a billion litres per year.

High-speed rail, with intercity passenger trains capable of speeds of 250 kilometres per hour works well in 12 countries around the world. High-speed rail could well be viable between Brisbane, Sydney and Melbourne where it has the potential to reduce aviation fuel use by over a half billion litres a year.[40] However, high-speed rail would take at least 10 years for the first trains to start operation. In the meantime, there is no alternative but to upgrade our existing rail system.

It makes sense for Australia to follow the lead of New Zealand[41] and other countries to reduce dependence on imported oil. This will require an upgraded rail system and improved road pricing.

WHAT MIGHT HAVE BEEN

Suppose, as envisaged by Parkes in 1889, and again in 1926 by visiting British expert Sir George Buchanan,[42] railways after Federation were under the control of the Commonwealth, as opposed to the states. How different would Australian railways be from what they are now?

- In line with the findings of the 1921 royal commission, it is likely that the gauge questions would have been resolved within a few decades. As seen by Mr Whitlam (*Hansard*, 30 October 1956) 'If one authority were in charge of the railways, the break-of-gauge would be intolerable and the responsibility would swiftly be sheeted home to the appropriate minister.'
- Cost shifting between the state and Commonwealth governments, and putting off much needed investment in rail, would have been avoided.
- There would have been more balance between federal rail and road investment.
- Commonwealth control of railways would have likely resulted in better-quality interstate links meeting Canadian and US Class I railroad standards in terms of alignment, speed weight characteristics, clearances and signalling.
- An inland route between Melbourne, Parkes and Brisbane,[43] would have been built during the 20th century. It is still to be built.
- Early Commonwealth control of railways would have prevented the excessive diversity of locomotives and rolling stock. For all of the 20th century, these were made, at much extra cost, to different specifications.[44]
- The different management of interstate rail freight operations would have been addressed well before the early 1990s.
- Privatisation of rail assets would have been better handled; in some cases, such as Tasmania, they were costly and failed experiments.
- Rail deficits, which occurred during the second half of the 20th century, would have been much smaller.
- Road deficits would have been reduced.
- Less oil would need to have been imported.
- The burden of operating trains under different state-based safety regulators would have been lifted long ago. Only in 2011 was approval given by the Council of Australia Governments, or COAG, for a national rail safety regulator.

As noted earlier this year by federal Infrastructure Minister Albanese: 'It is 110 years since Federation … yet …on some issues it's as if Federation is as elusive as it was for Henry Parkes.'[45]

MAKING FEDERATION WORK

One solution to problems of federation on many fronts favoured during the early 20th century was to establish more states. In 1939 Sir Isaac Isaacs considered that two reform options warranted attention: 'The first is the abolition of State Parliaments. The second while leaving State Parliaments undisturbed, to implement Commonwealth powers to meet modern circumstances.'

Gordon Greenwood, writing in 1946, went further and found that 'Yet, despite its achievements, the evidence points decisively to the conclusion that the federal system has outlived its usefulness, … and … It is time to recognise that the Federation should be replaced by a unified state.'[46]

Support for this view continues and it is costly to the nation to maintain the state governments with their present functions.[47] Today, the preferred option appears to be to make COAG work more effectively. However, even with some progress by COAG, a long-standing Australian Transport Council of Ministers, and a National Road Transport Commission since 1992, transport reform continues to be unacceptably slow.

WHERE TO NOW?

In conclusion, although Federation has conferred many benefits, the failure during the 1890s to include railways along with defence and communications as a federal responsibility has been costly to the nation. The railway gauge question, resolved in the late 19th century in Britain, Canada, the United States and New Zealand, still awaits resolution in Australia.

There is now a major backlog of rail capital works on several fronts this decade. This demands a national approach rather than a state-centric one.

If Parkes were living today as premier or prime minister, he would urge that action be taken to give Australia a uniform railway gauge.

Secondly, Parkes would be concerned for Australia's ability to respond to any threat from overseas and this would include a need to lessen dependence on imported oil. In turn, this will require:

- expansion and upgrading of urban rail in Sydney and other large cities,
- bringing mainline interstate track towards Canadian and US Class I railroad standards by straightening and strengthening the track with better clearances,
- residual gauge standardisation, particularly of broad to standard gauge,

- rehabilitation of branch lines and completion of better rail links to ports,
- construction of an inland route, and,
- road pricing reform.

Some of these measures would be assisted by giving the Australian Rail Track Corporation a firm legislative basis for getting more freight and passengers onto rail.

In this regard, there has been a legislative basis for a National Highway System since 1974 with a federal *National Roads Act*.

Parkes would likely seek, in the absence of a total revision of the Constitution, a transfer of all national transport functions to the Commonwealth. He would also press for adequate rail investment to remedy decades of neglect.

Only by such means will Australia finally gain a rail network fit for the 21st century.

The author would like to thank the School of Mathematics and Applied Statistics of the University of Wollongong (UOW), the Henry Parkes Foundation, the Sir Henry Parkes Memorial School of Arts, and his family. My thanks are due to my father, Mr John Laird, of Ravenshoe, Queensland, Professor Rodney Nillsen (UOW) and Mr Scott Martin, Research Officer Economic Development and Infrastructure Committee of the Parliament of Victoria for reviewing drafts of this paper and to Ms Sarah Satchel UOW for research assistance. The views expressed are my own.

Notes:

1 In the words of Sir Robert Garran, the 1889 Tenterfield speech of Parkes 'turned a vague ideal into a practical working program for Federation'; http://www.nationaltrust.com.au/placestovisit/shp/

2 Richmond T., *Brooklyn – Federation Village*, Deerubbin Press, 2010, p. 20. Also *Sydney Morning Herald*, Thursday 2 May 1889; http://trove.nla.gov.au/ndp/del/article/13744429

3 *Sydney Morning Herald*, Thursday 2 May 1889; http://trove.nla.gov.au/ndp/del/article/13744429

4 Parliament of Victoria, *Report by Major-General Edwards, C.B. on the Military Forces and Defences of Victoria, with a memorandum containing proposals for the re-organisation of the Australian Forces*, Government Printer, Melbourne, 1889, pp. 8–9. Edwards also urged that '…the railways to connect Port Darwin and Western Australia with the other Colonies should be made as soon as possible'.

5 Parkes, Sir Henry, *The federal government of Australasia: speeches delivered on various occasions*, 1890. Sir Henry revisited rail issues in November at St Leonards, December at Albury and February 1890 at Melbourne. On the gauge question '… if the four colonies could only combine to adopt a uniform gauge, it would be an immense advantage in the movement of troops, as well as in the operations of commerce and the various pursuits of society'.

6 See Stevenson, R., *Rail transport and Australian federalism,* Australian National University, Canberra, 1987, and Puffert, D., 'The standardization of track gauge on North American railways, 1830-1890', *The Journal of Economic History,* Vol. 4, 2000, pp. 933–960.

7 White M. and Rahemtula A., *Sir Samuel Griffith: The law and the constitution*, Lawbook Co, 2002, which notes refinement of drafts on the Queensland Government ship 'Lucinda' not far from the Hawkesbury River Bridge by Sir Samuel Griffith and others.

8 Livingston K. T., *The wired nation continent*, Oxford, 1996, p. 163; see also Moyal, A. *Clear across Australia*, Nelson, Melbourne, 1984, which outlines the challenges between 1 March 1901 and 1910 of merging six colonial post and telegraph services into one.

9 Quick and Garran, *The annotated constitution of the Australian Commonwealth*, Legal Books, 1901 (1976 edition), pp. 169, 176 re vote 18 to 12; also pp. 642–643.

10 Section 51: (xxxii) the control of railways with respect to transport for the naval and military purposes of the Commonwealth; (xxxiii) the acquisition, with the consent of a state, of any railways of the state on terms arranged between the Commonwealth and the state; (xxxiv) railway construction and extension in any state with the consent of that state.

11 Keating, P., '… a big strike for rail but an even bigger strike for the country' to mark the 10th Anniversary of Melbourne Adelaide Rail Gauge Standardisation, *Railway Digest*, July 2005, p. 29.

12 Burke, D., *Road through the wilderness,* UNSW Press, Sydney, 1991. This notes railway agreements with South Australia and Western Australia and the Commonwealth *Kalgoorlie to Port Augusta Railway Act 1911*.

13 Fischer T., *Trains unlimited*, ABC Books, 2011, which notes (p. 169), inter alia, Kitchener's concern about break of gauge and that the Australian railway system would favour an enemy more than the defenders.

14 The no fewer than 11 breaks of gauge required an annual average transfer of about 1.8 million tonnes of freight to be transferred during WWII (peaking at 2.3 million tonnes), and added immense costs to the war effort (Brigadier L.G. Binns, as cited in Appendix 1, *Government Members Rail Standardisation Committee [1956] Report)*.

15 Harding, E., *Uniform railway gauge*, Lothian Publishing, Melbourne, 1958; Stevenson, R. (see footnote 6); and Laird P. 'The legacy of Sir Harold Clapp', *Railway Digest* (NSW ARHS), July 2005, pp. 34–38.

16 See, for example, Laird P., 'A half-century of highway subsidisation – or 50 years after Hughes and Vale', *Railway Digest*, November 2004 pp. 26–29; and 'The Wentworth and ALP standardization reports', *Railway Digest*, November 2006 pp. 35–40. The formation of the two committees was also prompted by a meeting held in January 1956 by the Australian Institute of Political Science leading to a book *Australia's transport crisis*. Plus a call by Malcolm Fraser MHR (Vic, Lib) for a national transport plan and to overcome anomalies '…created by the break in railway gauge in the various states'.

17 From 30-year-old Federal Cabinet records, Casino–Brisbane CTC signalling had also been proposed and rejected for limited federal loan funds under the *National Railway Network (Financial Assistance) Act 1978*. The cost estimate is based on traffic data and estimates of stopping a freight train (then $104) to exchange staff (Michell, M. and Laird, P. 'Smooth running – a route of cost reduction', 2002 Conference on Railway Engineering, Wollongong Proceedings, pp. 227–237)

18 Perth's rail electrification, like Brisbane and Central Queensland was at 25,000 volts AC as opposed to the older 1500 volts DC system in use in Melbourne and Sydney.

19 This railway, agreed to by the Commonwealth in 1908, and long delayed over the decades, was commenced by Prime Minister Fraser in the early 1980s and stopped in 1983 by Prime Minister Hawke. It was ultimately revived due to the persistence of each Chief Minister of the Northern Territory and the strong support of the Government of South Australia.

20 Fischer, T. *Trains unlimited*, ABC Books, 2011, p. 189.
In addition, the Chief Minister, Paul Henderson, of the Northern Territory Government (personal communication, letter 19 July 2011) notes that the new railway has provided 'immediate economic benefit' and facilitated a number of new mining projects; also a 2008 study has found that '… economic benefits of $211 million were derived between 2004 and 2008 … also future benefits from 2009 to 2015 of $548 million are expected'.

21 Michell, M. 'Great railway setbacks of the 20th Century', *Railway Digest*, April 2001.

22 House of Representatives Standing Committee on Transport, Communications and Infrastructure (HORSC Transport etc), *Rail: five systems, one solution*, Canberra, 1989. This committee called for a national approach and noted that: '... Rail has been starved of funds and rendered inefficient'.

23 HORSC Transport etc, *The great freight task: is Australia's transport network up to the challenge?* Canberra, 2007. This report again noted, inter alia, a need for a national approach. Plus more investment.

24 Laird, P., 'East coast mainline rail track: options for 2014', Conference on Railway Engineering 2008, Perth, Proceedings, pp. 357–368.

25 Harper, L., Chartered Institute of Logistics and Transport, 'The major task of increasing rail traffic on the East Coast, *Track and Signal*, Oct-Nov-Dec 2008, pp. 9–13. This assessment is supported by earlier Engineers Australia Infrastructure Report Cards.

26 Laird, P., Adorni-Braccesi, G. and Collett, M., 'Australian land transport – is it sustainable?', Towards Sustainable Land Transport Conference, Wellington New Zealand, 2004. See also Senate Rural and Regional Affairs and Transport Committee (2009) Inquiry into the investment of Commonwealth and state funds in public passenger transport infrastructure and services. Over the 30 years to 2004, federal funds for all roads were about $58 billion, and for all rail $4 billion; a ratio of over 14 to one.

27 'Call this a rail system? – "Third world" branch lines driving freight onto roads', *The Land*, 11 August 2011, re round table conference held by the Independent Pricing and Regulatory Tribunal (IPART) as part of its review of access pricing on the NSW grain rail network.

28 Bureau of Infrastructure, Transport and Regional Economics (BITRE), *Information Sheet 40 – Public Road-Related Expenditure and Revenue in Australia*, 2011.

29 Allen Consulting Group, *Land transport infrastructure, maximising the contribution to economic growth*, Australian Automobile Association, 1993. Canberra estimated these costs at about $80 billion per annum. From GDP data at http://www.rba.gov.au/statistics/tables this was about 11 per cent of GDP. This is now about $150 million per year.

30 'Roads lobby has it all wrong', *Australian Financial Review*, 24 January 2011. See also http://www.mtf.org.au/Events-MTF/Transport-of-Economics-Forum-June22nd-2010.aspx

31 Laird, P., Newman, P., Bachels, M. and Kenworthy, J., *Back on track: Rethinking transport policy in Australia and New Zealand*, UNSW Press, 2001.

32 Laird, P., *Freight transport cost recovery in Australia*, Australasian Transport Research Forum, 2006. The Henry Tax review in 2010 had a number of recommendations that if implemented would see an improvement in road pricing for heavy trucks.

33 Australian Bureau of Statistics, *Survey of motor vehicle usage (SMVU) for 12 months ended 31 October 2010*. Cat. No. 9208.0, Canberra, 2011; and Australasian Railway Association, *Australian Rail Industry Report 2010*. Earlier SMVU data notes that in 1991 Australian road vehicles used about 21 billion litres of fuel and in 2001, about 26 billion litres.

34 Chartered Institute of Transport, statement from their 1998 National Symposium; and Institution of Engineers Australia, *Report on sustainable transport*, 1999.

35 Henry, K., address to the Transport Policy Colloquium, 3 October 2002; http://archive.treasury.gov.au/contentitem.asp?NavId=&ContentID=440

36 Gargett, D., *Petrol prices in Australia*, Australasian Transport Research Forum, 2010 (www.patrec.org)

37 Gilbert, R. and Perl, A., *Transport revolutions: moving people and freight without oil*, New Society Publishers, Gabriola Island BC Canada, 2010; and Rubin, J., *Why your world is about to get a whole lot smaller: oil and the end of globalization*, Random House, 2009.

38 Garnaut, R., *Garnaut Climate Change Review 2008*, Chapter 21 'Transforming transport', at http://www.garnautreview.org.au. Garnaut also suggested that various governments may now like 'to examine why intercity passenger train services in Australia are inferior to those in European and high-income Asian countries, with a view to removing barriers to the emergence of high-quality inter-regional rail services in Australia.'

39 Australian Bureau of Statistics, *Survey of motor vehicle usage for 12 months ended 31 October 2010*. Cat. No. 9208.0, Canberra, 2011; shows passenger vehicles using 18.4 billion litres of fuel to move 164.4 billion kilometres. Of this, 95.6 billion was in capital cities using at least 10.7 billion litres of fuel.

40 Laird, P., *Potential reduction in energy use from a high speed rail network in Australia*, Australasian Transport Research Forum, Adelaide, 2011.

41 New Zealand excise on petrol is 48.524 cents per litre (as of October 2010) and has been increased many times since Australia froze fuel excise indexation in 2001 at 38.143 cents per litre; also New Zealand has had mass distance pricing for heavy trucks since 1978, works to get more freight onto rail and sea, and in 2011 committed $36 billion over 10 years to road and rail upgrades.

42 Page, Sir Earle, *Truant Surgeon*, Angus and Robertson, 1963, p. 145. Sir George Buchanan was retained by the Bruce–Page government and found, drawing on overseas experience, that transport, which would include railways, main roads, major ports, shipping, pilotage and aviation, should be taken over by the Commonwealth Government and that a new department should be created expressly for the purpose of its administration.

43 Day, D., *Andrew Fisher, Prime Minister of Australia*, HarperCollins Publishers (Australia), 2008. This book notes that an inland route was recommended by Prime Minister Fisher during the mid 1910s.

44 The Bruce–Page government proposed joint Commonwealth mainland state uniform standards for the construction of railway lines and rolling stock, and gauge unification.

45 Albanese, A. 'COAG today to be asked to complete Federation dream', Opinion, *Canberra Times*, 13 February 2011.

46 Greenwood, G., *The future of Australian federalism,* 1946. Some 30 years later, Greenwood's book was republished. In the 1976 edition, whilst acknowledging that he had earlier underestimated the degree to which federalism was entrenched, 'the central argument of the book has not been damaged but indeed has been strengthened by time.'

47 Drummond, M., 'Abolish the states and save $50 billion', *The Order*, Summer 2009–2010.

"We aspire to be a country that treats people fairly and equally. Yet we still have a Constitution that expressly recognises that people can be denied the vote or subject to different treatment because of their race. It is hard to describe us as a free and tolerant democracy when this possibility remains. … Australia needs to recapture Parkes' vision for achieving social justice through constitutional reform."

Social justice through constitutional change: mission impossible?

George Williams
24 October 2012

*Museum of Australian Democracy at Old Parliament House, Canberra ACT.**

AS A CONSTITUTIONAL lawyer, I am well aware of the large debt I owe to the life and works of Henry Parkes. More than any other person, he kick-started the process of drafting the Australian Constitution, and so put us on the road to federation and nationhood.

He did so when on 24 October 1889 at Tenterfield he called for the colonies to 'unite and create a great national government for all Australia'. He then wrote to the other colonial premiers proposing a meeting to devise a constitution for the new nation.

This began a decade of conventions and public debate in which the community and our leaders were seized with a bold spirit of reform. The outcome was a Constitution and the Australian Federation in 1901.

---

* Following the presentation of this speech for the Henry Parkes Foundation in 2012, a version was subsequently published in *Project republic: plans and arguments for a new Australia*, Black Inc, 2013.

People today often remember Parkes as the 'Father of Federation', without recognising that his Tenterfield speech came towards the end of a four-decade political career in what was his fifth, and final, stint as premier of New South Wales.

His contribution to the founding of Australia was remarkable, but no less so than his extraordinary achievements in democratic and social reform. These included:

- the introduction of universal male suffrage;
- free secular education for children;
- the training of nurses for public hospitals;
- funding the colony's first public library; and
- establishing areas for public enjoyment, such as Centennial Park in Sydney.

Parkes' vision for social justice and equal opportunity infused his work, including when it came to federation. He saw that the new nation should serve the common good, as reflected in his proposal that it be known as the 'Commonwealth' of Australia.

Across many fields, Parkes was a reformer, and an extremely successful one at that. He demonstrated the qualities needed to achieve social justice in a tumultuous and unforgiving political process. He showed that this can be realised when it is backed by a clear vision, sound political judgement, persistence and a willingness to convince the community of the need for change.

These lessons can be too easily forgotten, and we can still learn much from Parkes today. This is particularly true when it comes to changing the Australian Constitution.

Parkes was embroiled in a number of constitutional debates, beginning with the creation of self-government in New South Wales in 1856. He recognised that longer-term goals such as equality and justice demand a continuing commitment to democratic and constitutional reform.

This insight was true in Parkes' time, and it is just as true today. Unfortunately, we have lost sight of this to our detriment.

Rather than being seen as a living document that fosters our national aspirations, the Constitution has faded into the background of public debate. As a result, we maintain a structure of government that is generally sturdy, but which reflects popular values and common understandings of government that made sense in the 1890s, but not today. These include the idea, written into Australia's constitutional DNA, that governments should discriminate between people on the basis of their race.

GEORGE WILLIAMS

George Williams AO is one of Australia's leading constitutional lawyers. He is the Anthony Mason Professor, a Scientia Professor and the Foundation Director of the Gilbert + Tobin Centre of Public Law at the Faculty of Law, University of New South Wales. He is a well known media commentator on legal issues, and has written and edited 28 books, including *Australian constitutional law and theory* and *The Oxford companion to the High Court of Australia.*

By not updating and improving the Constitution, we have failed to ensure that we have the structure of government that best meets our needs. This has many costs, including especially when it comes to social justice.

THE CONSTITUTION

At first blush, the Australian Constitution is a dry and boring document. Indeed, former federal attorney-general and High Court judge Lionel Murphy remarked that he kept a copy of the Constitution by his bedside. If he found himself sleepless in the middle of the night, the document was a perfect antidote.

Murphy had a point. Our national Constitution is hard to read and often obscure, and much of it is now seemingly irrelevant to the issues of the day. After all, how could a set of rules written at the end of the century before last still be relevant today?

Part of the problem is that it was not written as a people's constitution. Parkes may have propelled the federal movement forward, but he had little influence over its drafting.

The Constitution produced by the end of the 1890s was a lawyers' document containing the nuts and bolts of how our system of government was to operate. This is reflected in its preamble which, tellingly, opens with the word 'whereas':

> *WHEREAS the people of New South Wales, Victoria, South Australia, Queensland, and Tasmania, humbly relying on the blessing of Almighty God, have agreed to unite in one indissoluble Federal Commonwealth under the Crown of the United Kingdom of Great Britain and Ireland, and under the Constitution hereby established:*

By contrast, the United States Constitution opens:

> *We the People of the United States, in Order to form a more perfect Union, establish Justice, insure domestic Tranquility, provide for the common defence, promote the general Welfare, and secure the Blessings of Liberty to ourselves and our Posterity, do ordain and establish this Constitution for the United States of America.*

On the surface, Australia's 111-year-old Constitution would seem to have little to do with current questions of public policy such as how to fix the Murray–Darling Basin, or matters of social justice such as the human rights of asylum seekers or how to provide everyone in the community with access to first-rate schools and hospitals.

In fact, the Constitution has everything to do with these things. We must simply look deeper, often beyond the dry words on the page, to understand how fundamentally the Constitution continues to shape the nation and our capacity to realise our collective goals. Among other things, the Constitution:

- establishes lines of power in our society (such as who can do what to whom);
- establishes relationships and the legitimacy of people and organisations; and
- provides recognition of groups and national aspirations.

In these ways, as Parkes would have anticipated, the Constitution has a profound, ongoing impact on the nation and community well-being. This is rarely noticed.

When it comes to government, people tend to be aware of sudden shifts and things that draw high levels of media attention, such as elections or High Court decisions that frustrate party policy.

By contrast, the influence wrought by the Constitution may only produce glacial change. Recording and explaining things that produce changes over the course of years and decades, even where they are of great importance, is not something that is well captured by today's 24-hour news cycle.

CONSTITUTIONAL CHANGE

Parkes recognised the link between constitutional reform and his political aspirations. He understood that structures of government and democratic processes are fundamental to achieving social justice.

This is reflected in at least one respect in the Constitution itself. Even though the Constitution was enacted by the British Parliament, it embodied the egalitarian notion that it should only be altered by the Australian people.

In a radical experiment for the time, this was not to be done by their representatives in parliament, but by the people directly. Hence, section 128 of the Constitution requires that any change to its text be approved at a popular referendum.

Unfortunately, the Australian politicians who have since championed the cause of constitutional reform have found this hurdle almost impossible to surmount. They have only rarely been able to translate the success they have achieved in elections to winning referendums.

Constitutional change has always been hard to achieve, with only eight out of 44 referendums succeeding. Disturbingly, however, change has become more difficult and less likely to be achieved as time has gone on, with no referendum passing since 1977.

As at 2012, 35 years have passed since Australia changed its Constitution. At around one-third of the life of the nation, this is by far the longest period that Australia has gone without amending the document. The next longest period was 21 years between the 1946 and 1967 referendums.

It seems that as the necessity of changing the Constitution increases, so does our inability to bring this about.

When it comes to constitutional reform in Australia, we have lost the plot.

Rather than seeking to re-engage, our politicians seek to avoid the whole topic whenever they can. After all, if something is doomed to failure, why bother making the attempt and risking not just defeat, but a public backlash? Even the idea of an Australian republic has seemingly been put off by its political backers until the death of our current monarch.

Australia has not held a referendum since 1999, when the people voted 'No' to becoming a republic and inserting a new preamble in the Constitution. This made the first 10 years of the 21st century the first decade in Australian history in which no referendum was held.

It looked like this drought might be broken when the Gillard government was cornered into promising one, and possibly two, referendums in 2013 on recognising Aboriginal Australians and local government in the Constitution.

These polls were put on the political agenda not because they represented a priority for the government, but as a result of the commitments the Prime Minister had to make to Greens and Independent members to secure power after the August 2010 federal election.

Since 2010, the government has not deployed the energy and resources required to hold the referendums successfully in 2013. Expert panels have been convened, but have yet to be responded to. Ministers have also failed to promote the referendums with any vigour in public debate. Most Australians remain unaware even that referendums have been proposed for next year.

Not surprisingly, the Aboriginal recognition referendum has been postponed for two to three years, and the prospects of holding a referendum on recognising local government are looking extremely shaky.

All this serves to reaffirm the perception that winning a referendum is 'mission impossible'. This also reinforces the destructive cycle whereby a strong political aversion to holding a referendum means that referendums are unlikely to be held, and also less likely to succeed, thereby in turn further strengthening the aversion to constitutional change in the first place.

This has major costs. In order to explain this, I will explore two examples where the Constitution must be changed in order to achieve important social justice goals. These are areas that Parkes himself engaged with: the idea that Australia should adopt a federal system of government, and justice for Australia's first peoples.

FEDERALISM

When it comes to federalism, the problem is not that we have a federal system, but that the one we have is broken.

It is broken because we have a system designed for the needs of 1901, not one that has been updated for those of 2012.

Australia's federal system was drafted in the age of the horse and buggy, and it shows. In the 1890s, it was thought by the framers that the new nation would best be served by six strong state governments and a weak central Commonwealth, and the Constitution was drafted to reflect this.

This vision has since unravelled, while the text of the Constitution has remained largely static. Two world wars have demonstrated the need for national leadership and centralised regulatory control over many aspects of business and daily life. Australia's integration into the global economy has also shown the need for national laws that support competition with other countries, and not just competition between the states.

The result today is a Constitution and federal system that distorts government priorities and policy outcomes to the great cost of the community.

Matters such as service delivery are often determined not by which tier of government can do the best job, but which tier of government has managed to raise the funds to take control. In our system of government, who has the money matters more than who should do the job. It is often just a matter of good fortune if the two happen to coincide. In this respect, the financial dominance of the Commonwealth is all pervasive. It has the money to run the Federation, with or without state consent.

This issue is not a function of who is in government. Indeed, recognition of the magnitude of problem is bipartisan, as is the failure to champion a solution.

Unfortunately, by seeing the referendum as a no-go zone, governments have avoided tackling these important areas, and have seemingly given up on any prospect of holistic federal reform.

The referendum has a continuing, necessary, role to play because the text of the Constitution continues to shape Australia's system of government in inescapable ways. At the most basic level, the Constitution establishes a set of binding rules for Australia's federal system that cannot be ignored.

These rules have an, often unacknowledged, impact upon federal–state relations in almost every policy area, including those of greatest contemporary concern, such as health, the environment, education, Indigenous disadvantage, taxation, business regulation and water policy.

In many areas, the constitutional rules enable effective and efficient governance. In others, they impose a set of values and principles derived from 1901 that can be an awkward, almost impossible fit for the solving of current problems.

This can stop reform in its tracks, or put sufficient obstacles in the way that the political price becomes too high for the reform to proceed, or it may permit reform to be achieved only in a second best manner. There are many examples of where the Constitution has driven policy development down wrong turnings or less desirable paths. For example, the attempt to meet the environmental and other problems besetting the Murray–Darling basin has been shaped by the Australian Constitution. It affects everything from the chances of achieving a national solution for the basin, through to the environmental, social, economic and other factors that may or may not be taken into account in developing a new Murray–Darling Basin Plan.

The Constitution, and in particular its division of legislative and other responsibilities between the Commonwealth and the states, has made what might seem a desirable national approach exceedingly difficult to achieve. It is also a key reason why the current attempt to achieve a plan for the Murray–Darling Basin has become mired in confusion and political controversy, and faces years of High Court litigation.

The root of many such problems lies in the age of Australia's Constitution and the failure to adapt it to changing circumstances. To continue the water example, Australia's Constitution remains based upon the desire of the framers of the 1890s to reach a settlement that accommodated the now non-existent riverboat trade from South Australia. It is not surprising that constitutional text derived from such concerns is out of kilter with contemporary needs.

The result is a system that can produce major failures of public policy. This has a major financial impact.

One recent study has found that problems with our federal system mean that every Australian family pays an unnecessary $1,100 in tax each year. This is wasted money. Overall, we are taxed a pointless $9 billion. This is the amount being used to prop up the Australian federal system. The figure is the conservative estimate of the Business Council of Australia. It is how much the community pays for the duplication of services, buck-passing and inefficiency that bedevils the relationship between our federal and state governments.

Even this understates the true cost. It is only the amount of extra tax we pay and does not include the money lost to businesses in having to comply with unnecessary red tape and extra regulation from multiple layers of government.

Taking some of these other costs into account, it has been estimated that the duplication and extra coordination costs in Australia's federation are an astonishing $20 billion a year, or 9 per cent of all general government expenses or 3 per cent of GDP.

This is an enormous strain upon the economy and the public purse. It also represents a massive lost opportunity. A federal system will never operate at peak efficiency, but even if some of this money could be clawed back, it would represent an enormous pool of money that could be directed to things like improved funding for education and a national disability insurance scheme.

Our dysfunctional federal system necessarily impacts upon the quality of government services and our capacity to meet the needs and welfare of the most vulnerable in the community. A consequence is that we have lower standards in health and education than we could otherwise attain.

The bottom line is: if you care about Australia's schools and hospitals, you also need to care about the poor state of our federal system of government.

ABORIGINAL PEOPLES

Aboriginal peoples have long sought recognition in Australia's national and state Constitutions. They have done so because these fundamental laws have either ignored their existence or permitted discrimination against them. They rightly argue that the story of our nation is incomplete without the histories of the peoples who inhabited this continent before white settlement.

Parkes himself was not silent about the injustice being done to Aboriginal peoples. He was known not just as a politician and statesman, but also as a poet. One of his poems from 1857, entitled 'The murdered wild boy', was written about the torture and death of a young Aboriginal boy by settlers on the Hawkesbury River near Sydney. It opens:

Loud talk ye of the savages,
As they were beasts of prey! –
But men of English birth have done
More savage things than they.

He then describes the 'horrid' and 'cowardly' deed, which he says 'haunts' him 'day and night'.

What sympathy Parkes had for Aboriginal Australians ran largely against the grain of his time.

The Australian Constitution was drafted to deny Aboriginal people their rights, their voice and even their identity as peoples. It was drafted against a backdrop of racism that led to the White Australia Policy and a range of other discriminatory laws and practices.

The 1890s Conventions that wrote the Constitution did not include representatives of Australia's Indigenous peoples. In many cases, Aboriginal people were not even allowed to vote for the delegates to the Convention. It is not surprising then that the Constitution did not reflect their interests or aspirations.

In fact, the Constitution was premised upon their exclusion. They were not conceived of as citizens (and even the term second-class citizens would be to put their status too high), but as a dying race lacking a long-term place in the Federation. This was reflected in the terms of Australia's 1901 Constitution:

- Section 25 recognised that the states could disqualify people from voting in the elections on account of their race. Headed 'Provision as to races disqualified from voting', the section provides that if a state disqualifies the people of a race from voting in its elections, the people of that race are not to be counted as part of the state's population in determining its level of representation in the federal parliament.
- Section 51(xxvi) provided that the Commonwealth could legislate with respect to 'the people of any race, other than the aboriginal race in any state, for whom it is deemed necessary to make special laws'. This was the so-called 'races power'.

- Section 127 provided: 'In reckoning the numbers of the people of the Commonwealth, or of a state or other part of the Commonwealth, aboriginal natives shall not be counted'.
- Section 51(xxvi) was inserted to allow the Commonwealth to discriminate against sections of the community on account of their race. Aboriginal people were not originally subject to this section. However, this was not because they were to be protected, but because it was thought that the Aboriginal issues were a matter for the states and not the federal government.

By today's standards, the reasoning behind s 51(xxvi) was clearly racist. Edmund Barton, the Leader of the 1897–1898 Convention and later Australia's first Prime Minister and one of the first members of the High Court, stated at the 1898 Convention in Melbourne that the power was necessary to enable the Commonwealth to 'regulate the affairs of the people of coloured or inferior races who are in the Commonwealth'.

Given the drafting history of the Constitution, it is not surprising that legislation enacted by the Commonwealth Parliament has been based on racially discriminatory policies. For example:

- The White Australia Policy, as provided for by the *Immigration Restriction Act 1901* (Cwlth).
- The denial of the vote in federal elections to Aboriginal people. The federal franchise determined by the *Commonwealth Franchise Act 1902* (Cwlth) extended the vote to women, but denied it to any 'aboriginal native of Australia'. Aboriginal people are finally granted the vote in 1962. Even then, full equality did not occur until 1983, when the law was amended to make enrolment for and voting in federal elections compulsory for Indigenous people as it is for other Australians.
- The suspension of the *Racial Discrimination Act 1975* (Cwlth) in order to facilitate 'bucketloads of extinguishment' of native title in 1998 and the Northern Territory intervention in 2007.

In 1967, a referendum proposal was put before the Australian people under which the words 'other than the aboriginal race in any State' in s 51(xxvi) would be struck out and s 127 deleted entirely. The people overwhelming voted 'Yes'. The proposal was supported in every state and nationally by 90 per cent of Australians.

The 1967 referendum was an important turning point in the place of Aboriginal people within the Australian legal system. However, it is important to note that, while the referendum deleted an obviously discriminatory provision in the form of s 127, it did not insert anything in its place. Nor did it remove the recognition of state race-based voting in section 25.

The change left the Constitution, including the preamble, devoid of any reference to Indigenous peoples. In addition, while the objective of the 1967 referendum was to remove discriminatory references to Aboriginal people from the Constitution and to allow the Commonwealth to take over responsibility for their welfare, it may be that, in failing to set this intention into the words of the Constitution, the change actually laid the seeds for the Commonwealth to pass laws that impose a disadvantage upon them.

This is because the racially discriminatory underpinnings of s 51(xxvi) were extended to Aboriginal people, but without any textual indication that the power could be applied only for their benefit.

The possibility that the races power, as extended to Aboriginal peoples, might be applied to their detriment was raised in the High Court *Hindmarsh Island Bridge Case* in 1998.

The Commonwealth argued in the case that there are no limits to the races power: that is, provided that the law affixes a consequence based upon race, it is not for the High Court to examine the positive or negative impact of the law. On the afternoon of the first day of the hearing, the Commonwealth Solicitor-General, Gavan Griffith, suggested that the races power 'is infused with a power of adverse operation'. He acknowledged 'the direct racist content of this provision' in the sense of 'a capacity for adverse operation'. The following exchange then occurred:

> *Kirby J: Can I just get clear in my mind, is the Commonwealth's submission that it is entirely and exclusively for the Parliament to determine the matter upon which special laws are deemed necessary … or is there a point at which there is a justiciable question for the Court? I mean, it seems unthinkable that a law such as the Nazi race laws could be enacted under the race power and that this Court could do nothing about it.*
>
> *Griffith QC: Your Honour, if there was a reason why the Court could do something about it, a Nazi law, it would, in our submission, be for a reason external to the races power. It would be for some wider over-arching reason.*

Of course, without a national Bill of Rights or express protection from racial discrimination, there was no such over-arching reason.

The overall effect of the judgments was inconclusive. The Court split 2:2 on the scope of the races power, with a further two other judges not deciding. The Court thus left open the possibility that the Commonwealth still possesses the power to enact racially discriminatory laws.

The ongoing recognition of racial discrimination in Australia's Constitution and the fact the concepts of race remain embedded in our Constitution has again produced a movement for constitutional change. Both of Australia's major parties support recognising Aboriginal peoples in the Constitution, and removing references to race from the document. While a referendum to bring these changes about has been put off for some years, grassroots activism for change continues to build.

CHANGING THE CONSTITUTION

In our book *People power: the history and future of the referendum in Australia*, David Hume and I examine all of Australia's 44 referendums. We ask why so many have failed, and what needs to be done to achieve success?

We find that Australia's poor referendum record reflects the fact that our political leaders make the same mistakes time and time again. Rather than learning from the last failure, they tend to simply follow the same flawed path.

The upside of this is that if these mistakes are recognised and avoided, there are realistic prospects that the Australian people will vote Yes to the right proposal.

One of the main problems is that referendums are usually approached in an ad hoc, one-off way. Australia has never put in place the long-term machinery to identify and refine the right proposals for reform, and to build popular support for change. Instead, referendums tend to emerge somewhat randomly out of the hurly-burly of daily politics and, not surprisingly, then founder.

Putting referendums on a stronger foundation could start with the simple act of updating the legislation that establishes how referendums are run. These rules are set out in the *Referendum (Machinery Provisions) Act 1984* (Cwlth). That law was adopted in 1912, and has changed little since.

It was written at a time when voting was not compulsory, Australia's population was far smaller and far less diverse, and the print media and public speeches were the dominant modes of communication. The system is showing its age and is not suited to contemporary Australia. The law does not even permit voters to receive information about a referendum via electronic means. It must be posted to them.

To modernise Australia's referendum process, the Act should be changed to:

- abolish restrictions on expenditure by the Commonwealth Government;
- rethink the official Yes/No pamphlet, by which the Electoral Commissioner must send each elector a pamphlet showing the proposed amendment to the Constitution, with arguments 'for' and 'against' the proposal of not more than 2,000 words each, authorised by members of Parliament on each side of the debate; and
- continue the Yes and No committees from the 1999 referendum by which the cases 'for' and 'against' were championed by two opposed committees funded by the Commonwealth.

These changes are reflected in the recommendations of the House of Representatives Standing Committee on Legal and Constitutional Affairs made in 2009 in its inquiry into the holding of referendums. They have yet to be implemented.

In addition, we need to recognise that tens of millions of dollars of taxpayers' money are being wasted on inadequately conceived and poorly run proposals. Rather than wasting public funds and energy in this way, we should invest funds earlier in the process to generate better ideas more likely to attract popular support. Just as we have bodies like the Productivity Commission to help identify and refine economic reforms, so too do we need such institutions in the constitutional area.

In particular, I would like to see Australia adopt a system whereby:

- A small, ongoing Constitutional Review Commission is charged with reviewing the Constitution, generating proposals for constitutional reform, consulting with the public on draft proposals and recommending them to Parliament.
- The recommendations of the Commission are fed into a regular, popular Constitutional Convention, convened once each decade or 'half-generation'. It should consider the recommendations of the Commission as well as proposals put to it by the federal parliament, a majority of the states or by petition of a large number of Australians. The Convention should debate reform ideas and recommend proposals to the federal parliament for submission to a referendum.

These changes would improve how Australia goes about the process of changing its Constitution.

Even with this, a successful referendum will still be a major challenge, and will require the conviction and persistence of Parkes. It must also be based upon the following principles distilled from Australia's long referendum record:

1. Bipartisanship

Bipartisan support has proven to be essential to referendum success. Referendums need support from the major parties at the Commonwealth level. They also need broad support from the major parties at the state level. The history of referendums in Australia provides many examples of proposals defeated by committed opposition from a major party at either level.

This has been a particular feature of the referendums put by the Australian Labor Party, which has lost 24 out of its 25 referendum attempts. Only its one successful proposal, put in 1946, had Opposition support.

2. Popular ownership

Just as deadly as partisan opposition is to constitutional reform is the perception that a reform idea is a 'politicians' proposal'. From the 1967 nexus proposal, which was felled by the cry of 'no more politicians', to the Republic referendum, which was killed off by the claim that it was the 'politicians' republic', Australians have consistently voted 'No' when they believe a proposal is motivated by politicians' self-interest.

The design of Australia's reform process exacerbates this problem. Politicians, and only politicians, can initiate constitutional reform through the federal parliament. This renders every referendum proposal at risk of being perceived as self-serving.

3. Popular education

Surveys of the Australian public show a disturbing lack of knowledge about the Constitution and Australian government. Rather than being engaged and active citizens, many Australians know little of even the most basic aspects of government. This is often a reflection of the fact that disengaged citizens tend to have less knowledge about their system of government and the reform being proposed.

The problem has been demonstrated over many years. For example, a 1987 survey for the Constitutional Commission found that almost half the population did not realise Australia had a written Constitution.

These problems can be telling during a referendum campaign. A lack of knowledge, or false knowledge, on the part of the voter, can translate into a misunderstanding of a proposal, a potential to be manipulated by the Yes or No cases and even an unwillingness to consider change on the basis that 'don't know, vote No' is the best policy. Overall, the record shows that when voters do not understand or have no opinion on a proposal, they tend to vote 'No'.

4. A sound and sensible proposal

As important as it is to get the process of generating proposals right, it is equally important to get the proposals themselves right. Changes to the Constitution must be drafted to last 50 or 100 years. Just as we are living with the compromises and values of Parkes' time, so might generations to come have to live with ours.

CONCLUSION

Australia needs to recapture Parkes' vision for achieving social justice through constitutional reform. Our federal system has a habit of frustrating such goals, or of wasting enough money to make them difficult to achieve. This needs to change.

We also aspire to be a country that treats people fairly and equally. Yet we still have a Constitution that expressly recognises that people can be denied the vote or subject to different treatment because of their race. It is hard to describe us as a free and tolerant democracy when this possibility remains.

Australia's long record of failed attempts at constitutional reform does not mean that winning such referendums is 'mission impossible'. Instead, it shows that we should expect a referendum to fail whenever our major political parties disagree, or when poor management means that the Australian people feel left out or confused as to what is being changed. People will also vote 'No' to a proposal that is dangerous or has been poorly thought out.

We need to recognise this if we are to overcome the current political aversion to changing Australia's Constitution.

Indeed, my own view is that constitutional change in the name of social justice can, and must, be brought about.

"No serious observer of politics in Australia, except those with specific interests, can pretend that we do not have major problems with our system of government or that we are incapable of achieving any improvement after a century of experience."

State of the Federation

Ted Mack

26 October 2013

Sir Henry Parkes Memorial School of Arts, Tenterfield NSW.

I CAME TO POLITICS some 40 years ago having no previous involvement with political parties or organisations. I had worked as an architect for 20 years mostly on hospitals and public housing. I didn't have any burning desire to change the world – just a few simple principles like the workings of government should be open to public scrutiny. That elected representatives should enable people to not only participate in all decisions that affect them but ultimately find ways to have people make decisions for themselves. That the very basis of democracy is that a decision taken by the public as a whole will be right more often than decisions taken by an elite group no matter how wise that group. That people entrusted with the public purse should honour that trust and treat public money as they would want other people to treat their money. These ideas of course created an inevitable collision with the operations of political parties and most bureaucracies.

In any case over the next 20 odd years I was given the unique experience of having an independent inside view of 14 years in local government, seven in state government and six in federal government. This didn't happen because the electors of North Sydney were carbon monoxide affected or because I had discovered some magic secret of electoral success. It happened because people saw the benefits of three fundamental principles – open government, decentralised decision-making and financial probity demonstrated in North Sydney Council for some eight years.

My comments here will cover the state of our political system, some of the causes of the problems and to suggest possible directions for reform.

In 1992 the former secretary to the Office of Governor-General, Sir David Smith, wrote: 'There is much that is wrong with the way this nation is governed and administered: never before have we had so many royal commissions and other inquiries; never before have we had so many office-holders and other figures in, or facing the prospect of prison; never before have the electors registered their dissatisfaction with the political process by returning so many independent and minor party candidates to Parliament.'

In the Mackay Report of July 2001, social researcher Hugh Mackay stated: 'Australia's contempt for federal politics and its leaders has plumbed new depths. If it (the Mackay Report) was a family newspaper, we would scarcely be able to print the things Australian's are saying about their politicians … In the 22-year history of the Mackay Report political attitudes have never been quite as negative as this.'

On 16 June 2013 in *The Australian* newspaper Tony Fitzgerald QC (who chaired the 1987 Queensland Royal Commission) wrote an article 'The body politic is rotten'. He stated: 'There are about 800 politicians in Australia's parliaments. According to their assessments of each other, that quite small group includes role models for lying, cheating, deceiving, "rorting", bullying, rumour-mongering, back-stabbing, slander, "leaking", dog whistling, nepotism and corruption.'

He states, in effect, that the dominance of the major parties by little known and unimpressive faction leaders who have effective control of Australia's democracy and destiny … might be tolerable if the major parties acted with integrity but they do not. Their constant battles for power are venal, vicious and vulgar.

Over the last 30 years there has been a plethora of minor and major scandals, misuse of most forms of parliamentary allowances, interstate travel, overseas travel, telephone allowances, comcars, taxis, air charters and stamp allowances in addition to the revelations of major royal commissions. It seems that almost

TED MACK

Edward (Ted) Mack was named by the National Trust in 1998 as one of 100 National Living Treasures. Trained as an architect, he was first elected to North Sydney Council as an independent in 1974, serving for 14 years, including eight as Mayor. He held the state seat of North Sydney from 1981 to 1988, and the federal seat of North Sydney from 1990 to 1996. He was an elected delegate to the 1998 Constitutional Convention.

anything can and has been rorted. The number of resignations of ministers of state and federal parliaments shows that something is wrong with the selection process or the talent pool. One problem is that the ability to become a cabinet minister often has nothing to do with ability to be a minister.

- In 1984 there was the Costigan Royal Commission revealing extensive criminal activities, tax fraud and the notorious 'bottom-of-the-harbour schemes'. Cost $13.9 million.
- 1987 saw the Fitzgerald Inquiry in Queensland initiated, leading to the Premier being deposed, three former ministers and the Police Commissioner going to gaol. Cost $90 million.
- In 1991 we had WA Inc revealing enormous corruption in politics and business in that state. Both Liberal and Labor premiers went to gaol. Cost $30.5 million.
- In 1994 New South Wales had the Wood Royal Commission into the Police. This resulted in resignations and dismissals of the Police Commissioner and some 92 officers. Cost $70 million.

Yet after all this, the public watched in disgust at the collapse of the New South Wales – Iemma–Rees–Kenneally – governments in 2007–11 exposing the worst level of government corruption in Australian history.

The 2010–13 federal parliament saw the major parties virtually eliminate any real form of democratic debate, substituting little but character assassination of opponents. It was a three-year election campaign of personal abuse and fear mongering. It was debased even further with aggressive bullying by the media and special interests at unprecedented levels.

The same period saw both state and federal governments pandering to special interests allowing massive increases in the promotion of gambling and alcohol. Pandering to the development and mining industries and the seemingly endless privatisation of public assets often creating private monopolies, continued irrespective of public opinion.

The last decade has also seen a substantial escalation in the endless federal–state 'turf wars'. This seems to bedevil almost all main areas of government activities such as health, education, transport, agriculture and water policy. The massive overlap of functions results in huge increases in bureaucracy. The expansion of government, particularly the costs of expanding political staff and salaries, seems to be in inverse proportion to the levels of public satisfaction.

Recent increases bring the basic salary of the prime minister to $507,000 compared to the American president at US$400,000, and the English prime minister at £142,000. Salary packages for MPs have escalated at federal level with steady creation of new positions and extensions of fringe benefits. So much so that only a handful of backbench members of the government receive the lowest salary package. State governments have followed suit.

Salary packages for federal government members now range from around $325,000 to some $475,000 per year for ministers. However, extremely generous superannuation schemes can effectively double that depending on age at retirement. For example, recently retired after nine years in the New South Wales upper house, Eric Roozendaal aged 51 receives a pension of $120,000. This is indexed to future politicians' salaries. Given his life expectancy, this works out at around $500,000 per year for his nine years of office. Together with his annual salary he was rewarded with almost $1,000,000 for each year in parliament. This is for a job that the officials of political parties can bestow on people with no experience or qualification.

The 10 ex–prime ministers and governors-general each averaged around $500,000 per year in public costs for 2010–11 or around $10,000 per week in retirement but the annual appropriation available for the current Governor-General's office is approaching $13 million.

Over the last 30 years politicians' staff has increased dramatically. At federal level there are now some 1700 personal staff to ministers and members. The states probably account for over 2000 more. Add to this the direct political infiltration of federal–state public services and quangos with hundreds more jobs for the boys and girls, there is now a well-established political class.

This has provided the political parties with a career path for members. In many cases it often produces skilled, partisan, 'whatever it takes' warriors with a richly rewarded life through local state and federal governments to a well-funded retirement. Unfortunately, while this career path, as Tony Fitzgerald states, does 'include principled well-motivated people ... it also attracts professional politicians with little or no general life experience and unscrupulous opportunists, unburdened by ethics, who obsessively pursue power, money or both'.

Since the 1990s there have been endless calls by federal and state government for increased efficiency, no wage increases unless matched with productivity, for restructuring, downsizing and deregulation all in the name of increased competitiveness and facing the international community in the 21st century. Many thousands of jobs have disappeared, particularly those in federal and state bureaucracies at middle and lower incomes and in the general workforce.

Now there is little doubt some restructuring of the country is necessary but it is strange that the political-administrative structure and the legal system are somehow excluded from any need for reform – given both the massive costs and level of public dissatisfaction. It is surprising that while the media regularly exposes major and minor political misdemeanours, it rarely proposes any serious need for reform let alone suggests possible solutions. Our many publicly funded schools of government and politics also seem to be largely silent on the need for political or constitutional reform, with some individual honourable exceptions.

In an effort to increase public confidence in the political system a huge amount of legislation has been passed over recent years to ostensibly promote such things as open government, public participation and reduced reliance on private donations. Effectively the open government legislation has mainly meant freedom from information. Even this year the Labor government and the then opposition quietly combined to sneak through legislation that completely exempted the three government departments that supervise the running of the federal parliament from answering Freedom of Information requests.

As for public participation, virtually all government decisions are made in private by small groups of people who are in many cases not in parliament. Public funding of elections was first introduced into New South Wales in 1981 and federally in 1984 on the basis that it would reduce private donations. Neville Wran presented the bill and concluded his speech by saying 'this bill will remove the risk of parties selling political favours and declares to the world that the great political parties of New South Wales are not up for sale'. Since then an escalating 'arms war' of election spending has developed with public funding steadily increasing and private funding increasing even faster.

The taxpayer cost of federal elections has increased from $38 million in 1984 to $161 million in 2010. Of the latter $53 million was public funding to parties and candidates. Currently, in spite of massive increases, public funding is less than 20 per cent of about $350 million total election spending. We are now effectively the second best democracy money can buy.

There is an overwhelming need to reduce overall election spending. The United States democracy has been largely destroyed by the huge amount of money dedicated to this purpose and Australia is accelerating down the same tollway. Maximum spending limits must be applied to all elections. At present freedom of speech is only effectively available to the rich and those using other people's money. The Electoral Commission should produce booklets setting out candidates' biographies and policies as was done for the 1999 Constitutional Convention elections, with all advertising banned.

Organisations have been set up to monitor government's administration: ombudsmen of various varieties, royal commissions, anti-corruption bodies, competition commissions, auditors, the Remuneration Commission, the Electoral Commission, the Competition Commission, ASIC and many others. To an extent these so-called independent bodies have not been as successful as originally hoped for and only operate at a fearful cost. Codes of ethics are a favourite device as are claims of independent Speakers often made by incoming governments to address behaviour of members. History shows that codes of ethics and fair Speakers never last – the code is soon buried and the fair Speakers are sacked.

Political parties as they have developed over the last century seem like two mafia families seeking control of the public purse for distribution to themselves, supporters, the special interests who fund them and for buying votes at the next election. Political parties are not mentioned in the Constitution. They are effectively unregulated private organisations but they now control government treasuries.

When they unite with common interests, for example funding themselves, the public are mostly powerless except on the rare occasions when public outrage is too great – for example the attempted $60 million virtually secret increase in public funding for the parties earlier this year (2013).

Both parties have rightly suffered huge reductions in membership over the last few years almost in direct proportion to the centralisation of power in their organisations. Public election funding and huge allowances have reduced the party's need for workers for elections. Candidates now can rely on direct mail, general advertising and paid help.

By centralising power, as Tony Fitzgerald puts it, the public interest is subordinated to the pursuit of power, party objectives and personal ambitions, sometimes including the corrupt acquisition of financial benefit. Branch stacking has become endemic and as Fitzgerald says, 'The parties gift electorates to family connections, malleable party hacks and mediocre apparatchiks.'

The views of people like retired judge Tony Fitzgerald QC, Hugh Mackay, possibly Australia's leading social researcher, and Sir David Smith, Official Secretary to five governors-general, should be taken seriously. They have a long and rare experience of government in Australia. Their views are considered and well founded. They demand examination of the many problems of our system of government in order to establish directions for reform.

The Australian Constitution could only be based on conditions existing in the late 19th century. As Professor Helen Irving states in her recent book *Five things to know about the Australian Constitution*, '... it does not mean what it says ... it does not say what it means ... it says some things without actually saying them ... it fails to say things which might be important ... it says things that might be important'. Today it is not only obsolete but is an expensive handicap to the well-being of Australian society. In essence it was a parochial compromise between the states based on an amalgamation of the British system and the American Constitution.

We followed English parliamentary practice but without accepting English traditional restraints. For example in Westminster the Speaker is fair, in Australia fair Speakers are quickly dispensed with. The government must always win. This is why Question Time in Australia often descends to a schoolboy rabble. We have a system where the opposition almost always loses and has virtually no role in legislation. This forces members to extremes – to magnify differences – often reaching levels of mindless partisanship only seen at football matches.

The two-party system of government and opposition where the 'winner-takes-all' has inevitably resulted in mutual denigration with little or no sensible parliamentary debate. Frankly, in Australian parliaments opposition is a form of political death. The thought of it colours all decision-making. It entrenches the philosophy of 'whatever it takes'. It even means less salary for the members of the opposition – shock, horror.

The election of governments by parliamentary members, in the absence of fixed terms, means a rigid parliamentary discipline must be enforced to achieve stability. Extreme partisanship takes over and the public interest is irrelevant.

Parliament can never be a check on executive government except in rare situations. The domination of parliament by executive government effectively means it is an 'elected dictatorship', except in the rare cases of hung parliaments.

The two-party system stifles ideas, debate and decision-making within the parties. The faction system often ensures minority views triumph within both party rooms. In the case of the government, the minority view will then be taken into parliament and become an even greater minority law. Hence the shocking derailing of democratic government in New South Wales in 2007–11. Voting within parties is often based on what faction members belong to, who wants to become or stay a minister or who wants to be party leader. What the electors think is at best a secondary consideration. Party members almost always follow the party line and are often voting against what they really believe or what their electorates would want.

A classic example of this was the 1999 Republic Referendum where opinion polls showed that 70 per cent of the public wanted the right to vote for any future president but only three out of 225 members of federal parliament supported that position. A few years of regularly voting and speaking against what they believe in, I suspect some cease to believe in anything and take refuge in extreme partisanship following whatever is the party executive's position.

After 112 years the functions of Commonwealth and state governments as well as the financial arrangements are in chaos, resulting in endless dispute, waste and inefficiency. A century of debate and confusion over these issues shows that the problems are impossible to resolve without a rewrite of the Constitution.

Our founding fathers at the conventions of the 1890s must have been blinded by the magnificence of the British Empire at the zenith of its power to adopt the worst feature of the Constitution, that is, the single-member electorate system. Electing parliaments by voting for single members, then having the elected members elect a government, is a democratic travesty kept alive by politicians, academia and the press. There was little excuse for the founding fathers let alone today's political establishment. John Stuart Mill, known as the most influential English-speaking philosopher of the 19th century, set out the principles of democratic voting in 1861.

He clearly showed that the single-member electorate system results in only accidental relationship between seats won and the total actual votes. This occurs because it is possible to win 100 per cent of the seats with around 43 per cent of the vote. For example, the 2012 election in Queensland produced the bizarre result that the state government won 88 per cent of seats with 49.7 per cent of the vote. The other 50.3 per cent of voters were rewarded with 12 per cent of the seats.

This system also largely eliminates minorities unless their vote is concentrated in particular electorates. That is why such parties as the Australian Democrats and Greens get almost no lower house seats with often twice the vote of the National Party, while the latter generally receives around 10 members and three or four ministers and the deputy prime ministership.

It is fundamental to liberal democracy that while the majority should rule, minorities should be represented in proportion to their support. Even more essential is that the electoral system should represent the will of the people – the single-member electorate system does neither and in addition results in a maximum not minimum wastage of votes.

Since World War II federal elections have resulted in five governments elected with a minority of two-party preferred votes. Yet the fundamental rule of democracy is majority rule. Conversely only three governments out of 26 achieved over 50 per cent of the primary vote, as did one opposition. No wonder most governments are unpopular soon after the euphoria of an election fades.

So why do we keep the single-member electorate system? Because only the major parties can change it. But why should they? It helps preserve the two-party duopoly. It largely prevents the election of third-party candidates. An incumbent lower-house federal candidate today has effectively $400,000 worth of facilities and money to ward off challengers. Major parties can transfer a million or so extra dollars from safe seats if they really want to stop an outsider. It also enables the government parties to 'pork barrel' specific seats. It is hardly an equal opportunity for challengers whether they are individuals or new parties.

There have been many changes to electoral systems over the last century and almost all have been made for partisan reasons.

The Senate is also fundamentally flawed as a democratic organisation. In each election 42.3 per cent of the vote will elect 50 per cent of senators in each state for a start. Then there is the voting system that allows parties to transfer preferences effectively without the voters' knowledge. This system led to the infamous 1999 'tablecloth' election in the New South Wales upper house with dozens of new political parties created to take advantage of this undemocratic system. In that election a candidate was elected to the New South Wales upper house with a primary vote of 0.2 per cent, receiving preferences from most of the previously unknown parties.

This is known as the 'harvesting of preferences' and certainly distorted the result. Even the New South Wales Labor government that some would say was the epitome of political evil, reformed this system 14 years ago by ensuring that only the voter could transfer preferences. Yet similar distortions have been obvious at federal level at the 2004 and 2010 elections, and here we are in 2013 with the same rort. We now have some five senators with no democratic legitimacy, all because the major parties are so venal and are prepared to treat voters as mushrooms to obtain power. It is to Australia's shame that at least 99 per cent of voters at the recent elections had no idea where their Senate vote really went.

Certainly, the 1949 electoral reforms of the Senate providing for proportional representation (for the wrong reasons) do make the Senate more reflective of the Australian voter than the lower house. However, the unequal state and arbitrary territory representation is fundamentally undemocratic. It cannot be democratically acceptable to have for example, one Hobart vote to be equal to 14 Tenterfield votes or one Darwin vote worth almost three Bendigo votes when voting on issues that affect all Australians equally.

Australia's electoral systems at federal and state level, excluding the ACT and Tasmania, are in my view clearly in breach of Article 25 of the International Covenant on Civil and Political Rights to which Australia is a signatory and has ratified. They do not guarantee 'the free expression of the will of the electors' and federal elections are not by 'equal suffrage' and candidates are not 'freely chosen'.

As things stand, Australian democracy consists of voting in a rigged system every few years to elect others to make decisions for us. The voters mostly know little or nothing about most candidates after the 'faceless men' and 'branch stackers' have had their way. We are rarely permitted to have any say on policies. Cabinet ministers, premiers and prime ministers come and go without reference to us. We go to war and sign treaties without even our parliament having a say let alone the public. When the major parties agree, as they do when funding themselves and their mutual friends, we have no say whatsoever. It is a pretty minimalist democracy and a long way from Abraham Lincoln's 'government of the people, by the people, for the people'. We seem to have achieved 'government of the people by the powerbrokers, for the mates'.

Most people today believe they should have a right to have their say in all decisions that affect them. Yet the usual position of politicians is to say 'we were elected to make the decisions and if you don't like it vote against us at the next election'. This view is totally unsatisfactory. It is the decision people are interested in, not revenge some time later. In addition, general elections provide only a mandate to govern – they do not provide a mandate for all or any future decisions, except in rare circumstances.

Still there are only about 30 or so countries you could call partial democracies but only Switzerland that fulfils Lincoln's definition of democracy. This is not surprising considering democracy, while enjoying a brief starburst in Greece 2,500 years ago, really only took modern form in the 18th century after the French and American revolutions. Unfortunately writing constitutions has inherent problems – they can only reflect the values of their time, they are doomed to obsolescence and usually difficult to change. Bills of rights have the same problems in addition to politicising the judiciary and weakening democracy.

Constitutional problems have been obvious for many years and there have been many attempts at reform with little result. One of the virtues of the Australian Constitution is that the founding fathers gave the right to change it exclusively to the public by way of referendums. Unfortunately they gave the right to ask the question for public consideration exclusively to the government. Government, however, has generally only asked to be given more power.

Many party-oriented people decry the ignorance of the voter for the high failure rate of referendums. The real lesson of a century of mostly failed constitutional referendums is that generally any suggestion of centralised power will be rejected. This view is reinforced by the fact that 12 out of 16 referendums in New South Wales have been carried as they were about specific issues rather than centralisation of power to the government.

The fundamental problems of our system of government have not seriously ever been addressed since Federation. These problems can be summarised as:

- the level of over-government;
- the obsolescence of the constitutional relationships between the three levels of government
- the two party 'winner-take-all' executive domination of parliament and the associated corrupted voting systems;
- the domination of the political system and public service by the two private unregulated political parties and their largely self-regulated access to the public treasury; and
- almost a total absence in the school system and for new citizens of any education concerning the three levels of government, their function and voting systems.

In recent years there have been calls for the abolition of the states in response to the frustration of Commonwealth–state relations. This is understandable but misguided. As with other large countries such as the United States, Russia, India and Germany, all are federal, being too large to have acceptable unitary democratic arrangements.

In such countries, and others for particular reasons, there are national, regional and local issues and all should be represented. Australia's problem is no clarity in our Constitution as to what each level should do. Ideally each level should spend and raise its own finance. Deciding what functions each level should do is vital as it appears that historically the tendency is to centralise. Both Australia and the USA are suffering with bloated federal bureaucracies. Functions are best performed at the lowest practical level and here again Switzerland shows the way.

In Australia the states are the level of government most over-represented, with their 598 members of parliament. Their Westminster systems are wasteful and inefficient and should be replaced with single chambers and a generally increased number of voters per member with a minimum of say, 15 members.

There is also a good case for creating more states or regions than draftsmen in the British Foreign Office decided in the middle of the 19th century. One of the reasons decentralisation has never really worked in Australia is that all power resides in the six capital cities. New South Wales' boundaries with all three adjoining states are now inappropriate and it could well be broken into six or seven states. Queensland and Victoria lend themselves to about four states each. Logically Northern Territory and the Kimberly should be one state.

As to the basic structure of parliament, there are only two broad systems in use that are generally regarded as democracies. The first, developed in England substantially in the 18th century, is the one we have: parliaments elected using single-member electorates. The second is those elected by proportional representation developed in the 19th century – with usually five to 10 political parties. This not only allows more representative views to be aired, it also has more eyes watching the system, tending to reduce corruption.

In his book *Patterns of democracy* analysing governments and their performance in 36 countries, world-renowned political scientist Arend Lijphart concludes that consensual political systems using proportional representation stimulate economic growth, control inflation and unemployment and limit budget deficits as well as countries using single-member electorate systems. However, he also concludes that the consensual democracies clearly outperform single-member electorate systems on measures of political equality, women's representation, citizens' participation and proximity between government policies and voter preferences. He also demonstrates that the more consensual a democracy the kinder and gentler it is when addressing such issues as welfare, environment, criminal justice and foreign aid.

The single-member electorate system is confined largely to the English-speaking world, but overwhelmingly most democracies use proportional representation. Our system as indicated earlier has major defects and is promoted by claiming that it is necessary for the stability of government. It relies on manufacturing a false majority and preserving the two-party system. It is no accident that both the American and British systems are currently experiencing major problems stemming from their single-member electorates.

There are far better ways of preserving stability of government without compromising the electoral system. There is the American method of separately electing executive government or, if you really want stability, consider Switzerland. Its seven-member executive federal government has never been renewed entirely at the same time over 175 years. It is elected by the parliament every four years and only four members have been voted out in over 150 years. Most members retire after two or three terms. Since 1990 Switzerland has had some 22 ministers in federal government; in the same time we have had a kaleidoscope of around 300 ministers. If that is not enough to scare our political parties, there is the amazing fact that there are only seven full-time paid federal politicians in the Swiss executive and lower house for their eight and a half million people, compared to our 150.

The two-party system is essentially preserved by the single-member electorate system. In proportional representation countries there are an average of about five to 10 parties, allowing an increase in political ideas and a more democratic reflection of the voters.

There are a number of variations of proportional representation methods used around the world but surprisingly the most democratic yet devised is the Hare-Clarke system used in Tasmania. This was initiated largely by Andrew Inglis Clarke around 1900 as the Attorney-General in the Tasmanian Parliament. He also penned the first draft of the Australian Constitution.

This voting system accurately reflects the will of the people. To obtain 50 per cent of the seats you must receive 50 per cent of the vote. It gives the electors the choice of party candidates. The voters can replace unsatisfactory members with another candidate from the same party. Wastage of votes is minimal as is the practice of branch stacking. Minorities are represented according to their size. Donkey votes, how-to-vote cards and by-elections are eliminated. Ideally it uses seven- or nine-member electorates similar to the senate's six-member electorates and all preferences should be optional.

It also uses much larger electorates that if combined with electronic voting in parliament to adjust for population shifts, could be based on electorate boundaries that really reflect community of interests and would rarely need to change. This would eliminate the current horrendous costs of constantly adjusting federal and state electorate boundaries and the confusion that is created.

Possibly the greatest problem with governments around the world is that of self-regulation. History clearly demonstrates that when politicians have free access to treasuries the results are always, to put it mildly, unsatisfactory. The present Australian system of effective self-regulation for wages and fringe benefits for politicians, unlike the great majority of other employees, is totally unacceptable. This self-regulation produces a mutual waltz where the politicians tell senior public servants 'you're worth more money' and the public servants return the favour. This flows through all political and public service positions of the Commonwealth and the states, the respective judiciaries and quangos. The politicians hide behind a carefully selected 'Remuneration Committee' consisting of three persons drawn from the highest paid people in Australia.

A common problem is the confusion of the roles of representatives and government. Representatives' role is to represent the people. They do not require high management or technical skills and are unrepresentative if they are, as at present, among the top one per cent of wage earners. Government ministers however require a largely different and much greater set of skills. The failure rate of federal and state ministers is such that it is obviously being drawn from too small a pool. Ministers would be better if they could be drawn from the whole community, either appointed as in America or preferably elected as in Switzerland.

According to the *Sydney Morning Herald* of 10 January 2011, the highest-paid civil servant in New South Wales was the head of Energy Australia at $774,799, plus perks, no doubt. *The Australian* newspaper of 27 September 2011 reported that the salaries of a number of federal public service heads were expected to rise from the current $500,000 per annum to $800,000 per annum plus perks or around $56,000 per week. All this follows the pattern of private CEOs' pay. Recently Melbourne University economist Mike Pottinger reported that in 1900 the BHP Chief Executive's salary was around 50 times average Australian wages. By the 1980s this ratio had dropped to only six or seven times as much. The ratio then rapidly increased to 200 times by 1998, touching 250 times by 2005. It has fallen back these days to about 160 times, at only $12.58 million per annum plus perks.

Of course CEOs and company directors effectively set their own salaries. Frankly there is no evidence that executives, both public and private, are so superior to their counterparts prior to the 1980s that could justify the massive salary increases since then.

As things stand, politics in Australia is now the province of a political class that now offers a lifetime career path in federal and state parliaments, the public services and quangos. Entrance to this world often involves nepotism and cronyism. There can be few other legitimate jobs with salary packages over $300,000 that can often be obtained with virtually no experience and qualifications and little restrictions on second jobs or holidays.

Equating integrity with paying more money flies in the face of history. By paying politicians starting salary packages of over $300,000, more people are attracted who could not get that salary level elsewhere. In fact people pursuing material gain should be discouraged from entering politics.

There is certainly no evidence that the massive increases of salary packages in recent years has increased benefits to the public or improved the quality of members or ministers compared to governments of the past. Far from paying peanuts and getting monkeys, paying more peanuts seems to attract gorillas.

Avenues for ambition, financial advancement, offers of prestigious government appointments, indeed all possible inducements that could colour a member's voting, should be eliminated where possible. Limitation of office of say, three terms, should apply, with only inflation-indexed salaries. Using any political or government office for personal financial gain over and above the official salary should result in dismissal. Attempting to influence a member's voting with financial or any form of fringe benefit should be a criminal offence. The politicisation of Australia's public services over the last 30 years has degraded many public organisations and reduced government's ability to implement policy even when they are acting in the public interest. The notorious self-regulated politicians' superannuation scheme should be abolished. They should obtain superannuation in the same manner as the rest of the community.

The problem of self-regulation was well put by the former Clerk of the Senate, Harry Evans. He pointed out that our present system was like a cricket match where the captain of the batting side was also the umpire. When ministers or members of the batting side played false shots they are rarely and reluctantly given out. There really needs to be an independent umpire to not only monitor ministers and members but to also appoint the Speaker of Parliament from outside parliament.

A fully independent Public Service Board needs to be reinstated for all government appointments, particularly for bodies such as the Ombudsman, Corruption Commissions, Auditor-General, Police Integrity Commission, Electoral Commission and Remuneration Tribunal. Appointments must be based only on proven competence and integrity. The main reason many of these bodies at present fall short of public expectations is that the executives are appointed by, and their briefs are constrained by, government. Yet their role will often involve investigation of government.

In other words all those bodies that have no political functions but are there to ensure the integrity of the system should be independent of government.

One feature of our original federal Constitution that should be reinstated is a role for a directly elected Governor-General to fully umpire the system in addition to the traditional role as head of state. He or she could also head a fourth arm of government known as the Integrity Branch. Such a role for the Governor-General would be spelt out in the Constitution as having no power in relation to political policy but only power to ensure integrity of government and to ensure the Constitution is upheld.

The concept of a separate fourth branch of government has been canvassed in legal circles in recent years, particularly by James Spigelman in 2004, then Chief Justice of the New South Wales Supreme Court. It has been extensively examined in the October 2012 issue of the Australian Institute of Administrative Law's journal *AIAL Forum* (No. 70, 2012). As James Spigelman pointed out in his two lectures, the concept of a separate integrity level of government is an ancient Chinese concept. In the last three decades we have informally created this fourth branch as a means of stemming various problems but with only limited success. Formalising its independence from government would certainly improve its performance.

Earlier I made reference to various aspects of the Swiss Government from which we could learn. Its fundamental advantage over all other democratic systems is the use of direct democracy. In Switzerland the people are sovereign – they can overrule the government, the parliament and even the constitution at will. Referendums on the Constitution or policy can and are initiated by the people every three months. Government legislation can be cancelled or amended by the people. From 2000 to 2012 there have been some 104 referendums at federal level. That is an average of eight each year. There are many more at state and council levels. They have dealt with all sorts of issues that dominate our parliaments in angry, abusive debates. Swiss government seems to quietly get on with implementing public policy set by the public. This means that all government deliberations are mostly on a consensus basis. If it isn't, it generally means a referendum. There is also no formalised opposition.

At federal level there is a seven-member government elected proportionally by parliament, with candidates drawn from the whole community. The effect of this is calm deliberation, none of our daily chaos and accusations. The seven members of government take it in turn annually to be Prime Minister with no additional power or money. Apparently most people are unsure of who the prime minister is. There is no career path for federal members of parliament who are all part-time. No leadership fights, no minority government, no dramatic changes of governments, public policies or public servants after elections. Fundamentally the Swiss Government cannot enact any law without majority support. You can begin to see why the Swiss system has been kept secret for the last century.

It is informative that whereas many decry the difficulty of amending our Constitution because of the requirement for a referendum, the Swiss however have no trouble and have amended it constantly since 1848. The difference is the people ask the questions, not the politicians. It is government by the people.

It is very easy to sneer at the Swiss as most elitists do. It is often done with humour as in the movie *The Third Man* when Orson Wells said, 'In Italy for 30 years under the Borgias they had warfare, terror, murder and bloodshed, but they produced Michelangelo, Leonardo da Vinci and the Renaissance. In Switzerland they had brotherly love, five hundred years of democracy and peace and what did that produce? The cuckoo clock.' But that was only a movie. He did not say it was the leading democracy in the world, arguably the most successful multicultural society, with among the highest per capita income and life expectancy. They have not had a war since the French Revolutionaries invaded them. It is a land almost without tennis courts or an ocean, yet produced Roger Federer and won the America's Cup. Still while not perfect, their first university was founded in 1460 and we can learn from them.

No serious observer of politics in Australia, except those with specific interests, can pretend that we do not have major problems with our system of government or that we are incapable of achieving any improvement after a century of experience. 'Minimalism' in our approach to a new constitution would always be a mistake, as outstanding constitutional experts have documented, such as

Helen Irving in her 2001 Barton Lecture, David Solomon in his book *Coming of age, charter for a new Australia* and Harry Evans, former Clerk of the Senate, arguably Australia's leading expert on constitutions and government.

There have been many new constitutions written since the World War II. Most have been prepared in times of overwhelming crisis or the urgent aftermath of revolution or war. Fortunately we do not have this degree of urgency. In an analysis and survey of constitution-making in the book *Democracy's victory and crisis* (1997), Jon Elster formerly of the universities of Chicago and Oslo and now Columbia University, has distilled some basic principles:

- First, a democratic constitution is best formulated through a fully elected constitutional commission. Parliaments should not be allowed to be judges in their own cause. Serving politicians and bureaucrats will almost never have the public interest at heart when ceding or gaining 'turf', as evidenced by the last century of attempts at reform.
- Second, the role of experts and lawyers should be advisory rather than in actual decision-making.
- Third, constitutions should be evolved in calm, generally open, deliberate and measured conditions avoiding grandstanding and rhetorical over bidding. Secrecy should be minimised to avoid partisan interests and log rolling coming to the forefront and threat-based bargaining.
- Fourth, any constitution should not come into effect until some time after it has been adopted, so as to reduce the impact of short-term partisan motives.

Following these principles, a fully elected constitutional commission should be convened on the basis of one-vote-one-value on an Australia-wide proportional basis. It should be serviced by a technical secretariat and meet for short sessions over a substantial period of time. It should have the power to utilise polling and to put plebiscites to the people, ideally to coincide with elections to establish fundamental directions.

Eventually the commission should be authorised to institute a referendum on the basis that the new constitution will not come into effect for say, seven years.

Serious reform is, of course, perhaps many years into the future and the obstacles and enemies of democratic reform are many. The political parties and their partisan supporters' overwhelming interest is in gaining power and preserving the political duopoly.

Big business is implacably opposed to more democracy. It wants more centralisation of power. It currently employs more than 600 registered lobbyists in Canberra and spends millions of dollars to subvert democracy.

Big media is always constrained by its owners' interests. Since World War II there has been a growth of corporate propaganda to protect corporate power against democracy. Nevertheless given authoritarian government has been the norm for almost all of modern humans' 200,000-year history and democracy seriously arrived just over 200 hundred years ago, it is making reasonable progress – but there is a long way to go.

In conclusion I would like to thank the Henry Parkes Foundation for the opportunity of delivering the 2013 Oration. It is a major honour to help recognise Parkes' Tenterfield speech and pay homage to his pre-eminent career in Australian political history, both in longevity and achievement.

"Many of those characteristics for which Australians are renowned across the world – egalitarianism, the rewards of integrity, access to education, fine health services, and working towards the common good – can find these ideals in an examination of the example and leadership of Henry Parkes."

The enduring legacy of Henry Parkes

Dame Marie Bashir
25 July 2014

Government House, Sydney NSW, on the 175th anniversary of Parkes' arrival in Australia on board the 'Strathfieldsaye'.

IT IS A DEEPLY FELT privilege to have been asked to deliver an address on Sir Henry Parkes, 19th century English immigrant who was indeed a titan in the history of modern Australia. He stands as an individual who from any appraisal of qualities of character, and from his life history, his specific contribution to the building of a great nation, will continue to inspire thoughtful Australians with a sense of gratitude as well as admiration.

Modern Australia, often described as 'the lucky country', or 'the happy country', can attribute, I believe, these valid descriptions to the vision, the energy and the inspirational leadership of Henry Parkes. Many of those characteristics for which Australians are renowned across the world – egalitarianism, the rewards of integrity, access to education, fine health services, and working towards the common good – can find these ideals in an examination of the example and leadership of Henry Parkes.

It is fitting that the Henry Parkes Foundation desires that we might reflect upon the life history of the man, sometimes so aptly referred to as 'the Australian

Colossus', and that we appreciate the development of his outstanding contribution, a legacy from which so many Australians have continued to benefit throughout the 20th century and now beyond.

Since my appointment as Governor of New South Wales in 2001, I have indeed been privileged to occupy the fine office of the Colonial Secretary where I am surrounded by the superb furniture, and personal memorabilia of Sir Henry Parkes. His magnificent portrait by the artist Cecil Holmes hangs above the marble fireplace, looking down upon the occupant, evoking recollection of his prophetic exhortation 'one people, one destiny' – still so relevant to 21st century Australia.

A fine biography of this great man has been recently published in 2013. Written by an Australian writer, Stephen Dando-Collins, it is entitled *Sir Henry Parkes – the Australian Colossus*, and I am indebted to the author for enriching my knowledge further on this exceptional man.

HUMBLE BEGINNINGS

Henry Parkes was born in Warwickshire England in 1815, to a family of very limited means. The security, the livelihood of his father, a yeoman farmer, had been deeply affected by the Industrial Revolution, and as a consequence, young Henry was compelled to leave school between the ages of eight and 10 years in order to assist in supporting his family, securing work as an apprentice for a bone and ivory turner. Avid for education throughout his life, Henry later attended a Mechanics Institute. Ever enterprising, at 22 years he established his own bone and ivory carving business. But success continued to elude him, first in Birmingham and later when he moved to London.

In Birmingham, however, he had witnessed at close hand the political energy which resulted eventually in the passing of the reform bill in the British Parliament, legislation which aimed to improve the harsh lives of working class people. Impressed by these developments, Parkes joined the political union, the group which had successfully advocated for this humanitarian reform.

Becoming aware of the Australian colonies' desire for more British immigrants, Henry together with his pregnant wife Clarinda, set sail for Sydney in 1839. In Australian waters, two days before disembarking in Sydney, Clarinda gave birth to a baby girl, Clarinda Sarah. Her two previous children had died soon after birth.

Neither Henry nor Clarinda had any personal contacts in the colony to assist them in any way; but after disembarking, Henry found employment as a farm

DAME MARIE BASHIR

Professor the Hon. Dame Marie Bashir AD CVO is the former and second-longest-serving Governor of New South Wales. Born in Narrandera, New South Wales, she graduated from the University of Sydney in 1956 and held various medical positions, with a particular emphasis on psychiatry. In 1993 she was appointed the Clinical Director of Mental Health Services for the Central Sydney Area Health Service, a position she held until appointed Governor on 1 March 2001. She has also served as the Chancellor of the University of Sydney (2007–2012).

labourer with Sir John Jamison at his Regentville estate, but later he returned to work in a foundry and brass works.

Eventually, by 1845, six years after arriving in Australia, he was able to establish his ivory turning trade in a shop in Hunter Street, Sydney, residing above the shop with his wife and baby daughter.

Because of the gracious generosity of members of the Parkes family descendants, I have the unique honour of displaying quietly in my office, Sir Henry's office, a letter opener of bone, created by Sir Henry, which he has decorated in most delicate carving a small scene of South Head Lighthouse, the Francis Greenway lighthouse of Governor Macquarie's period. This historic treasure will be returned to the care of the family following my retirement from the office of the Governor.

DEDICATED TO SOCIAL PROGRESS

Able to understand and to identify with those who had experienced social deprivation in their formative years, Parkes gave much consideration to social progress and opportunity, and he began to attend such meetings regularly, thus gaining further insight, and the opportunity to present *his* opinion on behalf of the free immigrants and working classes.

As with a number of other committed citizens, such as the Reverend John Dunmore Lang, he was strongly opposed to the transportation of convicts to the colony, but he favoured an extension of a limited franchise being granted to free settlers. Clearly, he was already demonstrating significant political insight.

It has been said that – and I quote – 'his views offered a more-or-less middle course between liberalism and radicalism through much of the 19th century'.[1] In 1850, he established a newspaper, named *The Empire*, which he believed would be able to offer a different perspective to John Fairfax's *Sydney Morning Herald*.

This publication was said to provide a combination of liberal and radical thought, in contra distinction to the conservative viewpoint. However, Parkes' financial management was, like that of many idealists, never sharply astute, and *The Empire* finally ceased publication within eight years – in 1858.

With the retirement from the Parliament in 1854 of William Charles Wentworth, however, Parkes was able to stand for election in Wentworth's former seat. Elected by a 2:1 majority, Parkes had decisively defeated Charles Kemp, who had been a co-owner of the *Sydney Morning Herald*.

Parkes' historic parliamentary career had now begun, with his major support essentially coming from free immigrants of middle and working class background, whose interests he had been promoting for some time.

Unfortunately, with the high cost of supporting the continuing publication of *The Empire*, which had been absorbing significant sums of borrowed money, and with a young family to support, Parkes' difficulties in financial management continued to mount. Across the following years, he would have no option but to be declared bankrupt.

Nevertheless, his parliamentary career, with some intermittent periods of electoral loss, would span four decades.

An early public responsibility assigned to Parkes once elected, was to chair a Parliamentary Select Committee from 1860 into the condition of the working classes. Housing conditions were described as appalling, rents were high, overcrowding was common, and a significant number of homeless children, said to be around 1000, were roaming the streets at considerable risk, some young girls. Indeed young women were being forced into the sex industry.

It seems that Parkes' excellent chairmanship of that Select Committee resulted in greater attention being drawn to these issues by the wider community, and importantly by his fellow parliamentarians.

He was subsequently elevated to the important post of colonial secretary in the ministry of James Martin in 1866.

Consistent in his concern for the well-being of vulnerable young people and aware of their potential strength to a nation, Parkes established a nautical school (one could say 'a small naval college' perhaps) for male orphans, utilising a hulk moored in Sydney Harbour for their training experience.

And when the inadequacies of the critical care of hospitalised patients were brought to his attention, he approached Florence Nightingale (of Crimean War renown) to arrange assistance. This resulted in the decision of Miss Nightingale to despatch Miss Lucy Osborn, as matron, with five other nurses from London, arriving in March 1868, to establish at Sydney Hospital an Australian nurse training school. Indeed within a few years, Osborn-trained nurses would be found contributing significantly to better health care across all New South Wales hospitals. (Many of you would be aware of the Nightingale wing and the Lucy Osborn Museum at Sydney Hospital, which honour that vital contribution to the development of early health services in Australia, and especially to the noble profession of nursing.)

And in direct response to a decisive decision by Parkes, emanating from a royal visit with dramatic and unexpected consequences, the citizens of Sydney acquired a great hospital, renowned today for clinical and teaching excellence across Australia and also internationally – the Royal Prince Alfred Hospital.

As history records, on 12 March 1868, the second son of Queen Victoria, HRH Prince Alfred, during a visit to Australia and whilst attending a picnic at Clontarf in his honour, became the intended victim of an audacious assassination attempt by a gunman of Irish origin – one James O'Farrell.

As the gunman was speedily apprehended, the Prince fell to the ground, wounded but free from spinal injury. The Prince was transported across the harbour to Government House, where Lucy Osborn and her team of splendid nurses ensured that recovery would be full and speedy.

An indication of Parkes' extraordinary insight and diligence can be noted in the fact that, as news of the assassination attempt reached him in his office, he himself set off to lead a search of the rooms where O'Farrell had lodged. Amongst the items examined, Parkes' appraisal of the assassin's notes and behaviour could not convince him that O'Farrell, despite his past history of epilepsy, heavy alcohol use and suicidal thoughts, was of unsound mind.

Refusal by the Governor to approve calls for clemency followed, and O'Farrell was sentenced to death by hanging.

The citizens of Sydney however, jubilant and grateful that the prince had not perished, thus also sparing the loyal colony's reputation as a responsible member of Queen Victoria's empire, were determined to endow a lasting memorial. In generous outpourings of thanksgiving, a substantial sum of money was collected by the citizens, which Parkes and his advisers believed should be directed to upgrade deteriorating conditions of Sydney Hospital.

However, the citizens resolutely directed that an entirely new hospital should be established in the Prince's name. And the University of Sydney, newly established in the Camperdown district, adjacent to the city, readily provided the land on their western boundary, aware of the potential of a well-endowed teaching hospital with Australia's first university. Thus Royal Prince Alfred Hospital, centre of excellence in many medical, surgical and research streams, today continues to fulfil the hopes with which it was inaugurated.

In the impressive 19th century entrance hall of Royal Prince Alfred Hospital, magnificent and extensive glass murals record the Prince's image and that dramatic relationship with the hospital's foundation.

But certainly, one of the greatest and most enduring contributions of Parkes to our nation, I believe, was the high priority which he placed on education – education for all children – ever mindful of his own years of deprivation. And driven also by his intellectual strengths and energy, ever wishing to rectify this, he would endeavour to ensure the education of all children.

As premier, Parkes speedily established a special council to oversee denominational and religious schools. Parkes believed that children of *all* denominations should be educated together, and separated only for specific scripture classes.

Indeed, as chairman of the Parliamentary Select Committee, Parkes had learnt a great deal about the circumstances of children, especially children from poor families. And I believe that a determination was thus developed within his mind to provide opportunities to rectify their appalling and unfair disadvantage. (Because of his concern for adequate health services, for education for all young people, and his advocacy for the poor and marginalised, you may understand why I consider it the greatest honour to occupy his office, to sit at his desk, appreciate his richly carved furniture around me and have his great portrait looking down from above the fireplace, monitoring everything I say and do.)

CONSUMMATE POLITICIAN

It is well established that Henry Parkes possessed in abundance, impressive physical, intellectual and psychological strengths. A handsome man of proud stature and perhaps leonine features. Most significantly also, he had developed – because of his devotion to learning and no doubt to reading and self-improvement – powerful gifts of oratory which would command even demand attention from all sides.

After some years away from parliament, essentially the result of his financial difficulties and ever-mounting debt from loans awaiting payment, Parkes in 1872 made a dramatic return to the political arena and was elected forthwith as premier of New South Wales, thereby providing an opportunity to promote his free-trade policies and also to initiate a major public works program.

But within three years, Henry Parkes no longer occupied this high office, the consequence of heated parliamentary conflict arising from divided opinion regarding the right of the New South Wales Governor to remit the length of a gaol sentence imposed upon a certain Frank Gardiner, a notorious bushranger of the period. Allow me to note that this prerogative of mercy of the governor exists to this day, and on very infrequent occasions in consultation with the attorney-general of the day, the submission is presented with significant supportive material to justify such request.

Whilst the Governor and the Premier agreed on this policy, public opinion was strongly against remission of the sentence, even though the bushranger had served 10 years of his sentence in an exemplary and trouble-free manner, demonstrating, the Governor and Premier Parkes believed, that he possessed 'a capacity to abide by the law'. Parkes' political opponents, however, fomented public opinion, it is believed, and thus loosing control of the legislative assembly, he ceased to be premier for another three years.

However, on his return to the leadership, Parkes vigorously set about strengthening the education system, always an issue of high priority for him, in the light of his childhood experience and relative educational deprivation. This would have been a major personal issue for an individual with high intellectual ability and an ever enquiring mind.

Under Parkes' strong and persuasive leadership, enriched by his considerable powers of reason and oratory, education became free for all children; indeed, it was to be compulsory and secular. The passage in 1866 of Henry Parkes' *Public Schools Act* was a landmark event, I believe, in the nation's history and was adopted with the opposition's support.

State Aid was withdrawn from religious schools, which understandably would become a sensitive issue for such schools over many subsequent decades. And further, this gave rise to a sense of anger from the affected section of the community, some of whom believed that it was a direct form of religious discrimination. But both secular and denomination systems of education were placed 'under a council of education' which would also oversee teacher training and the content of secular lessons. By contemporary world expectations, these developments were insightful and visionary.

In 1877, Parkes was appointed a Knight Commander of St Michael and St George by Her Majesty Queen Victoria.

Free libraries had been established in the previous decade; in 1878, a working man's college was inaugurated, and within 14 years there were 2000 enrolments, the institution developing later into Sydney Technical College. This college was further comprehensively expanded some decades later into the splendid University of New South Wales, officially inaugurated in 1949.

However, in 1883, a period when Australia had been adjudged by overseas banks (including Scotland) to have the most buoyant economy in the world and the highest per capita income, Parkes' government lost office.

His reputation, however, as an outstanding politician had spread as far as great Britain with *The Times* newspaper describing him as the 'most commanding figure in Australian politics'.

Ever resilient, Parkes continued to advocate for free trade and honest government, raising also the need for a bridge across the harbour and a railway line going inland from the north shore of Sydney. Returning to victory, he led New South Wales again from 1887 to 1891. And during the maritime strike of 1890, he undertook the control of the police and also the military.

VISION FOR A FEDERATED LAND

Looking back over his career at this point, one can surely identify so many significant achievements from which the vast majority of New South Wales citizens would benefit and thus enshrine his reputation as one of the greatest leaders in the history of modern Australia.

However, one major issue was now in the forefront of his mind, one which would bequeath an incomparable legacy to all Australians. This was his avowed, unshakeable dedication to a federated land – a united land, one which would bring all Australian states and territories together as one nation.

It is not easy to imagine today this great south land as being composed of distinct separate colonies, each independent from one another. Indeed, when crossing the Murray River to enter Victoria, prior to Federation it was necessary to pass through Customs and to pay a toll.

Furthermore, the adequate provision of military services and Australia's security were increasingly under consideration, given the regularity of conflict and war in other parts of the world, and concerns about Russia's increasing interest in the region. Therefore, the colony of Victoria, in its independent wisdom, had moved to establish its own navy and had already acquired some naval vessels. Victoria was 'always acutely conscious of being less under the protection of Royal Navy guns than their northern cousins'.

Consequently earnest discussions were now taking place around unity, around federation and it is noteworthy also that they were proceeding towards this goal in a respectful and inclusive way.

So in 1889, following Parkes' fifth re-election as premier, he resumed his determined advocacy for federation. It is recorded that 'as far back as 1867, Parkes at an intercolonial conference had said – 'I think the time has arrived when these colonies should be united by some federal bond of connexion'.[2] This was soon followed by an appropriately worded bill which was approved by both parliamentary houses. But subsequently it had been put aside by the secretary for the colonies in Britain. Thus for the next 20 years, this highly important initiative did not develop further.

However, in late 1889, an ever more confident Parkes responded to a critical report on national defence, which put forward the notion of the federation of all the defence forces of the Australian colonies, and also a uniform gauge for railways.

The time had come for more decisive, more definitive action.

In October 1889, Parkes telegraphed his fellow state premiers, suggesting a conference, which would take place later in Melbourne.

Enshrined as one of the most significant days in Australia's history, on 24 October 1889 at the Tenterfield School of Arts, Parkes delivered the Tenterfield Oration, a resounding clarion call for a convention, and I quote his words verbatim,[3] 'to devise the constitution which would be necessary for bringing into existence a federal government with a federal parliament for the conduct of national undertaking'.

And in a passionate comparison with the United States' move to confederation, Parkes noted that the populations of both Australia and the United States of America were comparatively equal, and declared 'surely what the Americans had done by war, the Australians could bring about in peace'.

Within a few months, in February 1890, the Australasian Federation Conference took place in Melbourne, and it was followed the next year in Sydney at the 1891 national Australasian Convention, at which Parkes was appointed Convention President and Sir Samuel Griffith of Queensland, the Vice President.

It was at this convention that the first draft of a bill to constitute the Commonwealth of Australia was developed. And it must ever be acknowledged that it was Henry Parkes himself who put forward the name 'Commonwealth of Australia'.

PARKES THE MAN

In regard to Parkes' towering and complex personality, limited attention is given to the more tender aspect of his character, except perhaps it is implied in various allusions to his virility, his three marriages and indeed the comments, sometimes insensitive, regarding the speedy nature of his third marriage to Julia Lynch, so soon after the death of his second wife Eleanor Dixon.

Despite the many assertive, even leonine aspects to his energetic character, I consider that beneath so many undoubted strengths, there was, in Henry Parkes, a deep, powerful and enduring need for being nurtured.

Despite the material impoverishment of the Parkes family during Henry's years of childhood and adolescence, the love and supportive encouragement from Martha, his mother, and from Sarah, his older sister, were undoubted. Indeed, Stephen Dando-Collins' splendid biography relates that 'Henry's mother would take him by the hand, and sitting in front of the fire, would re-tell Daniel Defoe's *Robinson Crusoe* to amuse him until Sarah came home from work (at Allsops). Although Martha was illiterate, she had succeeded in committing whole slabs of the text of the novel to memory, word for word. As for Sarah, Henry would say that she increasingly became like a second mother to him, and he felt able to confide his innermost thoughts to her.'

Little wonder that Henry had an enduring love for, and an enduring need for nurturing women in his life.

And this softer aspect of his character can be observed in his relationship with many of his children, who numbered a total of 17!

During a visit to the United States in late 1881, hoping to negotiate improved trade issues, Parkes went on to Europe, dining with royalty and then to the town of his birth, Stoneleigh.

There he met with a gathering of local school children to whom he delivered some stirring advice. 'You will not all rise to a position of power, honour, influence and responsibility such as that I now fill. But by resolving to discharge the duties of life, in being of use and service in your day and generation, you will do far better than I have done'.

Words of wisdom to children perhaps, but 175 years after Henry Parkes began his life of contribution to Australia, he continues in so many ways to inspire and to enrich the nation.

Notes

1 Lucy Hughes Turnbull, *Dictionary of Sydney*

2 'Banquet to the New South Wales Delegates', *The Argus*, Melbourne, 18 March 1867; http://trove.nla.gov.au/ndp/del/article/5788716

3 *Sydney Morning Herald*, 26 October 1889. National Library of Australia's Trove database: http://trove.nla.gov.au/ndp/del/article/13746899

The text of what became known as the 'Tenterfield Oration' was reported in the Sydney Morning Herald of 25 October 1889, the day after Parkes delivered the speech at a banquet in his honour at the Tenterfield School of Arts.

The Tenterfield Oration

Sir Henry Parkes

BANQUET TO THE PREMIER. A BRILLIANT RECEPTION.

| *By Telegraph.*| *(From our special reporter.)*

Tenterfield, Thursday

SIR HENRY PARKES left Brisbane at 7 o'clock this morning, and travelled by special train to Wallangarra on the Border, which place was reached about 6 p.m. He was met there by a special train, under the charge of Mr. Richardson, general outdoor Superintendent, and Mr. C. H. Strange, locomotive engineer. The Premier was then brought to Tenterfield, where great preparations had been made for his reception. The whole town was en fete. All the stores were closed, and half the population gathered at the station to greet him on his arrival. Flags and banners were plentifully displayed, and the local brass band played an active part in the proceedings.

Sir Henry, who was accompanied by Mr. David Christie Murray, was met on the platform by Mr. Lee, M.L.A., Mr. E. R. Whereat, Mayor of Tenterfield, Aldermen W. Read, W. Morrell, A. G. Weir, D. Corney, J. Whereat, J. Williams, C. Burgess, and A. B. Butler, and also many prominent local men. A detachment of the Tabulam Mounted Infantry, under Lieutenant Readford, acted as an escort.

THROUGH THE EYES OF A COMPANION ...

English writer David Christie Murray accompanied Parkes to Tenterfield and included a description of the event in his book *The Cockney Columbus, notes on travels in the United States, Canada, Australia and New Zealand* (Downey & Co., London, 1898).

It was my good fortune to be present at that now famous meeting at Tenterfield at which Sir Henry chose to make his pronunciamento with regard to Australian federation, and I shall not readily forget the enthusiasm his speech evoked. His utterance was plain, straightforward, and convincing, and the speaker's sterling belief in the greatness of his theme and the propitious character of the hour was strikingly evident. The excellent choice of words, the masterly elaboration of phrases which were obviously moulded whilst he stood there upon his feet, were in some contrast to the manner of his utterance. The voice was a little veiled by fatigue and age. The massive shoulders were a little bowed, but the huge head, with its streaming wave of silver hair and beard, was held as erect as ever. The rough, homely features were as eloquent as the words he spoke, and the instinct of the natural fighting-man lit up the ancient warrior's eye. The mere aspect and manner would have been remarkable to a stranger anywhere; but there, where for the first time the voice of an authoritative statesman gave soul and utterance to the aspiration of a people, it was truly memorable, and not without a touch of sublimity.

The MAYOR on welcoming Sir Henry Parkes, read the following address: 'The Hon. Sir Henry Parkes, G.C.M.G., Premier and Colonial Secretary, New South Wales. Sir, – We beg, on behalf of the people of Tenterfield, to convey to you the welcome which we, its inhabitants, desire to accord you. It is not often we have the opportunity of meeting with a gentleman who has been entrusted by his country with the highest position which that country can confer upon him. All classes of the community, no matter on what side their opinions in politics may be, join in welcoming the Premier of New South Wales. We are fully cognisant of the talent and energy that have been displayed through your political life, which has received throughout a recognition than which there can be no higher, viz., that you are once again the head of the Government. In welcoming you, we desire to exclude all political considerations, and we feel that the harmony that should be attendant upon the welcome that we have an opportunity of giving you might be marred by allusions to any burning political subject. We trust that your short sojourn here may remain in your remembrance as a mark of the pleasant feeling that your presence creates wherever you go. We wish that in the present and in the future you may continue to be what all of us believe you are — a man who consistently does his best for his country, and a gentleman whose pleasing qualities are an ornament and delight to society. We trust that as years roll on you may long hold a position as one of the first and most earnest of our legislators, and we offer you, as a tribute to your long and faithful exertions in the service of our country, our best thanks and our very hearty welcome.'

Sir HENRY PARKES, in reply, said that he had received their address with feelings of peculiar pleasure, and he did not think that he could find language in which to express all that he felt on revisiting their beautiful town and happy district. The kind things which they had been good enough to say to him he took exception to, as being more in the shape of compliment than reality. (*No, no.*) He knew well himself how far he had fallen below the standard which he had set up for his public life, but he knew equally well that he had at all times studiously tried to perform the duties which he had taken in hand. He knew in the inmost depths of his conscience that he had never allowed any consideration but that of what he believed to be the public good to influence him in the course which he had taken. It afforded him much gratification to know that the results of his labour were appreciated so highly above their value. He had come there with a sincere desire to make himself better acquainted with the town, although nothing which he could possibly learn now could assure him more than the circumstances of the past had done, of the generous confidence and honesty of the people of Tenterfield. (*Hear, hear.*)

The Premier was then escorted to Mr. Curley's Commercial Hotel, where he is to stay during the remainder of his visit.

With regard to his visit to Queensland, Sir Henry expressed himself as being extremely satisfied as to its results. Unfortunately, owing to Mr. Morehead's illness, he was not able to have a personal interview with that gentleman, but from conversations with the leading politicians of both parties, Sir Henry has come to the conclusion that the Queenslanders are by no means satisfied with the Federal Council. It is pointed out that the council does not really represent colonial opinion, and that it is very doubtful whether it has, under the Imperial Act, any power to deal with such an important question as the proposed scheme for federal defence. In order to bring about any united action in this direction a bill would bare to be passed through the Imperial Parliament, and even then there would be no central executive authority qualified to take control of an army. Sir Henry Parkes, therefore, considers that some scheme of federal government should be agreed upon, and he has mainly devoted his efforts whilst in Brisbane to bring this about. Of course, nothing definite has been done as yet, but the Premier hopes that he has paved the way for future action in this direction.

THE BANQUET

Sir Henry was entertained at a banquet held in the School of Arts in the evening. Upwards of 80 persons were present, including a number of ladies. The chair was occupied by Mr. Whereat, Mayor of Tenterfield, and the vice-chairs by Messrs. J. B. Graham and J. H. Reid. Mr. Leo, M.L.A., Mr. David Christie Murray, and most of the prominent tradesmen were present. The usual loyal toasts were disposed of, and the chairman proposed 'The Ministry,' coupled with the name of their guest, Sir Henry Parkes. He spoke in eulogistic terms of the various members of the present Ministry, and especially referred to Sir Henry Parkes, who, on account of his long and arduous services, deserved the gratitude of the whole community. He also referred to the Local Government Bill, the differential railway rates, and concluded by tendering the warmest of welcomes to the Premier.

Sir HENRY PARKES, who was received with applause, said, in reply, that he could assure them he could not find words with which to acknowledge the toast, without recurring to the time when he had stood for a short period in intimate relations to them. This was one of the passages in his life which was not likely to fade away, for he remembered how generously they had elected him within a few hours after his defeat for East Sydney. He remembered also the generous confidence which they had displayed in refusing to accept his resignation on the occasion of his visit to England. He had afterwards felt compelled to suddenly resign his seat, but this arose from the same causes which had recently led to the appointment of the Public Works Committee. He had seen what had appeared to him such an utter profligacy in voting away large sums of money for public purposes, that he felt it was time he should refuse to sit in a Parliament where such things took place, although he saw occasion afterwards to return.

The Premier then referred to the appointment of the Public Works Committee, pointing out the valuable services which it was likely to render, and he also dealt at some length with the constitution of the present Government, showing in detail the ability of its different members. The late session would, if it had come to a conclusion ten days earlier, have been one of the most creditable ever held in this colony. He then traced briefly the work of the session, and went on to refer to what the Government intended to do. They intended as soon as possible to ask Parliament to sanction a Local Government Bill — (*Applause*) — which would be framed on a comprehensive scale, and they would also introduce a new Mining Bill.

They would also do their best to carry out as perfectly as possible the organisation of the defence force of the colony. He thought that they should by every means in their power encourage young men to enter the service, and to learn the use of arms, so that they might be of service to their country in case of need. They would do all they could to improve the organisation of the military forces of the colony in accordance with latest recommendations. They would doubtless be aware that a short time ago an Imperial officer inspected the forces of this colony and of the other colonies, and this officer's opinion of our men was that they were calculated to make as fine soldiers as any in the world. Although he pointed out some defects, on the whole his report was favourable. General Edwards had also advised that the forces of the various colonies should be federated together for operation in union in the event of war, so as to act as one great federal army. If an attack were made upon any of the colonies, it might be necessary for us to bring all our power to bear on one spot of the coast sometimes. More, however, was necessary if they were to have the federal system, so strongly recommended, and which must appeal to the senses of every intelligent man. The Government also proposed during the next session to introduce, if they possibly could, a measure to readjust the electoral system of the colony. (*Hear, hear.*) The policy of the Government was that taxation should only be imposed for tariff purposes.

The Premier then proceeded to deal briefly with the question of free trade, quoting statistics from Mulhall to show how the trade of England had increased during the past fifty years, and to what extent the savings of the people had increased. He also compared the commerce of England with that of other nations, and stated that as long as he lived and could exercise power, he would use it to perpetuate the freedom which they inherited from their forefathers. (*Applause.*)

The Imperial General who had inspected the forces of the colony had recommended that the whole of the forces of Australia should be united into one army. It would have pleased him greatly if they could rely on being safe without taking warlike measures, but as this was impossible, they must take measures to defended themselves, and the knowledge of this fact would be spread all over the world and make them additionally secure. There were two very important questions towards which their attention ought to be directed. They must have heard something of the Federal Council, on which New South Wales had not yet taken a place and which sat in Tasmania, and hold sessions which never appeared to interest any one; but if they were to carry out these recommendations of General Edwards, it would be absolutely necessary for them to have one central authority, which could bring all the forces of the different colonies into one army. Some colonial statesman had said that this might be done by means of the Federal Council, but this Federal Council had no power to do anything of the sort, as it was not an elective body, but merely a body appointed by the Governments of the various colonies It was therefore necessarily weak, and under the Imperial Act which appointed it no such tremendous power was given as that of originating and controlling a great Australian army. The Federal Council, also, had no executive power. It could propose, but could not execute. He would like to know what was to become of an army without a central executive power to guide its movements.

One way which had been suggested out of the difficulty was that the Imperial Parliament should be asked to pass a measure authorising the troops of the colonies to unite in one federal army, but still, even if this were done, there would be an absence of the necessary central executive government. The colonies would object to the army being under the control of the Imperial Government, and none of the other colonies could direct it.

The great question which they had to consider was, whether the time had not now arisen for the creation on this Australian continent of an Australian Government, as distinct from a local Government and an Australian Parliament (*Applause.*) In other words, to make himself as plain as possible, Australia had now a population of three and a half millions, and the American people numbered only between three and four millions when they formed the great commonwealth of the United States. The numbers were about the same, and surely what the Americans had done by war, the Australians could bring about in peace. (*Cheers.*) Believing as he did that it was essential to preserve the security and integrity of these colonies that the whole of their forces should be amalgamated into one great federal army, feeling this, and seeing no other means of attaining the end, it seemed to him that the time was close at hand when they ought to set about creating this great national government for all Australia. This subject brought them face to face with another subject. They had now, from South Australia to Queensland, a stretch of about 2000 miles of railway, and if the four colonies could only combine to adopt a uniform gauge, it would be an immense advantage in the movement of troops.

These were the two great national questions which he wished to lay before them. He had just returned from Brisbane, and the object of his visit had been not to force his advice on the authorities there but to discuss with them these matters. Unfortunately, owing to the illness of the head of the Ministry, his communications were rather more of a private character than otherwise; but, without disclosing any confidences, he thought he must state that he understood both sides in politics sympathised warmly and closely with the views which had been expressed by him. As to the steps which should be taken to bring this about, a conference of the authorities had been pointed to, but they must take broader and more powerful action in the initiation of this great Council; they must appoint a convention of leading men from all the colonies, delegates appointed by the authority of Parliament, who would fully represent the opinion of the different Parliaments of the colonies. This convention would have to devise the constitution which would be necessary for bringing into existence a federal government with a federal parliament for the conduct of this great national undertaking. (*Applause.*) The only argument which could be advanced in opposition to the views he had put forward was that the time had not come, and they must remain isolated colonies just in the same way as they were now. He believed, however, that the time had come, and, in the words of Brunton Stephens, the Queensland poet —

Not yet her day. How long 'not yet?' …
There comes a flush of violet!
And heavenward faces, all aflame
With sanguine imminence of morn
Wait but the sun-kiss to proclaim
The Day of The Dominion born.

(*Applause.*) He believed that the time had come, and if two Governments set an example, the others must soon of necessity follow, and they would have an uprising in this fair land of a goodly fabric of free Government, and all great national questions of magnitude affecting the welfare of the colonies would be disposed of by a fully authorised constitutional authority, which would be the only one which could give satisfaction to the people represented. This meant a distinct executive and a distinct parliamentary power, a government for the whole of Australia, and it meant a parliament of two houses, a house of commons and a senate, which would legislate on these great subjects. The Government and Parliament of New South Wales would be just as effective as now in all local matters, and so would the Parliament of Queensland. All great questions would be dealt with in a broad manner, just as Congress dealt with the national affairs of the United States, and as the Parliament of the Dominion of Canada dealt with similar questions. He, therefore, took advantage of the opportunity which had arisen for the consideration of this great subject, for he believed that the time was at hand when this should be done. One great thing to be accomplished was the massing together of their military forces, and this could not be controlled by any other power than one representing all the colonies. In conclusion, he thanked them for the kindness which they had shown him, and said that he had no fear but the federal parliament would rise to a just conception of the necessities of the case. The thing would have to be done, and to put it off would only tend to make the difficulties which stood in the way greater. In the meantime, there was this substantial work which they could not do by any other means to be carried out, and it could not be done by any existing machinery.

A number of other toasts were proposed, and responded to, and in reply to the toast of 'The Press,' Mr Murray delivered an interesting speech.

Sir Henry will visit the various public buildings in the town tomorrow, and will be driven round the district, and he intends to leave for Sydney on Saturday morning.

Acknowledgements

27 May 2015 marked the 200th anniversary of the birth of Henry Parkes, and provided the catalyst for the publication of this book dedicated to the reinvigoration of his legacy.

The Henry Parkes Foundation would like to thank its many contributors and supporters over the years.

As inaugural patron, the Hon. Gordon Samuels AC CVO QC launched the Foundation in 1999 at a ceremony in New South Wales Parliament House, and delivered the first oration at Tenterfield as part of Centenary of Federation celebrations in 2001. The indefatigable Professor the Hon. Dame Marie Bashir AD CVO became the Foundation's patron in 2001 and has continued in the role in a personal capacity after her term as Governor came to an end.

The Foundation's Board of Advisers all serve in a voluntary capacity. Since 1999, Parkes' great great grandson Ian Thom has managed the Foundation's finances, fund-raising logistics and governance with energy and professionalism, initially as Treasurer and since 2009 also as Chair; in addition, he is the keeper of the (very extensive) Parkes family tree. Great grand-daughter Jane Gray has channelled Henry's spirit from the beginning to keep the Foundation's work focused on his vision for a just, egalitarian and socially progressive society, as well as running things efficiently for more than 10 years as Honorary Secretary. And Peter Webber, adviser and Deputy Chair since 1999, has carried these values through into the series of Henry Parkes orations, which he was largely responsible for driving.

The other members of the current Board are Catherine Gray, adviser since 2002, Graham Spindler since 2004 (Deputy Chair since 2009), Dianne Barnes since 2011, Greig Tillotson and Gillian Webber since 2012, and Alan Ventress, a founding member of the Board who served 1999–2008, including four years as Chair, and then again since 2013. In addition, Ken Gray and Val Thom provide indispensable practical assistance to the advisers both at and between Board meetings.

Thanks are also due to past advisers, who all made invaluable contributions in their time: Brian Fletcher 1999–2006 (Chair 1999–2004); Neal Blewett 1999–2011; Ellen Elsey 1999–2000; Mary Gray 2002–2008; Richard Hall 1999–2000; Helen Irving 1999–2006; and Richard Waterhouse 2009–2011.

Neil Hartley, along with Jane Gray and Graham Spindler, are the Foundation's trustees.

For assistance in turning the idea of *The Crimson Thread* into a reality, the Foundation particularly acknowledges the excellent advice of publisher Tom Thompson of ETT Imprint, and the patience and flair of designer Alison White. Catherine Gray edited the manuscript, and led the work of the Foundation subcommittee comprising Graham Spindler, Alan Ventress and Greig Tillotson. Greig also provided the bibliography. Ian Thom, Val Thom and Peter Webber also made invaluable contributions, as well as brought an eye for detail to the final stages.

And of course, heartfelt thanks are due to the orators, whose thoughtful contributions will go on to spark discussion and debate into the future.

Henry Parkes Foundation
www.parkesfoundation.org.au

Bibliography

PRINCIPAL WORKS BY HENRY PARKES

Stolen moments: a short series of poems, Sydney, James Tegg, 1842.

The Empire, newspaper, Sydney (founder and proprietor). Launched by Henry Parkes 28 December 1850 and published by him until 28 August 1858.

Murmurs of the stream, Sydney, James W. Waugh, 1857.

Retirement of Mr Parkes from the Legislative Assembly of New South Wales, Sydney, 1857.

The Electoral Act and how to work it, Sydney, Thornton, 1859.

Freehold homes in a gold country: two public addresses on the present condition and natural resources of the colony of New South Wales, delivered at Derby and Birmingham by Henry Parkes Esq. Late Member of the Legislative Assembly of New South Wales, Birmingham, Hidson and Ellis, 1861.

The mother of Australia: a lecture delivered before the Working Men's College, Great Ormond Street, London May 17 1862, London, J. Haddon, 1862.

Australian views of England: eleven letters written in 1861 and 1862, London, Macmillan, 1869.

Studies in rhyme: with notes, Sydney, J. Ferguson, 1870.

The Public Schools Act: speech of Henry Parkes, President of the Council of Education, on opening the public school at Dundas on Thursday September 4 1869, Sydney, *J. Ferguson*, 1870.

The case of the prisoner Gardiner: the prerogative of pardon: a chapter of history, Melbourne, George Robertson, 1876.

Speeches on various occasions connected with the public affairs of New South Wales: 1848–1874, Melbourne, George Robertson, 1876.

Mr Gladstone and English liberalism from the Australian point of view: a speech by Sir Henry Parkes; and an address to the Right Hon. W. E. Gladstone, adopted at the public meeting at the Masonic Hall, Sydney New South Wales, Tuesday August 27 1878, Sydney, *Lee and Ross*, 1878.

Public instruction: speech delivered on the opening of the public school, Blayney, May 25 1880, Sydney, reprinted, with corrections, from the special report of the *Sydney Morning Herald*, Sydney, George Robertson, 1880.

The present condition and future prospects of Australia: a speech delivered by Sir Henry Parkes at Albury on 21 September 1880, Melbourne, George Robertson, 1880.

'Our growing Australian empire', *Nineteenth Century*, vol. 15, London, January 1884.

'Australia and the imperial connection', *Nineteenth Century*, vol. 15, London, May 1884.

The beauteous terrorist and other poems, by a wanderer, Melbourne, George Robertson, 1885.

Present state of public affairs: speech given by Sir Henry Parkes KCMG delivered at Granville, August 16 1886, Sydney, Turner and Henderson, 1886.

To the electors of St Leonards, Sydney, 1887.

Fragmentary thoughts, Sydney, S. E. Lees, 1889.

The Federal Government of Australasia: speeches delivered on various occasions November 1889 – May 1890, Sydney, Turner and Henderson, 1890.

One people, one destiny: speech of the Hon. Sir Henry Parkes GCMG to the citizens of Sydney, Sydney, Turner and Henderson, 1891.

Fifty years in the making of Australian history, London, Longmans, Green, and Co.,1892.

'The Protectionists of New South Wales', *Contemporary Review* 1892, pp. 621–628.

Sonnets and other verses, Kegan Paul, Trench, London, Trubner, & Co., 1895.

The 'Mandate of the People' and the Reid fraud, Sydney, Turner and Henderson, 1895.

The Reid ministry: speech by Henry Parkes GCMG in the Temperance Hall on Saturday July 20 1895, Sydney, Turner and Henderson, 1895.

An emigrant's home letters, Sydney, Angus & Robertson, 1896.

The bridge: with interesting speeches and prophecies (with E.W. Sullivan and Lord Hampden), Sydney, Hahn, 1932.

Letters from Menie: Sir Henry Parkes and his daughter, A. W. Martin (ed.), Melbourne, Melbourne University Press, 1983.

PUBLICATIONS ABOUT SIR HENRY PARKES

Bolton, Geoffrey, 'Sir Henry Parkes' in David Clune and Ken Turner (eds), *The Premiers of New South Wales 1856–2005, Volume One: 1856–1901*, Sydney, Federation Press, 2006.

Dando-Collins, Stephen, *Sir Henry Parkes: the Australian colossus*, Sydney, Knopff (Random House), 2013.

Lyne, C. E., *The life of Sir Henry Parkes, Australian statesman*, Sydney, George Robertson, 1896.

Martin, A. W., *'Henry Parkes and electoral manipulation: 1872–1882'*, *Historical Studies*, no. 31, November 1958.

Martin A. W., 'Sir Henry Parkes and public education in New South Wales', in E. L. French ed., *Melbourne Studies in Education 1960–61*, Melbourne, 1962.

Martin A. W., *Great Australians: Henry Parkes*, Melbourne, Oxford University Press, 1964.

Martin A. W., *Henry Parkes: a biography*, Melbourne, Melbourne University Press, 1980.

Murray, David Christie, *The Cockney Columbus*, London, Downey & Co., 1898.

Nairn, N. B., 'The political mastery of Sir Henry Parkes', *Journal of the Royal Australian Historical Society*, vol. 53, part 1, 1967.

Walker, W., *Recollections of Sir Henry Parkes*, Windsor, C. M. Davies, 1896.

Index

Pages with contributor biographies are indicated in **bold** text.

Aboriginal Australians *see* Indigenous Australians
Adult Migrant English Program 69
'Advance Australia Fair' 17
Advisory Committee on Executive Government 39
Albanese, Anthony 134
Alfred, Duke of Edinburgh, attempted assassination of 10, 23, 179
Anglo-Celtic heritage
  declining importance of 21
  early predominance of 14, 18
  future of 25–26
  unifying nature of 60
ANZUS Treaty 15–16
assimilation policy 20
Australasian Convention 1891 125, 183
Australasian Federal Convention 1897 125–126
Australasian Federation Conference 1890 183
Australia
  see also Commonwealth government; ethnic composition of Australia; Indigenous Australians; state governments
  Anglo-Celtic heritage 14, 18, 25–26, 60
  colonies seen as 'nations' in 99
  costs to of federal system 146
  democracy in 49–58
  diversification of 60
  education system 5–11, 109–121
  elected dictatorship in 42, 162
  electoral reform for 155–173
  head of state, republican options for 29–47
  in breach of ICCPR 164
  low school completion rates 112
  multiculturalism in 19–21
  poetic imagery of 17
  poor knowledge of civics in 152–153
  radicalism in 73–84
  railways in 123–138
  republican movement in 29–47, 76, 80
  social cohesion in 22–23
  subsidiarity in 98–107
  symbols of 64
  transport options in 130–131
  votes down republic proposal 33–34, 80, 143, 162
  what unites Australians? 59–72
  White Australia Policy 18–19, 62, 148
Australia Acts 1986 21, 77
Australian Capital Territory, Charter of Rights 83
Australian Constitution
  see Constitution of Australia
Australian Democrats 55, 163
Australian Electoral Commission 70
Australian identity 63–65
Australian Institute of Administrative Law 170
Australian Labor Party
  declining membership of 53
  education policies 9
  joint federalist agenda 83
  party system created by emergence of 52
  radical traditions 78–79
  referendums proposed by 152
  reform proposals for 55–56, 93
Australian National Railways Commission 127
Australian Rail Track Corporation 128, 135
Australian Republican Movement 34–36
Australian Transport Council of Ministers 134

Balfour Declaration 77
banking, attempts to nationalise 78
Bannon, John 97–107, **99**
Bardsley, Warren 90
Barton, Edmund, on 'races power' 148
Baruch, Bernard 54
Bashir, Marie 175–184, **177**
Baxters Well memorial 90
BHP Chief Executive, salary of 168
Birmingham, UK 176
Birrell, Robert 16
Bismark, Otto von 50
Blackburn, Jean 112
Blair, Tony 42, 66
Blewett, Neal 29–47, **31**
Bradley Review of Higher Education 112
Bradman, Don 23, 63
Brisbane, Thomas 94
Britain *see also* Anglo-Celtic heritage
  'devolution' in 105
  Parkes' early life in 176
  radical ideas from 75
  terrorist attacks in 67–68
  values of 66
Buchanan, George 133
Bulletin, The, motto of 19
Burney, Linda 85–96, **87**
Bush, George W. 42
Business Council of Australia 146

Cain, John 78
Canada
  growth as confederation 105
  immigration policies 62
  railways a federal responsibility in 125
Carr, Bob 86

Carrington, Lord 101, 124
Centennial Park 69, 86
Central Queensland railway 129
centralised service delivery, over-valuation of 106
Centralised Traffic Control on Sydney–Brisbane line 128
Charter of Rights proposed 82
Chartered Institute of Transport 132
Chifley, Ben 20, 77
Chinese Exclusion Bill of 1888 (NSW) 104
Churchill, Winston 91
citizenship test 66–68
Clapp, Harold 127
Clarke, Andrew Inglis 167
Clendinnen, Inga 95
Cleveland Street School 119
climate change concerns 132
COAG Reform Council 121
Coalition parties *see also* Liberal Party of Australia; National Party
  education policies 9
  codes of ethics 160
Coming of age, charter for a new Australia 172
Commonwealth Electoral Act, amendments to 70–71
Commonwealth Franchise Act 1902 (Cwlth) 148
Commonwealth government
  appointments made by 170
  benefits from control of railways 133
  Department of Immigration and Multicultural Affairs 20–21
  education funding from 9, 114–117, 120
  financial dominance of 105, 144–145
  funding role extended under Whitlam 78
  racially discriminatory policies 148–150
  reform proposals 49–58, 159
  special purpose payments by 117
  takes over non-metropolitan rail in SA and Tasmania 127
  tax powers ceded to 115
  'turf wars' with states 157
'Commonwealth of Australia' coined by Parkes 76, 140, 183
Commonwealth of Nations 15
compulsory voting 52, 64
Coniston massacre 90
Connors, Lyndsay 109–121, **111**
conscription referendums 77
consensual democracy 166–167
Constitution of Australia *see also* referendums
  Commonwealth funding powers under 120
  education policy in 109
  federal control of railways limited by 126
  limitations of 77–78, 161
  monarchical powers in 38
  'other powers' in 104
  preamble to 141–142
  proposed reforms to 58, 139–153
  provides for representative government 71
  race powers in 147–150
  requires free trade between states 126
  secularism in 7
Constitutional Commission, proposed 58, 172
Constitutional Conventions
  outcomes of 32–33
  Parkes' support for 57, 98
  proposals for 151
  reforms proposed by 39
Constitutional Council, proposed 32
Constitutional Review Commission, proposed 151
cooperative federalism 83
Costello, Peter 36
Costigan Royal Commission 157
Council of Australian Governments 121, 133
Council of Public Education NSW 111
Crean, Simon 56
'crimson thread of kinship' 20, 59–72
Cronulla, race riots at 67, 95
Curtin, John 15, 77

Dando-Collins, Stephen 176, 184
Dawn: A Journal for Australian Women 89, 91
democracy
  commitment to 65–67
  education and 109–121
  implementing 172
  in Switzerland 165–167, 170–171
  proportional representation and 166–167
Democracy's victory and crisis 172
denominational schools *see* private schools
Department of Immigration and Multicultural Affairs 20–21
Department of Public Instruction NSW 109
Dibbs, George 101
Dixon, Eleanor 184
Downer, John 119
Dundas speech by Parkes 110–111, 113
Dunstan, Don 79

Eddy, E. M. G. 124
education policies
  civics education required 152, 165
  impact of federal system on 112, 115–117
  importance of public education 5–11, 68–69, 109–121
  Parkes' contribution to 3, 5–11, 109–113, 119–120, 180
  secularism in 113–114
Edwards, Bevan 14, 124–125
Electoral Commission 160
Electoral Law Committee (NZ) 46–47
electoral reform
  preferential voting 163
  recommendations for 55
  single-member electorates 162–163, 167
  to federal system 106
  under Labor administrations 79
Elizabeth II, Queen, as Australian head of state 15, 21, 35

Elster, Jon 172
Empire, The newspaper 56, 178
Energy Australia, salary of CEO 168
English classes for immigrants 69
ethnic composition of Australia
see also Anglo-Celtic heritage; immigration to Australia; multiculturalism
'crimson thread' and 60
from waves of immigration 95
growing diversity in 25, 62–68
European Union, governments in 39, 105
Evans, Harry 169, 172
Evatt, Herbert De Vere 77

factionalism 55–56, 162
Faulkner, John 49–58, **51**, 91–92
Federal Council of Australasia 100
Federal Financial Relations Act 2009 (Cwlth) 120
federalism
costs and burdens of 144–146
criticisms of 134
Harold Holt definition of 107
problems with 115, 155–173
then and now 97–107
Federation
Australia at the time of 14
military reasons for 14–15
railways benefit from 126–127
role of radicalism in 74–75
female suffrage, Parkes declares for 18
Fenian conspiracy 23
Fifty years in the making of Australia 61
First Australians, The 94
First Fleet 95–96
Fischer, Tim 129
Fitzgerald Inquiry 157
Fitzgerald, Tony 156, 159, 161
Five things to know about the Australian Constitution 161
'flag, The' 13, 17
Fletcher, Brian H. 1–3
Fragmentary thoughts 13
Fraser Coalition government, offers to electrify Sydney–Melbourne rail line 129
free market policies 54, 80
freedom, living in 13–27
Freedom of Information requests 159
frontier wars 17

Gadigal people 95–96
Gallop, Geoff 36, 73–84, **75**
Game, Philip 78
Gardiner, Frank 180–181
Garnaut Climate Change Review 132
Gillard Labor government, referendums 143
Gillies, Duncan 101
Governor-General 158, 170
see also head of state
grain transport, road preferred to rail for 131
Grants Commission 105
Great Western rail line 124
Greens Party 55, 80, 143, 163
Greenwood, Gordon 134
Griffith, Gavan 149
Griffith, Samuel 183

Hanson, Pauline 54–55, 87
Hare-Clarke voting system 167–168
harvesting of preferences 163–164
Hawke Labor government, State Aid paid to private schools by 11
Hawkesbury River rail bridge 124
head of state
Governor-General as 170
parliamentary executive and 38
republican options for 29–47
Queen Elizabeth as 15, 21, 35
Henry, Ken 132
Henry Parkes Act proposed 120
Hewson, John 36
High Court
blocks attempts to nationalise banks 78
establishment of 40, 42
Hindmarsh Island Bridge Case 149
high-speed rail, potential for 132–133
Hindmarsh Island Bridge Case 149
Hirst, John 16
Hogan, Paul 63
Hollis, Colin 129–130
Holmes, Cecil 176
Holt, Harold, on federalism 107
Home Rule for Ireland bills 31
Horne, Donald 19, 23, 40
House of Representatives
see also Commonwealth government
functions and performance of 42–43
Standing Committee on Legal and Constitutional Affairs 151
Howard Coalition government 9, 82, 107, 117–118
Howard, John
control of House of Representatives 42
election campaigns 49–50
invokes ANZUS Treaty 16
on ethnic diversity 66
on federalism 81
on head of state 38
republic proposals opposed by 36
Hume, David 150

idealism 16–17
Immigration and Multicultural Affairs, Department of 21
Immigration Restriction Act 1901 (Cwlth) 148
immigration to Australia
see also ethnic composition of Australia; multiculturalism; racial discrimination
Anglo-Celtic focus of 19–20
anticipated prior to Federation 60
English classes for immigrants 69

Indigenous Australians
  education policy and 112
  excluded from Federation 7
  frontier wars with 17
  massacres of 90
  numbers of 18
  Parkes on 102
  proposed referendums on recognition of 143–144
  reconciliation with needed 22
  role in Australian nation 85–96
  storytelling skills 88
  under federalism 146–150
  voting by optional until 1984 92
Indigenous Labor Network 93
Institution of Engineers Australia 132
Integrity Branch proposed 170
Inter-State Commission on rail transport 126–128
International Covenant on Civil and Political Rights 164
Ireland, independence achieved by 31
Irving, Helen 59–72, **61**
  2001 Barton Lecture 172
  on the Constitution 161
Isaacs, Isaac 134

Jamison, John 177
Jupp, James 20, 23

Kalgoorlie, linked to Perth by rail 126
Keating Labor government 115
Keating, Paul 34–36, 38, 126
Kemp, Charles 178
Kerr, John 39
Kirby, Michael 7–8, 83, 150
Kitchener, Lord 126

Labor *see* Australian Labor Party
Lachlan Swamps 69
Laing, Nina and Billy 88
Laird, Philip 123–138, **125**
Land, The 131
Lang, John Dunmore 29, 74–75, 177–178
Lang NSW Labor government, sacking of 78
Lange, David 46
Langton, Marcia 95
Latham, Mark 49–50, 55–56
Lawson, Henry 90
Lawson, Louisa 88–91
Liberal Party *see also* Coalition parties
  fails to support republic proposals 35–36
Lijphart, Arend 166–167
Lincoln, Abraham 164
Lynch, Julia 184

Mack, Ted 155–173, **157**
Mackay, Hugh 156, 161
Mackellar, Dorothea 95–96
Malouf, David 115
Marsh, Jack 88, 90
Martin, A. W. 10–11
Martin, James 178
McCormick, Peter 17
McGarvie republic model 32, 39
McKenna, Mark 76
McMullin, Ross 79
media
  coverage of politics 52
  lobbying by 173
  reforms required in 56–57
Menzies, Robert, proclaims war with Germany 16
military threats to Australia 14–16, 103
Mill, John Stuart 162
'minimalist' republic model 31–37
ministerial responsibility 43, 168
Ministry of Public Instruction 11
MMP (mixed member proportional) voting system *see* proportional representation
monarchists, oppose republic proposals 35–36
Muggeridge, Malcolm 52
multiculturalism 19–21, 26
  see also cultural issues; immigration to Australia
'murdered wild boy, The' 147
Murphy, Lionel, on Constitution 141
Murray–Darling Basin Plan, administrative obstacles to 145
Murray, David Christie 186
Murray, Les 25

nation-states 53–54, 99
National Australasian Convention 1891 125, 183
National Goals of Schooling 120
National Highway System 130, 135
National Party 163 *see also* Coalition parties
National Party of New Zealand 47
National Rail Corporation 128
National Road Transport Commission 134
National Roads Act 1974 (Cwlth) 135
nationalism, idealistic 16–17
nautical school established by Parkes 179
Neville, Paul 130
New Guinea, annexed by colonial Queensland 100
New South Wales
  ARTC leases rail lines in 128
  colonial history of 100–101
  education system 9, 109
  first federation vote defeated in 102–103
  harvesting of preferences in 163–164
  military threats to 14
  perceived dominance of 102
  political cynicism in 91–92
  proposed name change to 'Australia' 101
  public funding for election campaigns 159
  rail transport in 124, 129–130
  self government achieved by 141
  state government corruption in 157, 162
  state referendums carried in 165
  under Parkes 5–6, 178–182

New South Wales Typographers Union 89
New Zealand, electoral reforms in 46–47
Newman, Peter 131
Nightingale, Florence 179
non-government schools *see* private schools
North Sydney Council 156
Northern Territory, railway modernisation in 129
nurse training school at Sydney Hospital 179

Obama, Barack 86
O'Farrell, Henry James 23, 179
oil shortages, road traffic vulnerable to 131–132
Olympics, Sydney 2000 64
'On the wave' initiative 95
One Nation Party, brief success of 54–55
Osborn, Lucy 179

Parkes, Clarinda Sarah 176
Parkes, Clarinda (Varney) 2, 176
Parkes, Henry
  see also Public Instruction Act 1880 (NSW); *Public Schools Act 1866* (NSW); Tenterfield Oration
  achievements as premier 140
  advice to schoolchildren 184
  as colonial secretary 178–179
  as president of the Council of Public Education 111
  Australasian Convention headed by 183
  bankruptcies 52, 178
  bone carvings by 177
  Burney's view of 89
  Chinese immigrants taxed by 89
  'crimson thread' speech 59
  'crowned republic' comment 35
  defence policies 14–15, 103
  descendants of 1, 120, 177
  Dundas speech 110–111, 113
  early career of 2–3, 176–177
  education policies 3, 5–11, 109–113, 119, 120, 180
  family life of 184
  female suffrage supported by 18
  Fenian conspiracy claims by 23
  immigration policies 60
  institutions designed by 51
  involved in creation of Centennial Park 69
  knighthood awarded to 182
  lays foundation stone at Cleveland Street School 119
  legacy of 1, 175–184
  nautical school established by 179
  offers to distribute food parcels 102
  on Indigenous Australians 147
  on planned federal government 98
  on White Australia Policy 20
  poetry by 13, 17, 89, 147
  political career 5, 177–183
  portraits of 89, 176, 180
  premierships of 2, 180–182
  proposes renaming NSW 'Australia' 101
  radicalism of 74–75
  railway policies 123–124
  role in Constitution 139
  runs *The Empire* 56, 178
  support for federation proposal 183
  'The Murdered Wild Boy' 147
  US trip by 60–62, 71
  view of US 17
  wins seat in NSW Parliament 178
Parkes, Martha 184
Parkes, Sarah 184
parks and reserves 69–70, 86
parliamentary republics 30, 37–39
party politics
  declining public trust in 54, 160
  emergence of 52
  MPs controlled by 41–42
  referendums and 152
  reform proposals 55
  results of 156, 162
Paterson, Banjo 17
Patterns of democracy 166–167
Patterson, James 101
peace, living in 13–27
People power: the history and future of the referendum in Australia 150
Phillip, Arthur 89
Pilbara region railways 128–129
plebiscites *see* referendums
poetry by Parkes 13, 17, 89, 147
politicians
  campaigning by 54
  public opinion of 156
  remuneration of 158, 168–169
  self-regulation of a failure 168–169
politics
  see names of political parties; party politics
Port Augusta–Kalgoorlie rail 126
Pottinger, Mike 168
presidential republic proposals 29–47
  see also republican movement
Press Council, role of 57
Priority Public, campaigns by 7
private schools
  Commonwealth funding for 11, 114–117, 120
  Parkes withdraws State Aid from 181
Privy Council, favours trucking over rail 127
proportional representation voting 46, 166–167
public education *see* education policies
public funding for election campaigns 53, 70, 159
public institutions, unity fostered by 70–71
Public Instruction Act 1880 (NSW) 3, 11, 68–69, 109–110
Public Instruction, NSW Department of 109
Public Schools Act 1866 (NSW) 119, 181
Public Schools Bill 1866 (NSW) 70
public servants, salary levels of 168–169
Public Service Board proposal 170
public service, politicisation of 169
public spaces, unity fostered by 69–70

Queensland
colonial history of 100
corruption enquiries 157
indentured labourers in 104
limited support for federation 102–103
railway construction in 127–129
state elections in 162–163
Question Time 43, 161

racial discrimination
anti-Irish sentiment 10
Federation and 7
in Constitution 147–148
in cricket team selection 90
institutional, in colonial Australia 104
White Australia Policy 18–19, 62, 148
Racial Discrimination Act 1975 (Cwlth) 148
racism *see* racial discrimination
radicalism 2, 73–84
railways in Australia 103, 123–138
Rees, Nathan 91–92
Referendum (Machinery Provisions) Act 1984 (Cwlth) 150–151
referendums
Australia early adopter of 76–77
bipartisan support required 152
Constitutional provisions for 142–143
Gillard government promises 143
high failure rate of 34–35, 106, 143
in Switzerland 170–171
on removing special reference to Aborigines in Constitution 148
on republic proposals 162
proposed reforms to process 57, 150–153
reject centralisation of power 165
voting patterns for federation proposal 102
Remuneration Commission 168
Republic Advisory Committee 35, 39
republican movement
Faulkner supports 57
Gallop supports 83
in 19th century 76
reasons for recent failure 33–34, 80, 162
republican models, presidential vs parliamentary 29–47
Reynolds, Henry 95
right-wing policies 80–81
rights, protection of 82
road transport, costs of 130–131
Roberts, Tom, portrait of Parkes by 89
Robertson, John 101
Robinson, Aunty May 94
Robinson, Hercules 181
Roosevelt, Franklin Delano 54
Roozendaal, Eric 158
Rowley, C. D. 95
royal commission into uniform rail gauge 126, 133
Royal Prince Alfred Hospital, establishment of 179–180
Rudd, Kevin, Apology to Indigenous peoples 94–95
Rudd Labor government 107, 120
Ryan, Susan 5–11, **7**

Samuels, Gordon 13–27, **15**
scepticism 64
schoolchildren 2, 184
see also education policies
schools *see* education policies; private schools
Schools Assistance Act (Cwlth) 120
sectarianism
anti-Catholic sentiment 10
Parkes opposed to 3
reduction in over time 23
secularism in education 113–114
Senate *see also* Commonwealth government
flaws in 163–164
future role of 80
power of to block Supply 39, 42–43, 57
separation of powers 41, 45, 167
service delivery, localisation of 106
Service, James 59
Sir Henry Parkes: the Australian Colossus 176
Smith, David 156, 161
Socceroos 64
social cohesion 22–23
social justice policies 139–153
Solomon, David 35, 172
Solon, Vivian 82
South African Truth and Reconciliation Commission 87–88
South Australia
colonial history of 100
Commonwealth takes over non-metropolitan rail in 127
objects to federal control of communications 125–126
railway construction in 127, 129
riverboat trade with eastern states 145–146
support for federation proposal 102
Speakers, selection of 160–161, 170
Spigelman, James 170
Spirit of Progress train 128
standard gauge
see uniform rail gauge, campaign for
Stanley, John 131
State Aid to private schools
see private schools, Commonwealth funding for
state governments
corruption inquiries in 157, 162
education policies 121
failure to develop long-distance rail 128
over-representation in 166
Parkes chairs Select Committee 178
reforms to needed 78, 134
retain responsibility for railways 125–126
'turf wars' with Commonwealth 157
Statute of Westminster 77
Stephens, James Brunton 16

subsidiarity in Australia 98–107
Switzerland, democracy in 165–167, 170–171
Sydney–Brisbane rail line 130–131
Sydney Hospital, nurse training school at 179
Sydney–Melbourne rail line 129–131
Sydney Technical College 182

Tasmania
  colonial history of 100
  Commonwealth takes over non-metropolitan rail in 127
  Hare-Clarke voting system 167–168
  support for federation proposal 102–103
taxes, unnecessary 146
teachers, importance of 110, 114
technological change, impact of on politics 52
Teese, Richard 117
telecommunications policy 125–126
Tennyson, Alfred Lord 16
Tenterfield Oration
  arguments set out in 57
  calls for more than Federation 73
  effects of 3
  Herald report on 185–192
  on rail gauges 125
  role in Federation 73, 97, 139, 183
The Bulletin, motto of 19
The Empire newspaper 56, 178
The First Australians 94
'The flag' 13, 17
The Land 131
'The murdered wild boy' 147
The Third Man 171
Third Wave of National Reform 83
tolerance vs unity 65
Truth and Reconciliation Commission (South Africa) 87–88
truth-telling, power of 86–87, 95
Turnbull, Malcolm 33–35, 40
Tutu, Desmond 87

uniform rail gauge, campaign for 124, 126–127
'uniformity', over-valuation of 106
United Australia proposal 101
United Kingdom *see* Britain
United States
  as presidential republic 30
  Australian alliance with 15–16
  Australian federal system borrows from 40
  bureaucracy in 166
  Constitution of 142
  election costs in 160
  interest in politics in 86
  lessons for Australia from 62–63, 71, 104
  Parkes' views of 60–62, 71, 183
  population growth through immigration 62
  railway regulation in 125
  role of Congress in 30–31, 42–44
  separation of powers in 45
  Vegemite banned in 64
universal manhood suffrage, Australia early adopter of 76
universities, Commonwealth funding for cut 115
University of New South Wales 182
University of Sydney, provides land for RPAH 180
upper houses, obstructionism of 78
  see also Senate
urban rail systems, electrification of 128

values, shared 66–68
Varney, Clarinda 2, 176
vertical fiscal imbalance 115
Victoria
  Charter of Rights 83
  colonial history of 100, 182–183
  Regional Fast Rail service 128
  support for federation proposal 102–103
  upper house blocks Supply in 78
voting, compulsory *see* compulsory voting

WA Inc 157
Walker, James 126
Waverley Cemetery, Fenian memorial in 25
Welles, Orson 171
Wentworth committee 127
Wentworth, William Charles 178
Western Australia
  colonial history of 100
  corruption enquiries 157
  railways in 126, 128–129
  support for federation proposal 102–103
Westminster system
  Australianisation of 40, 104
  decay of parliamentary authority in 44
  executive accountable to parliament 43–44
  focus on localism 51–52
  mistakenly perceived as ideal 35
  state governments and 166
White Australia Policy 18–19, 62, 82, 148
'white picket fence' view of history 23
Whitlam, Gough 78, 133
Whitlam Labor government
  abolishes White Australia Policy 19
  National Highway System 130
  rail transport policies 127–128
  State Aid paid to private schools by 11
Williams, George 2, 139–153, **141**
Windradyne 94
Wiradjuri people 85–86, 94
Wise, Bernhard 126
women
  involvement in Federation 18
  Parkes' relationship with 184
  struggle for equal rights 91
  suffrage for 18
Wood Royal Commission 157
working classes, Select Committee inquiry into 178
Wran, Neville 32, 159

www.ingramcontent.com/pod-product-compliance
Ingram Content Group UK Ltd.
Pitfield, Milton Keynes, MK11 3LW, UK
UKHW051128260726
13967UKWH00010B/2917